Research Series on the Chinese Dream and China's Development Path

Drawing on a large body of empirical studies done over the last two decades, this Series provides its readers with in-depth analyses of the past and present and forecasts for the future course of China's development. It contains the latest research results made by members of the Chinese Academy of Social Sciences. This series is an invaluable companion to every researcher who is trying to gain a deeper understanding of the development model, path and experience unique to China. Thanks to the adoption of Socialism with Chinese characteristics, and the implementation of comprehensive reform and opening-up, China has made tremendous achievements in areas such as political reform, economic development, and social construction, and is making great strides towards the realization of the Chinese dream of national rejuvenation. In addition to presenting a detailed account of many of these achievements, the authors also discuss what lessons other countries can learn from China's experience.

Guogang Wang

A Study on Interest Rate Liberalization in China

SSAP

Springer

Guogang Wang
Chinese Academy of Social Sciences
Beijing, China

Translated by Sai Pan
Polished by Zhiwei Song

ISSN 2363-6866 ISSN 2363-6874 (electronic)
Research Series on the Chinese Dream and China's Development Path
ISBN 978-981-97-3643-0 ISBN 978-981-97-3644-7 (eBook)
https://doi.org/10.1007/978-981-97-3644-7

Jointly published with Social Sciences Academic Press
The print edition is not for sale in China (Mainland). Customers from China (Mainland). Please order the print book from: Social Sciences Academic Press.

Published with financial support of the Innovation Program of the Chinese Academy of Social Sciences.

This Springer imprint is published by the registered company Springer Nature Singapore Pte Ltd.
The registered company address is: 152 Beach Road, #21-01/04 Gateway East, Singapore 189721, Singapore

Series Preface

Since China's reform and opening began in 1978, the country has come a long way on the path of Socialism with Chinese characteristics, under the leadership of the Communist Party of China. Over 30 years of reform, efforts and sustained spectacular economic growth have turned China into the world's second largest economy, and wrought many profound changes in the Chinese society. These historically significant developments have been garnering increasing attention from scholars, governments, and the general public alike around the world since the 1990s, when the newest wave of China studies began to gather steam. Some of the hottest topics have included the so-called "China miracle", "Chinese phenomenon", "Chinese experience", "Chinese path", and the "Chinese model". Homegrown researchers have soon followed suit. Already hugely productive, this vibrant field is putting out a large number of books each year, with Social Sciences Academic Press alone having published hundreds of titles on a wide range of subjects.

Because most of these books have been written and published in Chinese, however, readership has been limited outside China—even among many who study China—for whom English is still the lingua franca. This language barrier has been an impediment to efforts by academia, business communities, and policy-makers in other countries to form a thorough understanding of contemporary China, of what is distinct about China's past and present may mean not only for her future but also for the future of the world. The need to remove such an impediment is both real and urgent, and the *Research Series on the Chinese Dream and China's Development Path* is my answer to the call.

This series features some of the most notable achievements from the last 20 years by scholars in China in a variety of research topics related to reform and opening. They include both theoretical explorations and empirical studies, and cover economy, society, politics, law, culture, and ecology, the six areas in which reform and opening policies have had the deepest impact and farthest-reaching consequences for the country. Authors for the series have also tried to articulate their visions of the "Chinese Dream" and how the country can realize it in these fields and beyond.

All of the editors and authors for the *Research Series on the Chinese Dream and China's Development Path* are both longtime students of reform and opening and recognized authorities in their respective academic fields. Their credentials and expertise lend credibility to these books, each of which having been subject to a rigorous peer review process for inclusion in the series. As part of the Reform and Development Program under the State Administration of Press, Publication, Radio, Film, and Television of the People's Republic of China, the series is published by Springer, a Germany-based academic publisher of international repute, and distributed overseas. I am confident that it will help fill a lacuna in studies of China in the era of reform and opening.

Shouguang Xie

Contents

Chapter 1
Deposit and Lending Interest Rate Liberalization Reforms: Challenges, Pathways, and Policy Options

"Steadily advancing interest rate liberalization reforms"[1] is a strategic initiative for adjusting China's financial system and improving the monetary policy regulation. It is also a priority and challenge in deepening financial reforms. The idea of interest rate liberalization reforms in China was put forth as early as in 1993.[2] Since 1996, China has implemented interest rate liberalization reforms by following the approach of "taking the first step of reform for foreign currencies before the home currency, loan interest rate before deposit interest rate, long-maturity before short-maturity, and large-sum transactions before small-sum ones."

By 2004, China had cumulatively deregulated, consolidated, or canceled 118 types of home and foreign interest rate management.[3] On October 28, 2004, the People's Bank of China (hereinafter "PBoC" or the "Central Bank") released the *Circular on Adjusting Renminbi Benchmark Interest Rates*, which marks the first step of Renminbi deposit and lending interest rate[4] liberalization reforms. In the following 19 years, however, the Central Bank frequently resorted to administrative interventions to regulate deposit and loan benchmark interest rates, failing to achieve the reform goal of establishing market-based deposit and lending interest rates and market-based allocation of financial resources.

---

[1] Cited from Outline of the 12th Five-Year Plan for National Economic and Social Development, Chapter 48.

[2] In 1983, which was prior to this reform, the State Council granted the PBoC the right to adjust the statutory loan interest rate within a ±20% band. However, this right was not exercised until 1987 for working capital loans. Released in 1993, the Decisions of the CPC Central Committee on Matters concerning the Establishment of the Socialist Market Economic System and the Decisions of the State Council on Financial Reforms unequivocally laid out the basic vision for interest rate liberalization reform.

[3] See the PboC's Report on Monetary Policy Implementation in Q4 2004.

[4] Unless otherwise specified, "deposit and lending interest rates" in this paper refers to "Renminbi deposit and lending interest rates", "deposit interest rate" refers to "Renminbi deposit interest rates", "loan interest rate" refers to "Renminbi loan interest rate".

G. Wang, *A Study on Interest Rate Liberalization in China*, Research Series on the Chinese Dream and China's Development Path,
https://doi.org/10.1007/978-981-97-3644-7_1

The interest rate is the price of capital. It not only sets the basic price for credit and debt financial products but also restrains the price level of equity financial products. Deposit and lending interest rates play a fundamental role in China's interest rate system, and their level of liberalization bears an immediate effect on the market-based pricing of various financial products. Being a complex and arduous systematic project, deposit and lending interest rate liberalization reform is fraught with a host of significant risks. Any misstep may lead to financial and economic turmoil or in the worst case, a financial crisis with inestimable losses. In this sense, deposit and lending interest rate liberalization reform marks a critical stage of China's interest rate liberalization and involves far more stakeholders, difficulties, risks, and complexities than any previous interest rate reforms. All stakeholders must be fully aware of the profundity of this reform, and more cautiously identify solutions and implementation pathways.

1.1 Literature Review on Interest Rate and Interest Rate Liberalization

Interest rate liberalization reform means a process in which the interest rate formation mechanism shifts from administrative regulation to a market-based mechanism and ultimately market-based interest rates. Put simply, interest rate liberalization is the process of realizing or achieving market-based interest rates. That is to say, on the one hand, the shift from regulated to market-based interest rate formation mechanism—irrespective of its stage and pace—is a process of interest rate liberalization. On the other hand, the process of interest rate liberalization will not conclude until market-based interest rates are established.

In the history of monetary economics, numerous studies have been carried out to discuss interest rates and market-based interest rates from different perspectives. Based on the idea of free-market competition, the classical school led by William Petty and Adam Smith underscores the rationality of capital supply and demand in determining interest rates. According to Carl Marx (1894), interest derives from surplus value and is the part of surplus value alienated by industrial capital to bank capital; interest rates are determined by both profitability and factors like intersectoral competition for capital and the supply and demand of capital. John Maynard Keynes (1993) identified differences between the supply and demand relationships of money and capital and introduced the money demand factor, stressing the role of liquidity preference.

Keynes's theory laid the foundation for interest rates to be used as an instrument for economic regulation. Following this approach, John Richard Hicks (1995) introduced interest rate into the IS-LM model as a key factor linking commodity market equilibrium with currency market equilibrium. Since then, the neoclassical school of economics has investigated the formation of interest rate as an economic variable concerning money supply and demand, national income, commodity market, and currency market equilibrium, and found that interest rate played an important role in regulating the economy.

After the 1970s, Keynesian theories and policies were systematically refuted by Ronald I. McKinnon (1998) and E. S. Shaw (1998). Based on such concepts as "financial repression" and "financial deepening", they examined government-regulated interest rate policies and consequences in developing countries, proposing that governments should relax interest rate regulation so that interest rates fully reflect capital demand and supply. Their arguments became an important theoretical basis for interest rate liberalization reforms. After the 1980s, Joseph Eugene Stiglitz (2007) et al. performed an analysis of the interest rate determination mechanism under credit rationing. They believed that in a market of information asymmetry, capital transactions might not always follow the auction principle of "whoever bids the highest gets the capital." As a result, interest rates had lost their function of information transmission. Given the investment risks under credit rationing, an interest rate determined by maximal bank profits does not equal an equilibrium interest rate determined by the supply and demand of capital or money.

Three things can be learned from interest rate theories in Western mainstream economics: First, though Western academics discussed various issues related to interest rates and put forth such concepts as "nominal interest rate", "real interest rate", "market-based interest rate" and "natural interest rate", they seldom performed any systematic analysis of interest rates as an integral system as if only one interest rate existed for various financial products. Second, despite their discussions of interest rate formation mechanisms from different angles and analysis of various interest rate effects, they did not delve further into how each specific interest rate was formed and its associated financial and economic effects from the perspective of an interest rate system. Hence, none of them recognized the uniqueness of deposit and lending interest rates in the market-based interest rates system and their effects, let alone discuss the challenges to deposit and lending interest rate liberalization. Third, the above-mentioned Western interest rate theories offer limited guidance for China's deposit and lending interest rate liberalization reforms.

As China started to implement interest rate liberalization reforms after the mid-1990s, Chinese scholars have focused their discussions on the following five aspects:

First, the implications of interest rate liberalization. In this respect, a representative view is Li Yang's (2003), i.e., interest rate liberalization offers two real implications for monetary authorities: 1. Market-based interest rate determination, i.e., the risk structure, maturity structure, and level of interest rates cease to be determined directly by monetary authorities and gradually become determined by sellers and buyers of financial assets independently according to financial market supply and demand. 2. Market-based interest rate management, i.e., instead of resorting to administrative interventions, monetary authorities act as a market participant, using financial resources and monetary policy means at their disposal to alter capital supply and demand in financial markets through currency market transactions and ultimately influence financial market interest rates by regulating benchmark interest rates. The above-mentioned two aspects of interest rate liberalization have been underscored in various studies. According to Wang Guosong (2001), for instance, market-based interest rates as the goal of interest rate liberalization are achieved when a country's interest rate level and structure are determined by market supply and demand and a combination of market factors such as risk level, inflation, and economic nature. Dai Genyou (2001) believed interest rate liberalization reforms should aim to create an interest rate system and formation mechanism that is underpinned by central bank interest rates, relies on the intermediary effects of currency market interest rates, and determines financial institutions' deposit and lending interest rates according to market supply and demand.

Second, the necessity of interest rate liberalization reforms. In this respect, the literature has focused on the role of interest rate as a macroeconomic policy instrument. As Wang Zhao (2001) noted, regulated interest rates hardly serve as a signal for change in investment in the economy as a whole, which limits their function as monetary policy instruments. Sheng Songcheng and Wu Peixin (2008) also believed that given the absence of market-based transmission between interest rates at various levels, China's monetary policy transmission mainly relied on credit instead of interest rate channels, so that credit scale became the de facto intermediate target of China's monetary policy. This view is supported by empirical studies by Fang Xianming et al. (2005) and Sheng Zhaohui (2006), et al., who found the role of interest rates as a vehicle of China's monetary policy transmission to be impeded and less effective than credit.

Third, conditions for interest rate liberalization. In discussing China's interest rate liberalization reforms, most academics identified the improvement of financial markets as a precondition. For instance, Xu Jian (2003a, b) stressed the importance of financial market fundamentals and financial regulation as the premise for interest rate liberalization. Qian Xiao'an (2003) also identified competitive financial markets, financial institutions' governance, sound corporate operations, and financial regulation as key conditions for interest rate liberalization. Similarly, Zhou Xiaochuan (2011) identified essential conditions for liberalizing interest rates: fair competition among financial institutions, the financial hard constraint for qualified financial institutions, complete monetary policy transmission mechanism, better risk pricing, market-based pricing for a host of financial products, including intermediary business, among others.

Fourth, the relationship between interest rate liberalization and capital account openness. In analyzing China's interest rate liberalization, many academics identified an open economic environment as the external condition, highlighting its coordination with capital account openness. For instance, Wang Xiaoya (2001) identified interest rate liberalization as a basic precondition for opening up the capital account through a combination of interest rate and exchange rate policies. Zhang Zongxin (2006), Wan Xieqiu and Sun Wenji (2004) also stressed the importance of interest rate liberalization reforms from similar perspectives. Yet controversies remain regarding which should be carried out first: interest rate liberalization reforms or capital account openness? A typical view put forth by the Task Force for the International Comparative Research on Interest Rate Liberalization (2002b) holds that the interest rate market must be supported by capital account control. On the contrary, the Task Force of the Survey and Statistics Department of the People's Bank of China (2012) believed that there was no clear-cut privatization between interest rate liberalization and capital account openness and rules in favor of using the latter to advance interest rate liberalization reforms.

Fifth, risks of interest rate liberalization reforms. Given the pivotal role of interest rates in the financial system, the risks of interest rate reforms have been extensively discussed in the literature. For instance, Wang Guosong (2001) identified three potential risks of interest rate liberalization from restrictive conditions, i.e., fiscal deficit, banking risks, and shrinking demand for investment and consumption. The Task Force of International Comparative Research on Interest Rate Liberalization (2002a) shared similar views but was more concerned with the risk of monetary policy incoherence under imperfect financial markets. Shao Fujun (2004) performed a more detailed analysis of the macro and micro-level risks of interest rate liberalization reforms, highlighting the potential shocks of rising interest rates to the economy. Many other studies such as Huang Jinlao (2001) and Wu Jian (2003a, b) focused on the potential risks of interest rate liberalization reforms to financial institutions, especially commercial banks, and countermeasures.

As can be learned from the above literature, Chinese scholars have discussed a broad range of issues relating to interest rate liberalization reforms extensively and insightfully and reached consensus in many areas. These studies, however, seldom touched upon the role of deposits and loans in China's financial system and the effects of and challenges to deposit and lending interest rate liberalization reforms as part of broader interest rate liberalization reforms.

1.2 Adjusting Resource Allocation in China's Financial System

Difficulties in China's deposit and lending interest rate liberalization reforms are determined by its financial system's traits. In the two-sector model of macroeconomics, the household sector is a surplus sector and the industrial sector is a deficit sector. These two sectors jointly constitute the real-economy sector. In economic operation, surplus capital flows from the household sector to the industrial sector to support wealth creation. Hence, financial activity was originally carried out between the household and industrial sectors (specifically, the household sector supplies capital, and the industrial sector receives capital). That is to say, all financial powers originally rested with the real-economy sector. Specific pathways of capital flow include: First, the household sector provides the industrial sector with equity capital through investment and provides debt capital through such means as bond purchase. Second, within the industrial sector, industrial enterprises provide each other with equity capital in the form of investment and provide debt capital through bond purchase, lending, and financial leasing. Third, the industrial sector returns part of its operating profit to the household sector in the form of dividends and interest. In the process of financial development, financial institutions were separated from the real-economy sector, becoming specialized in financial services. However, such specialization does not deprive the real-economy sector of its financial powers.

Yet in the decades-long planned economy era, capital supply in China was controlled by the government through fiscal mechanisms. As a result, capital and financial ties between the household and industrial sectors were severed, and so were direct financial ties between household and industrial sectors. Also, their financial powers were deprived. Meanwhile, the role of depository and lending financial institutions came into play: while accepting deposits of surplus funds from the household sector, they issued loans to the industrial sector. Over three decades of reform and opening up, this pattern of financial intermediation has experienced no substantial change despite China's rapid financial development, and showed three distinctive characteristics:

First, the real-economy sector (including industrial and household sectors) lacked basic financial powers. For the household sector, apart from savings, household consumption surplus capital barely had any alternative outlet for financial operation; for the industrial sector, there was little alternative access to capital other than loans from depository and lending financial institutions. Privileges of financial activity became exclusive to depository and lending financial institutions—without their approval, industrial enterprises barely had any access to capital supplied by the household sector.

Second, depository and lending financial institutions became monopolistic seller institutions embedded in the real-economy sector. While receiving capital from the household sector at very low interest rates, they issue expensive loans to the industrial sector, profiteering from a huge interest rate spread.

Third, the shift from direct finance to indirect finance. As a form of direct finance, corporate bonds link capital demand from bond-issuing companies with capital supply from bond-purchasing households. After direct ties of capital supply and demand were severed between the household sector and the industrial sector, depository and lending financial institutions became the dominant buyers of corporate bonds. The household sector deposited funds at depository and lending financial institutions, which then purchased corporate bonds with such depository funds, i.e., capital suppliers are not directly linked with capital users. Having adopted the principle of prudential operation, depository and lending financial institutions are risk-averse and much less tolerant of corporate bond risks than the masses of average people in the household sector. Such risk aversion presents significant barriers to the issuance and sales of corporate bonds from the industrial sector.

Deposits and loans make up a lion's share of all financial products in China's financial system, and depository and lending financial institutions serve as a primary channel for fund allocation in the economy. Consequently, change in the total amount of deposits and loans significantly influences asset allocation and other financial products, money supply, and monetary policy. Moreover, depository and lending financial institutions also exert a significant influence on the financial system and the economy through their business operations. In comparison, the real-economy sector and financial markets are in a weak position in allocating financial resources.

Table 1.1 displays a change in the balance of deposits and loans as a share of assets held by financial institutions in 13 years from 2001 to 2013. First, deposits still represent a key source of operating funds for financial institutions despite a falling share over the period of 13 years (from 93.54% in 2001 to 88.86% in 2013). Compared with 2001, deposits in China had increased by 6.27 times in 2013. Second, loans still represent the most important use of funds for financial institutions despite a falling share over the same 13-year period (from 73.15% in 2001 to 61.12% in 2013). Compared with 2001, loans in China had increased by 5.4 times in 2013. Third, the most important business activity of financial institutions is to accept deposits and issue loans. Changes in deposits and loans, therefore, have a direct influence on the business performance of depository and lending financial institutions and their socio-economic effects.

Since the mid-1990s, China has been calling for vigorously developing direct finance and reversing the dominance of indirect finance. As can be seen from Table 1.2, on the one hand, the balance of each non-depository and non-lending credit financial product such as Treasury bonds and central bank bonds was far smaller than "balance of deposits" or "balance of loans." The total balance of non-depository and non-lending financial products only stood at 24,900.4 billion yuan in 2013, accounting for 23.85% of "balance of deposits" and 34.63% of "balance of loans." Deposits and loans, therefore, represent an indisputably dominant share of credit financial products (such dominance could not be fundamentally reversed by annual financing from share issuance and securities investment funds), and indirect finance still holds sway. On the other hand, other credit financial products have been purchased primarily by depository and lending financial institutions with depository funds received from the real-economy sector. They are supplements to rather than replacements of deposits and loans and fall basically into the category of indirect finance. As can be learned from Tables 1.2 and 1.1, various economic entities (such as the household, industrial and government sectors) consume and operate surplus funds that mainly derive from "depository savings" and receive capital from the financial system mainly in the form of "loans." In China's financial system, deposits and loans are a key mechanism for concentrating and allocating funds while depository and lending financial institutions are the immediate entities for the concentration and allocation of funds.

The dominance of deposits and loans in China's financial system directly influences the quantity of money and monetary policy operations. As can be seen from Table 1.3, in the 12 years from 2001 to 2012, deposits accounted for more than 90% of M2, and this share tends to further increase (from 93.94% in 2001 to 94.19% in 2012); corporate demand deposits as a share of M1 experienced little change, but remained above 60%. When total deposits and corporate demand deposits made up the majorities of M2 and M1, respectively, their growth rates also determine the growth rates of M2 and M1, respectively. Since the increases and decreases of deposits are determined by the income and spending relationships of economic entities, the increase and decrease of corporate demand deposits are determined by the source of funds for real-economy enterprises and how such funds are used. Corporate demand deposits are not primarily restricted by the quantity of money issued by the central bank. In

Table 1.1 Balance of deposits and loans as a share in financial institutions' assets (Unit: 100 million yuan, %)

Year	2001	2003	2005	2007	2009	2011	2012	2013
Total source (or use) of funds	153,539.78	225,313.26	302,042.84	454,267.97	681,874.78	913,226.33	10,24,067.49	1174,666.17
Various deposits	143,617.17	208,055.59	287,169.52	389,371.15	597,741.10	809,368.33	917,554.77	1,043,846.86
Financial bonds	51.38	2226.27	5672.79	11,505.04	16,203.41	10,038.83	8487.57	6681.0
Various loans	112,314.70	158,996.23	194,690.39	261,690.88	399,684.82	547,946.69	629,909.64	718,961.46
Marketable securities and investments	23,112.65	30,259.47	34,942.13	62,789.96	86,643.15	109,304.11	133,313.92	125,399.38
Share of deposits	93.54	92.32	95.08	85.71	87.66	88.63	89.60	88.86
Share of loans	73.15	70.57	64.46	57.61	58.62	60.00	61.51	61.12

Source Renminbi Credit Incomes and Expenditures of Financial Institutions, website of the People's Bank of China

Table 1.2 Amounts of China's credit and debt financial products from 2001 to 2012 (Unit: 100 million yuan)

Year	Balance of various deposits	Balance of various loans	Balance of treasury bonds	Balance of central bank bonds	Balance of financial bonds	Balance of corporate bonds	Balance of enterprise bonds	Balance of short-term financing bonds	Balance of mid-term notes
2001	143,617.17	112,314.70	10,973.18	—	8418.63	—	336.10	—	—
2002	170,917.40	131,293.93	16,326.93	1487.50	9875.14	—	643.00	—	—
2003	208,055.59	158,996.23	21,034.60	3376.80	11,789.69	—	917.00	—	—
2004	240,525.07	177,363.49	24,176.74	11,707.94	14,507.97	—	1232.50	—	—
2005	287,169.52	194,690.39	26,702.57	22,627.84	19,686.44	—	1801.50	1380.50	—
2006	335,434.10	225,285.28	29,048.17	32,299.65	25,387.92	—	2831.50	2667.10	—
2007	389,371.15	261,690.88	46,502.61	36,586.95	32,269.75	52	4422.10	3203.10	—
2008	466,203.32	303,394.64	48,753.36	48,120.95	40,968.34	400	6803.45	4203.10	1672.00
2009	597,741.10	399,684.82	55,411.38	42,326.11	50,952.26	1038.4	10,970.67	4561.05	8634.65
2010	718,237.93	479,195.55	62,628.29	40,908.83	59,355.94	1641.4	14,511.10	6530.35	13,591.12
2011	817,651.51	547,946.69	73,839.07	21,289.72	76,652.55	2896.6	16,799.49	5023.50	19,742.70
2012	943,943.14	629,909.64	80,735.93	13,439.72	95,197.93	5491.4	23,012.23	—	24,922.00
2013	1,043,846.86	718,961.46	91,780.65	5521.72	88,719.58	13,300.00	23,358.65		26,323.40

Notes Treasury bonds include book-entry Treasury bonds and (electronic) savings bonds; financial bonds include policy bank bonds, government-backed institutional bonds, commercial bank bonds, and bonds of non-banking financial institutions; corporate bonds include central SOE bonds, local enterprise bonds, and collective bonds

Source Data about various deposit and loan balances is from the PBoC's website; data about treasury bonds, central bank notes, financial bonds, and corporate bonds is from the ChinaBond website; corporate bond data is from Wind information the currency structure primarily consisted of various deposits, it becomes difficult for the central bank to use monetary policy instruments to influence the increase or decrease in the quantities of such deposits (Wang Guogang, 2011, 2012).

In economic operation, the growth rate of total investment in fixed assets has direct and increasingly strong effects on GDP growth. In 13 years from 2000 to 2012, China's final consumption rate dropped from 62.3% to 49.5%, and the capital formation rate rose from 35.3% to 47.8%.[5] Table 1.4 lists the source of funds for total investment in fixed assets in 13 years from 2000 to 2012, from which it can be learned that since 2003, the amounts of funds under the three accounts of "domestic loans", "self-raised funds" and "other funds" accounted for over 90% of total investment in fixed assets and tended to keep increasing (up from 88.51% in 2000 to 94.28% in 2012).

Without a doubt, some of "self-raised funds" and "other funds" are the self-owned funds of investment entities (for instance, a real-economy enterprise invests some of its operating profit, and urban and rural residents invest in business undertakings or housing). Judging by annual profits of real-economy enterprises and the amount of personal investments by urban and rural residents, however, most funds under these two accounts still derived from loans from depository and lending financial institutions in various ways. For instance, in the eight years from 2005 to 2012, the total profits of large industrial enterprises in China stood at 1480.254 billion yuan, 1950.444 billion yuan, 2715.518 billion yuan, 3056.237 billion yuan, 3454.222 billion yuan, 5304.966 billion yuan, 6139.6 billion yuan, and 6191 billion yuan, respectively. Rural household fixed asset investment and investment in housing construction amounted to 394.06 billion yuan, 443.62 billion yuan, 512.33 billion yuan, 595.18 billion yuan, 743.45 billion yuan, 788.6 billion yuan, 908.91 billion yuan, and 984.06 billion yuan. During the same period, however, the combined amount of "self-raised funds" and "other funds" reached 7013.875 billion yuan, 8946.02 billion yuan, 11,676.967 billion yuan, 14,320.487 billion yuan, 19,361.742 billion yuan, 22,404.202 billion yuan, 27,973.438 billion yuan, and 33,465.471 billion yuan, respectively, far eclipsing the total profits of industrial enterprises and the total fixed asset investments of rural households. Hence, the status of lending by depository and lending financial institutions is the key determinant of total investment in fixed assets and GDP growth rate.

The Third Plenary Session of the 18th CPC Central Committee called for giving play to the decisive role of the market in allocating resources. As can be learned from the dominance of savings and loans, depository and lending financial institutions play a decisive role in resource allocation under China's financial system. Thus, the following question can be raised: is the allocation of financial resources determined by depository and lending financial institutions or financial markets during China's establishment of a market economic system? Price is a basic mechanism of resource allocation. Deposit and lending interest rate liberalization reforms not only require a shift from administrative control to market-based interest rates but also entail an adjustment of non-market-based financial systems. In China, most financial resources

[5] China Statistical Yearbook (2013).

Table 1.3 Balance of savings and comparison with M2 and M1 (Unit: 100 million yuan, %)

Year	M2	Various deposits	Various deposits/M2	Growth rate of M 2	Growth rate of various deposits	M 1	Corporate demand deposits	Corporate demand deposits/M1	Growth rate of M 1	Growth rate of corporate demand deposits
2001	152,888.50	143,617.17	93.94	19.98	16.0	59,871.59	37,366.49	62.41	19.86	13.81
2002	183,246.94	170,917.40	93.27	19.86	19.01	70,882.19	45,352.99	63.98	18.39	21.14
2003	214,358.84	208,055.59	97.06	16.98	21.73	80,815.22	53,585.88	66.31	14.01	18.15
2004	250,802.79	240,525.07	95.90	17.0	15.61	95,971.01	61,833.98	64.43	18.75	15.39
2005	296,040.13	287,169.52	97.0	18.04	19.39	107,279.91	66,222.96	61.73	11.78	7.10
2006	345,577.91	335,434.10	97.06	16.73	16.81	126,028.05	77,744.82	61.69	17.48	17.40
2007	403,401.30	389,371.15	96.52	16.73	16.08	152,519.17	95,500.88	62.62	21.02	22.84
2008	475,166.60	466,203.32	98.11	17.79	19.73	166,217.13	101,790.78	61.24	8.98	6.59
2009	610,224.52	597,741.10	97.95	28.42	28.22	221,445.81	139,997.29	63.22	33.23	37.53
2010	725,851.79	718,237.93	98.95	18.95	20.16	266,621.54	164,536.07	61.71	20.40	17.53
2011	851,590.90	809,368.33	95.04	17.32	13.84	289,847.70	191,968.20	66.23	8.71	16.67
2012	974,148.80	917,554.77	94.19	14.39	15.45	308,664.23	203,448.39	65.91	6.49	5.98
2013	1,106,524.98	1,043,846.86	94.34	13.59	10.58	337,291.05	216,591.39	64.22	9.27	6.46

Source PBoC's website: Data on "corporate demand deposits" in 2001 and 2002 is from *China Financial Statistics (1949–2005)*

Table 1.4 Composition of funding sources for total investment in fixed assets (Unit: 100 million yuan, %)

Year	(1) Total amount of invest-ment funds	(2) National budgetary investment	(3) Domestic loans	(4) Use of foreign capital	(5) Self-raised funds	(6) Other funds	[(3) + (5) + (6)]/ (1)
2000	33,110.3	2109.5	6727.3	1696.31	16,317.3	6260.1	88.51
2001	37,987.0	2546.4	7239.8	1730.7	18,914.0	7556.1	88.74
2002	45,046.9	3161.0	8859.1	2085.0	22,816.7	8125.2	88.36
2003	58,616.3	2687.8	12,044.4	2599.4	31,449.8	9834.9	90.98
2004	74,564.88	3254.91	13,788.00	3285.70	41,272.59	12,963.7	91.23
2005	94,590.84	4154.29	16,319.01	3978.80	55,105.78	15,032.97	91.40
2006	118,956.99	4672.00	19,590.47	4334.32	71,076.45	19,283.75	92.43
2007	150,803.61	5857.06	23,044.20	5132.69	91,373.23	25,396.44	92.71
2008	182,915.29	7954.75	26,443.74	5311.94	118,510.45	24,694.42	92.75
2009	250,229.71	12,685.73	39,302.82	4623.73	153,514.80	40,102.62	93.08
2010	285,779.24	13,012.75	44,020.83	4703.64	178,744.34	45,297.68	93.80
2011	345,984.17	14,843.29	46,344.51	5061.99	229,346.84	50,387.54	94.24
2012	409,675.65	18,958.66	51,593.50	4468.78	277,792.36	56,862.35	94.28

Source Website of the National Bureau of Statistics (NBS)

are allocated by depository and lending financial institutions, from which such allocation should be diversified away. Households and enterprises should redeem their financial powers. Financial markets should be allowed to form interest rates for credit financial products. With broad implications for the real economy and financial sectors, these transformations will set off chain reactions and real changes in the above-mentioned conditions. Hence, deposit and lending interest rate liberalization reforms are a decisively important battle.

1.3 Difficulties in Deposit and Lending Interest Rate Liberalization Reforms

In 1992, China took the step towards establishing a new market-based economic system. In this context, it launched interest rate liberalization reforms, but the liberalization of deposit and lending interest rates as the backbone of China's interest rate system has stalled. The reasons are twofold: first, given its broad implications for the economy as a whole, the reform of deposit and lending interest rates must be carried out cautiously. Second, various prerequisites for liberalizing deposit and lending interest rates are not in place.[6] The lack of such prerequisites poses another challenge to deposit and lending interest rate liberalization reforms.

First, interest rate liberalization will sharply reduce the Central Bank's ability to regulate money supply and financial intermediation through the use of assets. When deposit and lending interest rates are determined by market mechanisms, the Central Bank should cease to use administrative mechanisms to directly regulate deposit and loan benchmark rates and the amount of newly issued loans. However, in the interest of stable financial and economic operations, deposit and loan rates should not be formed in a "completely laissez-faire" financial market. The key to solving this dilemma is that the Central Bank should have sufficient assets at its disposal and use such assets to influence the amount of funds available to depository and lending financial institutions and the price tendencies of various financial products. In this manner, these assets can be used to effectively influence interest rates in deposit and loan markets with broader effects on the economy to achieve expected monetary policy targets.

As can be seen from data inTable 1.5,[7] foreign exchange reserves have accounted for a significant share of the Central Bank's assets. In 11 years from 2003 to 2013, the Central Bank's total assets increased by 4.12 times. In the same period, China's "foreign exchange reserves" increased by 7.86 times. As a result, "foreign exchange reserves" as a share of the Central Bank's assets soared from 48.12% to 83.29%. The implication is that most of the Central Bank's assets are used for overseas allocations while less than 17% of the assets can be used for domestic allocations in China (as "foreign exchange reserves" assets continue to increase, the percentage of the Central Bank's assets that can be used for domestic allocation in China continues to shrink).

Second, "claims against other depository corporations", "other claims against financial corporations" and "claims against non-financial corporations" increased by rather small margins from 1944.541 billion yuan to 2208.025 billion yuan in 11 years from 2003 to 2013. As can be seen from Table 1.1, financial institutions saw their receipt of Renminbi funds increase from 15,353.978 billion yuan to 117,466.617 billion yuan (up 6.65 times) and the balance of various deposits rise from 14,361.717 billion yuan to 104,384.686 billion yuan (up 6.27 times) from 2001 to 2013, but the Central Bank's claims against these financial institutions only rose by 263.524 billion yuan. That is to say, the Central Bank is severely short of assets for domestic economic regulation, and accordingly, has lost much of its regulatory capacity over depository and lending financial institutions.

Lastly, "other assets" are funds directly available to the Central Bank. The amount of "other assets" rose from 2003 to 2005, but started to shrink thereafter, down from 1145.957 billion yuan in 2005 to 765.204 billion yuan in 2013. Their share in the Central Bank's total assets dropped from 10.30% in 2002 to 2.41% in 2013. Their proportion to the receipt of funds by these financial institutions dwindled from 3.78%

---

[6] The view that conditions for China's deposit and lending interest rate liberalization reforms are ready is questionable. See Yu Xuejun (2011), David Daokui Li (2012).

[7] Regarding the analysis of the Central Bank's balance sheet, please refer to Wang Guogang's (2010).

Table 1.5 Asset structure of the People's Bank of China (PBoC) (2001–2013) (Unit: 100 million yuan)

Year	2001	2003	2005	2007	2009	2011	2012	2013
Foreign assets	19,860.40	31,141.85	63,339.16	124,825.18	185,333.00	237,898.06	241,416.90	272,233.53
Foreign exchange	18,850.19	29,841.80	62,139.96	115,168.71	175,154.59	232,388.73	236,669.93	264,270.04
Monetary gold	256.00	337.24	337.24	337.24	669.84	669.84	669.84	669.84
Other foreign assets	754.21	962.81	861.96	9319.23	9508.57	4839.49	4077.13	7293.66
Claims against government	2821.33	2901.02	2892.43	16,317.71	15,661.97	15,399.73	15,313.69	15,312.73
Claims against other depository corporations	11,311.60	11,982.81	12,692.01	7862.80	7161.92	10,247.54	16,701.08	13,147.90
Claims against other financial corporations	8547.31	7255.95	13,226.11	12,972.34	11,530.15	10,643.97	10,038.62	8907.36
Claims against other non-financial corporations	—	206.25	66.73	63.59	43.96	24.99	24.99	24.99
Other assets	—	8516.19	11,459.57	7098.18	7804.03	6763.31	11,041.91	7652.04
Total assets	—	62,004.06	103,676.01	169,139.80	227,535.02	280,977.60	294,537.19	317,278.55

Source PBoC website. Where, "claims against other depository corporations" from 2003 to 2005 is the sum of "claims against depository banks" and "claims against specific depository institutions."

in 2003 to 0.65% in 2013. With assets at its disposal, the Central Bank has little real influence apart from fine-tuning depository and lending financial institutions' liquidity via open-market operations.

Regarding the use of monetary policy instruments, there is the following statement: "Money supply can be tightened by raising interest rates and relaxed by reducing interest rate." In practice, this statement means that the central bank may tighten the money supply to financial institutions and financial markets by raising central bank interest rates, and vice versa. Here, "money supply" refers to the central bank's issuance of money to depository and lending financial institutions and financial markets via such conduits as relending, rediscounting, or purchase of bonds. A basic precondition for the central bank's interest rates to exert guidance effects and influence the quantity of money in the financial system is that the central bank must have sufficient assets available for supporting regulation.

As can be seen from a comparison between Tables 1.1 and 1.5, however, the Central Bank (PBoC) was in severe shortage of such assets. With insufficient assets available for regulation, the Central Bank still had to operate without weakening its regulatory functions. In its monetary policy regulation after 2004, the Central Bank could only resort to such policy measures as the statutory reserve ratio, benchmark deposit and lending interest rates, administrative regulation over the amount of new loan issuance, among others. Funds obtained from raising the statutory reserve ratio were used to purchase foreign exchange and thus flowed back to depository and lending financial institutions. Although this approach may avoid inflation stemming from the massive issuance of Renminbi for the purchase of foreign exchange, it does little to increase financial resources available to the Central Bank for regulating those financial institutions. Despite the policy intention to "raise interest rates and tighten money supply", raising deposit and lending interest rates does not apply to the central bank interest rates and assets. Instead of creating a tightening effect, therefore, it increased the amount of lending and hardly achieved the Central Bank's regulatory targets. Due to the ineffectiveness of these policy instruments in achieving regulatory targets, the Central Bank could only resort to administrative control over the amount of newly issued loans instead of monetary policy maneuvers to regulate the amount of funds and loan growth rate in economic and financial operations.

Hence, the Central Bank is faced with a dilemma: On the one hand, in the context of deposit and lending interest rate liberalization reforms, the Central Bank would go against the principle of market-based deposit and lending interest rates if it continues to use administrative mechanisms to directly determine benchmark deposit and lending interest rates for depository and lending financial institutions and regulate the amount of their newly issued loans. On the other hand, without sufficient assets available for regulatory maneuvers, the Central Bank is not in a good position to regulate money supply through the use of the central bank interest rates, which is likely to cause market-based deposit and lending interest rates and other interest rates to lose control, causing serious uncertainties and instabilities to economic and financial operations. With insufficient assets available to the Central Bank for monetary policy regulation, deposit and lending interest rate liberalization would be an elusive goal.

Furthermore, market conditions cannot be effectively formed for the hard constraint of depository and lending financial institutions. Since depository and lending financial institutions have been corporatized and many of them have become listed companies, it appears that their financial hard constraint has already come into shape. Yet financial hard constraint is not just a question of profits and losses; it is subject to the business and profit models of these financial institutions. As can be seen from Table 1.1, deposits made up a lion's share of funds for deposit and loan financial institutions, which use funds primarily by issuing loans and wield a dominant market position with a seller's monopoly. That is to say, there is little for them to worry about their financial performance as long as they accept deposits and issue loans as much as possible.

First, in the depository market, depository and lending financial institutions sell certificates of deposit (CD), which are purchased by urban and rural households and real-economy enterprises. Since households and real-economy enterprises lack the basic powers of financial operation, depository and lending financial institutions are at a dominant position with a seller's monopoly. In Table 1.6, the Central Bank cut deposit interest rates for two consecutive times in June and July 2012, with one-year benchmark deposit interest rate down from 3.5% to 3%, but in the same year, urban and rural households saw their savings deposits increase by a record high of 5591.515 billion yuan. These savings deposits, often referred to as "mandatory savings", "passive savings" or "guaranteed savings", reflect a monopolistic advantage of depository and lending financial institutions in the depository and lending markets. Meanwhile, the "balance of various savings deposits" rose from 80.94 trillion yuan at the end of 2011 to 104.38 trillion yuan at the end of 2013, which reflects depository and lending financial institutions' monopolistic seller advantage in the overall depository market.

Second, in the lending market, depository and lending financial institutions sell certificates of loan, which are purchased by real-economy enterprises. In this market, depository and lending financial institutions are also at a dominant position of seller's monopoly. If government bonds (including treasury bonds, central bank bonds, etc.) are excluded from the credit and debt financial products as shown in Table 1.2, the balance of loans from the depository and lending financial institutions would account for a staggering 82.58% of total credit financial products to the industrial and household sectors by the end of 2013. Hence, loans have become a primary source of operating funds for real-economy enterprises. Under such conditions, the availability of loans matters more than loan interest rates for real-economy enterprises. As long as loan interest rates are still affordable (for instance, the profit margin is above loan interest rate), there will not be a sharp decrease in firms' demand for loans even if loan interest rates are raised (e.g., by one or two percentage points). When the money supply is tight, enterprises may continue to borrow and stay in business even if loan interest rates are higher than the operating profit margin. From 2003 to 2007, the one-year loan interest rate was raised by 2.16 percentage points from 5.31% to 7.47%, but the balance of various loans in the same period as shown in Table 1.2 increased sharply from 15.9 trillion yuan at the end of 2003 to 26.17 trillion yuan at the end of 2007, up by 64.59%.

Table 1.6 Adjustment of depository interest rates and change in savings deposits (Unit: 100 million yuan, %)

Year	1-year deposit interest rate	1- ear loan interest rate	Demand deposit interest rate	New savings deposits	Balance of savings deposits	Balance of various deposits
1995	10.98	12.06	3.15	8143.5	29,662.25	53,882.10
1996	7.47	10.08	1.98	8858.59	38,520.84	68,595.59
1997	5.67	8.64	1.71	7758.96	46,279.80	82,392.79
1998	3.78	6.39	1.44	7127.67	53,407.47	95,697.94
1999	2.25	5.85	0.99	6214.33	59,621.8	108,778.90
2000	2.25	5.85	0.99	4710.58	64,332.38	123,804.35
2001	2.25	5.85	0.99	9430.05	73,762.43	143,617.17
2002	1.98	5.31	0.72	13,148.22	86,910.65	170,917.40
2003	1.98	5.31	0.72	16,707.00	103,617.65	208,055.59
2004	2.25	5.58	0.72	15,937.74	119,555.39	240,525.07
2005	2.25	5.58	0.72	21,495.60	141,050.99	287,169.52
2006	2.52	6.12	0.72	20,536.31	161,587.30	335,434.10
2007	4.14	7.47	0.72	10,946.89	172,534.19	389,371.15
2008	2.25	5.31	0.36	45,351.16	217,885.35	466,203.32
2009	2.25	5.31	0.36	42,886.31	260,771.66	597,741.10
2010	2.75	5.81	0.36	42,530.83	303,302.49	718,237.93
2011	3.5	6.56	0.5	40,333.40	343,635.89	809,368.33
2012	3	6	0.35	55,915.15	399,551.04	917,554.77
2013	3	6	0.35	48,050.53	447,601.57	1,043,846.86

Notes In some years, there were multiple adjustments to deposit interest rates within a year, and in this case, this table only reflects the year-end value of the deposit interest rates
Source Website of the People's Bank of China (PBoC). In this table, data of 1995 to 1998 is from *China Financial Statistics (1949–2005)*

Third, for depository and lending financial institutions whose main business is deposit and loan business, their operating income primarily derives from deposit and lending interest rate spread. Deposit and lending interest rate spread minus operating cost is their primary source of profit. Under the assumptions that (i) all the loans issued by depository and lending financial institutions are from one-year deposits, (ii) the maturity of such loans is one year, and (iii) benchmark deposit and loan rates are at the same levels compared with the end of the previous year, we may arrive at the rough estimates of the interest rate spread income of such deposits and loans from 2005 to 2013: 648.319 billion yuan, 750.2 billion yuan, 942.087 billion yuan, 1010.304 billion yuan, 1223.036 billion yuan, 1466.338 billion yuan, 1676.717 billion yuan, 1889.729 billion yuan, and 2156.884 billion yuan, respectively.

Table 1.7 Depository structure of financial institutions (Unit: 100 million yuan, %)

Year	Corporate demand deposits	Demand savings deposits	Corporate time deposits	Time savings deposits	Total	Share of demand deposits
2004	74,502.52	41,416.53	25,382.15	78,138.86	219,440.06	52.83
2005	83,146.0	48,787.45	45,224.7	92,263.54	269,421.69	48.97
2006	98,802.64	58,575.92	52,767.10	103,011.38	313,157.04	50.26
2007	91,718.37	67,461.59	62,685.53	108,287.86	330,153.35	48.21
2008	97,499.04	78,336.79	80,702.58	143,668.84	400,207.25	43.94
2009	134,747.32	100,541.28	108,837.62	160,230.38	504,356.60	46.65
2010	164,536.07	126,264.39	88,424.20	180,902.00	560,126.66	51.92
2011	191,968.20	137,576.22	104,169.11	210,469.40	644,182.93	51.16
2012	203,448.39	158,271.76	125,446.87	247,919.83	735,086.85	49.21
2013	216,591.39	178,050.21	147,524.01	283,319.79	825,485.4	47.81

Source Website of the People's Bank of China (PBoC)

Such estimates are imprecise. As can be seen from the relationship between Tables 1.1 and 1.7, the balance of time deposits for real-economy enterprises and urban and rural residents was significantly smaller than the balance of loans during the same period. The spread between benchmark interest rates for one-year loans and demand deposits was far greater than one-year deposit and lending interest rate spread. If we consider that 3 to 5-year loan interest rates were higher than 1-year loan interest rate, among other factors, the actual interest rate spread incomes of depository and lending financial institutions should be higher than the above-mentioned rough estimates. But from those estimates alone, we still get a glimpse of the operating income received by depository and lending financial institutions from the real-economy sector.[8]

With depository and lending financial institutions still at a monopolistic position, premature deposit and lending interest rate liberalization (by abolishing administrative control over deposit and loan benchmark interest rates) may result in the following consequences: First, while competing to attract savings deposits with much higher depository interest rates, depository and lending financial institutions will use their lending monopoly to crank up loan interest rates (so that interest rates are high on both deposits and loans). In this manner, these financial institutions will offset the higher cost of capital resulting from high deposit interest rates and acquire sufficient operating profits. As a result, real-economy enterprises will see a sharp decline in their profitability. This is inconsistent with the requirement to "effectively reduce the cost of financing for the real economy."[9]

[8] In 2011, China's banking sector made a profit of 1041.2 billion yuan, which sparked public outcry against "monopolistic profiteering." The banking sector's high profitability is largely due to the monopolistic position of banks.

[9] *Communiqué of the Central Economic Working Conference held in December 2012.*

Second, if loan interest rates cannot keep up with rising deposit interest rates, depository and lending financial institutions may still earn sufficient operating profits by issuing more loans (similar to "quantity to make up for lower rates" in 2009), which may result in investment overheating, inflation, and economic overheating.

Third, with the total amount of loans and loan interest rate limited by the demand of real-economy enterprises, these financial institutions may cut deposit interest rates (by "following" rather than "colluding with" others in reducing deposit interest rates), so that interest rates are low on both deposits and loans at the expense of depositors. In all these cases, there is no substantive change to depository and lending financial institutions' business model, business structure, and asset portfolio, nor is it possible for their financial hard constraint to be formed in real earnest, and real-economy enterprises and urban and rural households are still deprived of financial powers. On the other hand, once instability, inflation, overheating, or other related problems occur in the economic and social life, the depository and lending interest rate liberalization reform process will be trapped in a stalemate.

The question is whether it is sustainable for banks to rely on deposits and loans in their business model? Particularly, in the process of deposit and lending interest rate liberalization reforms, if deposit and lending interest rate spread narrows, will such a business model still support depository and lending financial institutions' development? Over the years, such doubts were raised over the operational mode of China's financial institutions. The issue, however, is not about the correctness of such doubts, but the identification of financial market conditions essential for transforming the business model of depository and lending financial institutions. Assuming that the structure of China's credit financial products is the same as in Table 1.2, it would be almost impossible for such financial institutions to shift away from deposits and loans in their business model. In the formation of market-based deposit and lending interest rates, if numerous depository and lending financial institutions are trapped into severe operational difficulties due to narrowing deposit and lending interest rate spread, not only will significant systematic risks occur and bring unexpected shocks to the financial system and even trigger a financial crisis, but competent authorities may decide to suspend deposit and lending interest rate liberalization reforms due to concerns over above-mentioned consequences, causing the reforms to be abandoned halfway and even resulting in an institutional retrogression.

Third, real-economy enterprises and urban and rural households found it is hard to form the buyer's right of choice in financial markets. Depository and lending financial institutions still hold a seller's monopoly in the deposit and loan markets, indicating that real-economy enterprises and urban and rural households as their transaction counterparties lack the most basic right of choice in financial transactions. According to the market theory in microeconomics, in a market of perfect competition, price is neither determined by one-way competition among sellers nor determined by one-way competition among buyers but determined by two-way competition between buyers and sellers.

A key difference between a buyer's market and a seller's one can be described as follows: In a buyer's market, buyers have a sufficient right of choice in transactions, which restricts the seller's market choice, and forces sellers to change their business operations according to buyers' changing requirements. In a seller's market, buyers are deprived of this basic right of choice, and may only select from a range of products offered by sellers. In the financial system, various financial products are traded based on funds and are far more complementary and substitutable than the real economy requires. In this sense, real-economy enterprises and households should have a fairly sufficient right of choice. Due to institutional constraints, market mechanisms have yet to play a fundamental role in allocating financial resources. Securities issuance—which otherwise ought to be independently decided by real-economy enterprises—is subject to complex administrative review and approval and screening by financial regulators.

Most real-economy enterprises have no alternative access to capital other than loans from depository and lending financial institutions, which means that their right of choice for financing is lost. For most urban and rural households, there is little alternative to invest their savings in financial markets other than depositing them in banks (among various securities as shown in Table 1.2, except that the "balance of Treasury bonds" includes Treasury bonds held by households, other types of securities were almost entirely held by various financial institutions, and over 70% were held by depository and lending financial institutions). As a result, households' right of choice for financial products is also deprived. Without the right of choice for financial transactions, real-economy enterprises and urban and rural households are at a disadvantaged buyer's position in financial transactions.

Market-based deposit and lending interest rate reforms need to be supported by real-economy enterprises and urban and rural households. Buyers at a disadvantaged position are unable to form effective constraints on depository and lending financial institutions, and thus become vulnerable to adverse effects. With buyers and sellers at disparate market positions, it would be challenging to form make-based deposit and lending interest rates (the result is more likely to be distorted interest rates unfavorable to real-economy enterprises and urban and rural households).

Notably, for urban and rural households in China, deposit interest rates are more or less a matter of public welfare. Amid rising CPI over the years, the government has called for "positive deposit interest rates", reinforcing the public welfare attribute of deposit interest rates. In this context, if zero interest rate on demand deposits (in some instances, a management fee would have to be collected from depositors) as a common practice outside China is implemented during deposit interest rate liberalization, urban and rural households in China would feel betrayed (and possibly protest vehemently) and may trigger a backlash that destabilizes financial operations. The interest rate on demand deposits is the benchmark of various deposit interest rates, and once cut to zero, will trigger a dip in other deposit interest rates. This will affect depositors' interests more broadly.

Market-based reforms of deposit and lending interest rates will regulate the prices of dominant financial products in China's financial system. Not only will such reforms cause financial products to be repositioned and re-priced amid buyer–seller competition and financial systems to be re-engineered, but the relationship of economic entities involved in financial activities will undergo profound changes as well. Before the above-mentioned problems are resolved, "liberalization" may hardly achieve its intended goals. Market-based reforms of deposit and lending interest rates should, therefore, be a process of gradual "adjustment" to create conditions for further reforms.

1.4 Choice of Pathways for Deposit and Lending Interest Rate Liberalization Reforms

In the deposit and lending interest rate liberalization reforms after 2012, the Central Bank took the following reform initiatives: First, on June 8 and July 6, 2012, the Central Bank adjusted the lower limit on loan interest rates for financial institutions to 0.7 times the benchmark interest rate and the upper limit on deposit interest rates to 1.1 times the benchmark interest rate, which marks the first step to change the benchmark deposit and lending interest rate limits that had been in place since October 29, 2004. Given this progress, some argued that China had taken substantive steps in liberalizing deposit and lending interest rates, and that with a broadening band of benchmark deposit and loan rates, interest rate liberalization reforms would be close to completion.

Second, in its *Circular on Further Advancing Interest Rate Liberalization Reforms* ("*Circular*") released on July 20, 2013, the Central Bank removed the 0.7 times lower limit on loan rates for financial institutions, waived control over bill discount interest rates, and canceled the 2.3 times upper limit on loan rates for rural credit unions. Some hailed this circular as a milestone in deposit and lending interest rate liberalization reforms: over 90% of deposit and loan rates were liberalized, and as long as further steps were taken to relax the upper limit on deposit rates, China's deposit and lending interest rate liberalization reforms would be complete.

Third, the Central Bank announced the launch of the Loan Prime Rate (LPR) on October 25, 2013. The LPR was applauded by some as a sign that China's loan interest rate liberalization was accomplished. Without doubt, an increase in the floating band of deposit and loan benchmark interest rates makes those interest rates more resilient, and reinforces the pressure of change in deposit and loan rates on the business activities of depository and lending financial institutions, forcing them to closely follow supply and demand of deposits and loans. Yet deposit and lending interest rate adjustments based on administrative mechanisms are insufficient for liberalizing deposit and lending interest rates for the following reasons:

First, regarding the Central Bank's deregulation of the lower limit on loan interest rates on July 20, 2013, on the one hand, this initiative took effect de facto as of July 6, 2012. The intrinsic mechanism can be explained as follows: by the 3% benchmark rate for one-year deposits with a markup of up to 0.3 percentage points and the 6% benchmark interest rate for one-year loans with a markdown of up to 1.8 percentage points, the upper limit on one-year deposit rate would be 3.3%, and the lower limit for one-year loan rate would be 4.2%. In this manner, there is a mere 0.9 percentage points of deposit and loan rate spread while the cost of deposit and loan business was about

0.9 percentage points for state-controlled commercial banks such as the Industrial and Commercial Bank of China (ICBC), the Agricultural Bank of China (ABC), the Bank of China (BOC), and China Construction Bank (CCB). For small and medium-sized depository and lending financial institutions such as joint-stock commercial banks and city commercial banks, their business cost is above 0.9 percentage points without exception. Hence, almost no depository and lending financial institutions would issue loans at the lower limit of the benchmark loan interest rate. From this perspective, the Central Bank's relaxation of the lower limit of loan interest rates was of no substantive significance other than formalizing an operational practice that barely existed in reality.

On the other hand, the Central Bank did not abolish regulation over *benchmark* loan rates. As can be seen from the wording in the *Circular*, there is a noticeable difference between "relax" and "abolish". "Relax" is expediency. For instance, policymakers may decide to relax one specific matter while tightening another at one point in time and doing the opposite at a later stage (to either increase the net interest spread between deposits and loans or narrow it), and the decision to make such a change is highly subjective and rife with administrative uncertainties. "Abolish" means that the Central Bank will no longer possess and use a certain administrative power. The *Circular* made no mention of "abolishing" administrative control over benchmark loan rates, but stressed that "(the Central Bank) avoids adjusting the floating band of personal housing loan rate, maintains the previous floating band, and continues to enforce a differentiated housing credit policy." In this sense, policy relaxation was predicated upon weakening administrative regulation over loan rates.

Notably, the Central Bank also has the power to regulate the amount of newly issued loans each year in addition to its power to regulate the benchmark deposit and loan rates. As long as the amount of newly issued loans is still regulated under administrative mechanisms, the amount of loans will be a scarce resource, and loan price tends to go upward (above benchmark loan rate). Under such conditions, it would be unrealistic to expect the goal of liberalization to be achieved by relaxing the lower limit of loan interest rates.

Second, deposit and lending interest rates as capital prices should be formed through two-way competition between buyers and sellers. However, the three initiatives introduced in 2012 are focused on the seller side (i.e., depository and lending financial institutions) and of little real significance to increasing competitiveness (i.e., against depository and lending financial institutions) on the buyer side (i.e., real-economy enterprises and urban and rural households, the same below). Should deposit and lending interest rate liberalization reforms stay at this level, it would be impossible to achieve market-based deposit and lending interest rates and transform the financial system and financial resource allocation.

Third, in a mature market economy, benchmark interest rates refer to risk-free and arbitrage-free interest rates in financial markets and are formed in financial transactions according to the nature, maturities, risks and conditions of various financial products. Deposits and loans are not risk-free and arbitrage-free financial products, and therefore should not be subject to benchmark rates. In China, benchmark deposit and loan rates evolved from statutory deposit and loan rates that had existed before

2004. Despite a different name and a broader floating band of deposit and loan rates over the past decade, this policy instrument is still used by the government to price the major products of depository and lending financial institutions via administrative mandate. In a mature market economy, deposit and loan rates, tendencies, and even the amount of deposits and loans are strictly limited by interest rates and trading of various other credit and debt products in financial markets. Yet in China, it is the other way around: the interest rates and tendencies of other credit and debt products are determined by benchmark deposit and loan rates. This highlights the fundamental role of deposit and loan rates and a lack of various other credit and debt products competing with deposits and loans.

At a deeper level, real-economy enterprises and households are not competing against depository and lending financial institutions as much as they should by trading financial products. Under such conditions, no matter what it does to relax upper and lower limits on deposits and loans via administrative mechanisms, the Central Bank is unable to create financial market conditions in favor of buyer's competitiveness and form market-based interest rates.

In China, two pathways can be followed in liberalizing deposit and loan rates. One is the "regulatory approach", i.e., the use of administrative mechanisms by the Central Bank to directly adjust the Renminbi deposit and loan rates (including interest rates and floating band, etc.) of depository and lending financial institutions. The other approach is the "market-based approach", i.e., to develop alternative products such as corporate bonds, asset securitization securities, and wealth management products and use the institutional forces of financial markets to externally drive deposit and loan rate liberalization. The market-based approach requires financial institutions to transform their business model and offer innovative financial products and financial markets to keep up with those changes. China has followed the regulatory approach in liberalizing interest rates since 1996 and expanded the floating band for deposit and loan benchmark rates in 2013. Just as administrative diktats cannot beget a market-based mechanism, a full-fledged market-based deposit and lending interest rate system cannot be formed through interest rate adjustments under the regulatory approach.

As a key initiative of China's financial re-engineering, deposit and loan rate liberalization reforms are an integrated project aimed to achieve three correlated goals, including the market-based formation of deposit and lending interest rates, the business transition of depository and lending financial institutions, and financial market innovation and development. With the function of regulating benchmark deposit and loan rates, the Central Bank is unable to achieve these three goals with an administrative solution. Adjustment of benchmark deposit and loan rates through administrative mechanisms may increase the interest rate floating band, but does little to challenge financial institutions' monopoly in the depository and lending market, nor does it create market conditions for transform their business and profit models and adjust their asset structure; still less does it contribute to the innovation and development of financial markets.

For these reasons, deposit and lending interest rate liberalization reforms cannot be accomplished through administrative interventions. By developing alternatives to deposits and loans, the market-based approach satisfies, under consistent interest rates, both the requirement of capital suppliers (e.g., household, industrial and government sectors) for higher yields via direct finance, as well as the requirement of capital users for cheaper capital. Falling deposits from capital suppliers will reduce the share of loans in financial institutions' total assets, forcing them to transform their business structure and profit model. With increasing breadth and depth of direct finance, capital suppliers and users will both have more financial options with more bargaining powers against depository and lending financial institutions. Gradually, depository and lending financial institutions will lose their seller's monopoly, giving rise to a new pattern where sellers and buyers jointly determine deposit and loan rates and financial product structure via competition. In addition, financial market innovation and development provide external conditions for depository and lending financial institutions to transform their business and profit models, allowing them to implement the market law of "survival of the fittest" through differentiated business operations, product innovation, and service quality improvement.

In contrast, the "regulatory approach", which primarily relies on an administrative mandate, involves the coordination of multiple administrative mechanisms and interests under the separate supervision of different lines of financial business. Such red tape will add complexities and frictions to the market-based deposit and lending interest rate reforms. It may also cause the reforms to be marred by misunderstanding, policy shift, among other mishaps. The "market-based approach" is a solution to avoid administrative complexities and relies on systems and operational modes to ensure the smooth progress of the reforms.

Under the "regulatory approach", unexpected regulatory policies may cause abrupt shocks to market participants, which does little to iron out—and may even stir up—fluctuations in those reforms. Under the "market-based approach", in contrast, the reforms will be carried out in a gradual process over time, so that each direct financial product is issued and traded without disrupting market participants. Over time, however, these transactions will transform each party's inclination, choice, and behavioral modes. With an increase in the amount, categories, and price diversity of financial products as alternatives to deposits and loans, deposit and loan assets will cease to account for a majority of assets in China's financial system, and the yield curve of debt financial products will also come into shape. Hence, the cumulative effects of this approach will make a substantive difference for the Central Bank's monetary policy choice, the operations of financial institutions and financial markets, and the interests of real-economy enterprises and urban and rural households.

1.5 Strategies for Deposit and Lending Interest Rate Liberalization Reforms

Market-based reforms of deposit and lending interest rates should follow a market approach as the basic principle. With a "market-based approach", the reforms should be carried out gradually to create conditions and form market-based deposit and loan rates. Specifically, the reforms should comprise three elements:

First, the Central Bank should improve its asset structure by adjusting the amount of its foreign exchange assets and increasing the domestic allocation of its assets, so as to enhance its capabilities of monetary policy regulation.

It is also important to change the traditional concept about the Central Bank's holdings of foreign exchange reserve assets. First of all, we should establish a correct view on national foreign exchange assets. It is a misperception that only foreign exchange assets held by the government can be deemed as owned by the State. Theoretically, a country's foreign exchange assets should consist of foreign exchange assets held by the government, industrial and household sectors. Foreign exchange assets held by the government sector are only part of a country's foreign exchange assets. The quantity and structure of foreign exchange assets should be viewed from a national perspective instead of a government sector perspective. Furthermore, not all foreign exchange assets held by the government sector are reserve assets but include foreign exchange reserve and investment. Lastly, each entity's surplus or deficiency of foreign exchange assets can be regulated via foreign exchange transactions.

Based on a correct view of foreign exchange assets, we should divide foreign exchange assets owned by the Central Bank in the name of reserve assets. Such division can be achieved by: (i) estimating the amount of foreign exchange needed for current payments, taking into account all factors. Those foreign exchange assets should be defined as reserve assets and continue to be held by the Central Bank on the "asset side" of its balance sheet; (ii) estimating the amount of government foreign exchange assets for investment, and such assets can be obtained by setting up a foreign exchange investment fund or company and purchased by the central government from the Central Bank for the purpose of exporting productive capital; (iii) abolishing the system of foreign exchange settlement and sale to encourage real-economy enterprises to "go global" and allow them to keep and use some foreign exchange assets in exporting credit capital and productive capital; (iv) granting depository and lending financial institutions more autonomy and power to possess and use foreign exchange to encourage them to make effective use of foreign exchange assets by exporting credit capital; (v) allowing households to invest in foreign exchange and to keep and invest some foreign exchange assets via financial institutions (such as in wealth management products). Without a doubt, these institutional adjustments entail reforms to the foreign exchange administration system.

By the end of 2013, the Central Bank's total assets amounted to 31,727.855 billion yuan, including "foreign exchange" worth 26,427.004 billion yuan (accounting for 83.29% of total assets). According to the estimations of six-month import volume, non-trade spending, and profit expatriation by foreign investors, together with the needs for Renminbi exchange rate regulation and risk prevention, the Central Bank should retain some 1.2 trillion US dollars' worth of those reserves (about 7.4 trillion yuan by current exchange rate) and use the remaining foreign exchange assets worth 19 trillion yuan for domestic allocation. As a result, about 70% of the Central Bank's assets will be allocated domestically, up from 14.2%, which will give the Central Bank greater ammunitions for monetary policy regulation. Admittedly, such calculation is rough and simple (with increasing trade surpluses and foreign investments, more foreign exchange funds will flow into China, which is not reflected in the above-mentioned calculation). However, it can still be learned that the reduction of "foreign exchange" as a share of the Central Bank's total assets is a gradual process and cannot be achieved overnight.

With changing asset structure comes changing liability structure of the Central Bank. As an exclusive power of central banks, money issuance is an active liability and the cheapest source of funds for central banks. Before June 2008 (on the eve of the global financial crisis), money issuance accounted for 99.28%, 66.37%, and 36.74% of the liabilities of the US Federal Reserve, the European Central Bank (ECB), and the Japanese Central Bank, respectively. At the end of 2013, however, money issuance only accounted for 20.48% of the liability structure of China's Central Bank. Since 2003, the Central Bank (PBoC) amassed most of its numerous assets by raising the statutory reserve ratio, issuing central bank bonds, among other passive liabilities. The frequent use of these instruments not only points to a reduction in the Central Bank's proactive regulation capacity with a host of adverse effects on financial operation in China but also significantly increases the Central Bank's cost of capital. With a reduction of foreign exchange assets amid the restructuring of asset structure, the Central Bank will rely more on money issuance as a source of capital, beefing up its capacity to regulate the amount of capital in financial operation through price instruments such as central bank interest rates. In this context, the effects of financial market interest rates including deposit and loan rates will be brought into play under the guidance of central bank interest rates.

Second, there should be more issuance of alternatives to deposits and loans, such as corporate bonds, to force depository and lending financial institutions to change their business structure and model via financial disintermediation and reinforce their hard budgetary constraint under the forces of financial markets.

As a financial product, corporate bonds offer a basic substitute to deposits and loans. As a basic product of direct finance, corporate bonds have the function of linking capital suppliers with capital users. From a capital supply perspective, it appears that not much less capital is converted into deposits when real-economy enterprises raise capital from corporate bonds and then deposit such funds at depository and lending financial institutions, but this process avoids an increase in derivative deposits related to loans. For depository and lending financial institutions, corporate bonds reduce their balance of deposits. From a capital demand perspective, issuing corporate bonds is a privilege for real-economy enterprises. Frequent credit policy shifts may misalign capital supply volatility with real-economy enterprises' business operations. Such a mismatch can be avoided by firms' autonomy to issue bonds.

By issuing corporate bonds, real-economy enterprises rely less on loans from depository and lending financial institutions, forcing the latter into business transition. A corporate bond interest rate is the same for capital suppliers and users. It is higher than deposit interest rates and lower than the loan interest rates and free from the deposit and lending interest rate spread arising from the intermediation of depository and lending financial institutions. For this reason, corporate bond interest rates are favorable to both capital suppliers and users. The annual interest rate of five-year corporate bonds is two percentage points higher than the one-year deposit interest rate and 1.5 to 2 percentage points below the one-year loan interest rate. Without a doubt, corporate bonds will externally restrain depository and lending financial institutions' business structure dominated by deposits and loans and serve as a powerful external market mechanism for establishing their budgetary hard constraint.

Corporate bonds' effect on the balance of deposits and loans is subject to quantitative effects. As shown in Table 1.2, despite an increase in the balance of corporate bonds including "financial bonds", "corporate bonds", "enterprise bonds", "short-term financing bonds" and "mid-term notes" between 2008 and 2013, it is still much smaller than the balance of loans worth 71,896.146 billion yuan at the end of 2013. For corporate bonds to live up to the important task of financing for real-economy enterprises, the amount of corporate bonds must be large enough compared with loans. Considering the increase of newly issued loans each year, even with a rapid increase in the issuance of various corporate bonds, which may grow faster than loans, it is unrealistic for the balance of corporate bonds to be as large as the balance of loans in a short time. That is to say, the amount (and balance) of corporate bond issuance has a gradual effect on deposit and lending interest rates. Not only does it leave room for depository and lending financial institutions to modify their business structure and transform business model, but it also creates an environment for various economic entities in the financial markets to adapt to a new market environment. Fostering the corporate bond market is a less explicit "market-based approach" of reform more welcomed by economic entities with fewer repercussions and adverse effects.

The key is to restore the direct finance attribute of the corporate bond market. In this sense, corporate bonds should be issued primarily to capital suppliers, e.g., urban and rural households and real-economy enterprises, rather than financial institutions. To this end, we must focus on five priorities: (i) We should effectively adopt relevant rules of the *Company Law* and the *Securities Law* to safeguard companies' lawful rights of bond issuance. After 1994, the corporate bond market became an important priority for China securities market development. Chapter 5 of the *Company Law* effective as of July 1, 1994 prescribes rules on the issuance of corporate bonds. It stipulates that a joint-stock company with net assets worth 30 million yuan or a limited liability company with net assets worth 60 million yuan may issue corporate bonds, and that the balance of corporate bonds may reach 40% of the issuing company's net assets. In 2005, these rules were transferred into the *Securities Law* upon the amendment of the *Company Law* and the *Securities Law*. Nearly 20 years later, however, very few corporate bonds have been issued under these rules.

(ii) The current system of bond issuance review and approval, overseen by five competent authorities, should be abolished and replaced with a registration system.[10] Meanwhile, supervision over the transaction of corporate bonds should be enhanced.

(iii) Proactive efforts must be made to create market-based corporate bond interest rates that reflect the nature of corporate bonds and the conditions of issuers. On this basis, further efforts should be made to form a yield curve based on corporate bond rates and improve market-based securities pricing.

(iv) The role of credit rating in the securities market should be brought into full play to create conditions for the issuance and the transactions of corporate bonds of various types and levels.

(v) We should also develop debt acquisition to supplement equity acquisition and diffuse risks from the non-payment of principal and interest upon maturity.

Third, we should encourage financial product innovation and create options for depository and lending financial institutions to adjust their business structure and offer sufficient financial products for real-economy enterprises and households to convert deposits into "financial investments", thus driving the deposit and lending interest rate liberalization reforms.

Depository and lending financial institutions are not intended to specialize in deposit and loan business as their main business. Over the years, the homogeneous financial business portfolio in China has sparked much public criticism and restricted competition among depository and lending financial institutions. The financial business structure must be diversified for corporate bond development to achieve expected targets and depository and lending financial institutions to complete business transition, clearing obstacles to liberalizing deposit and loan rates. Also, depository and lending financial institutions and financial markets should offer enterprises and households multitiered and diverse financial services to meet their heterogeneous investment needs and risk appetites. In this sense, the development of corporate bonds is far from sufficient. Different types of financial products—including financial portfolio products—must also be offered to all types of investors. Runaway financial innovation in the US and some other Western countries is blamed for triggering the global financial crisis in 2008. Yet in China, the problem is a dearth of financial innovation rather than a glut of it.

Financial innovation is chiefly manifested in innovative financial products. Through the recombination of the equities, maturities, yields, and transaction and management modes of original financial products, financial product innovation is

[10] Five competent authorities are in charge of the review and approval of corporate bond issuance, including the National Development and Reform Commission (NDRC) responsible for approving corporate bonds, the Central Bank responsible for approving short-term financing bonds, mid-term notes and debt financing instruments, the China Banking Regulatory Commission (CBRC) responsible for approving financial bonds and various bank bonds, the China Securities Regulatory Commission (CSRC) responsible for approving bonds and convertible bonds issued by listed companies and bonds issued by securities companies, and the China Insurance Regulatory Commission (CIRC) responsible for approving bonds issued by insurance companies. The involvement of multiple competent authorities has resulted in a fragmentation in the involvement of multiple competent authorities has resulted in a fragmentation in the corporate bond issuance market.

carried out chiefly in the following three aspects: First, securities derivatives such as convertible corporate bonds, investment fund securities, equity certificates, and asset securitization securities; second, new products linked to such financial mechanisms as trust, leasing, guarantee, and insurance; third, depository and lending derivatives.

Financial innovation is intended to meet the needs of real-economy enterprises and households to invest in financial assets under market-based mechanisms. In the process of financial product innovation, enterprises and households will turn deposits into financial investments, thus reducing demand for loans. This shift in demand will force depository and lending financial institutions to adjust their asset structure and business model via financial product innovation. Innovation and competition will expedite deposit and lending interest rate liberalization in greater depth and scope. Without financial product innovation, deposit and lending interest rate liberalization reforms are likely to cause a lose-lose result for all and therefore enter a stalemate while effective financial product innovation will lead to a win–win result for all.

From a broader perspective, deposit and lending interest rate liberalization is linked with the creation of a deposit insurance system, exchange rate formation mechanism reform, and capital account openness as three equal priorities. In China's financial reforms, these priorities reinforce each other and should be carried out gradually and at the same time. In this sense, financial innovations are essential for China to create a deposit insurance system, improve the exchange rate formation mechanism, and further open up its capital account.

References

China Statistical Yearbook (2013), China Statistical Publishing House, 2014.

Dai Genyou: "Research Outline of Key Issues Related to China's Financial Reform and Development," *Journal of Financial Research*, Vol.9, 2001.

Fang Xianming, Sun Xuan, Xiong Peng, Zhang Yigao: "Empirical Study on the Effectiveness of China's Monetary Policy Interest Rate Transmission Mechanism, *Modern Economic Science*, Vol.4, 2005.

Huang Jinlao: "Interest Rate Liberalization and Risk Control for Commercial Banks, *Economic Research Journal*, Vol.1, 2001.

Hicks, John. R.: *Value and Capital*, The Commercial Press, 1995.

Keynes, J. M.: *The General Theory of Employment, Interest, and Money*, The Commercial Press, 1993.

Li Yang: "Interest Rate Liberalization in China: What Has Been Accomplished and What is Yet to Come, *Studies of International Finance*, Vol.9, 2003.

McKinnon, R. I.: Money and Capital in Economic Development, Shanghai Sanlian Bookstore, 1998.

Qian Xiao'an: "Motivations, Constraints and Steps of Interest Rate Liberalization under Open Financial Conditions", *The Journal of World Economy*, Vol.3, 2003.

Research Group of the Financial Survey and Statistics Department, the People's Bank of China: "Coordinated Implementation of Interest Rate and Exchange Rate Reforms and Capital Account Openness", *China Finance*, Vol.9, 2012.

Shao Fujun: "Interest Rate Liberalization and Risk Control for Commercial Banks, *Journal of Financial Research*, Vol.6, 2004.

Shaw, Edward S.: *Financial Deepening in Economic Development* (Translated Chinese Version), Shanghai Sanlian Bookstore, 1998.
Sheng Songcheng, Wu Peixin: "Dual Transmission Mechanism of China's Monetary Policy: Study on the 'Two Intermediate Goals, Two Regulatory Objects', *Economic Research Journal*, Vol.10, 2008.
Sheng Zhaohui: "Analysis of China's Monetary Policy Transmission's Channel Effects: 1994–2004, *Journal of Financial Research*, Vol.7, 2006.
Stiglitz, Joseph: "Imperfect Market and New Keynesian Economics", *Stiglitz Economics Papers*, Vol.4, China Financial Publishing House, 2007.
Task Force of International Comparative Research on Interest Rate Liberalization: "International Experiences and Lessons of Interest Rate Liberalization, *China Finance*, Vol.3, 2002a.
Task Force of International Comparative Research on Interest Rate Liberalization: "International Experiences and Lessons of Interest Rate Liberalization, *China Finance*, Vol.4, 2002b.
Wan Xieqiu, Sun Wenji: "Necessity and Institutional Analysis of Interest Rate Liberalization under Open Economy", *The Journal of World Economy*, Vol.4, 2004.
Wang Guogang: "A Brief Discussion of the Relationship among Money, Finance and Capital", *Chinese Review of Financial Studies*, Vol.2, 2011.
Wang Guogang: "Analysis of the Central Bank's Balance-Sheet-based Regulatory Capabilities", *Chinese Review of Financial Studies*, Vol.1, 2010.
Wang Guogang: "Operational Mechanism of China's Monetary Policy Regulation Instruments: 2001–2010", *Social Sciences in China*, Vol.4, 2012.
Wang Guosong: "Interest Rate Regulation and Liberalization in China", *Economic Research Journal*, Vol.6, 2001.
Wang Xiaoya: "China's Capital Account Openness and Interest Rate/Exchange Rate Policy Coordination," *Journal of Financial Research*, Vol.1, 2001.
Wang Zhao: "A Discussion on China's Monetary Policy Interest Rate Transmission Mechanism," *Economic Science*, Vol.5, 2001.
Wu Jian: "Interest Rate Risk Management in Interest Rate Liberalization in China", *Finance & Economics,* Vol.2, 2003.
Xu Jian: "Interest Rate Liberalization: Constraints and Practice", *Journal of Financial Research,* Vol.8, 2003.
Yu Xuejun: "Conditions Are Ready for Interest Rate Liberalization Reforms", *Financial Times,* November 7, 2011.
Zhang Zongxin: "Analysis of Interest Rate and Exchange Rate Reforms under Open Financial Conditions", *Studies of International Finance*, Vol.9, 2006.
Zhou Xiaochuan: "Reflections on China's Interest Rate Liberalization Reforms", *West China Finance*, Vol.2, 2011.

Chapter 2
Deposit and Lending Rates: Significance and Impacts of their Liberalization

The last step in interest rate liberation in China is the liberalization of deposit and lending rates. An analysis of the impact of deposit and lending rates liberalization presupposes an adequate understanding of the financial system as a whole: how it is set up, what problems it faces, and its development outlook. A study on these issues will shed light on the reasons for, goals of and how to achieve interest rate liberalization in China.

2.1 An Overview of the Chinese Financial System

Since the founding of the People's Republic of China in 1949, evolution of the country's financial system has undergone three major stages: high degree of centralization under a planned economy from 1949 to 1978; dominance of state-owned banks from 1979 to 1993; and dominance by the banking industry from 1994 onward.

Rapid economic development in China since the policy of reform and opening up was adopted has been accompanied by notable structural changes in the country's financial institutions, financial instruments and financial market. Financial institutions, which had been operating under a highly centralized system, were the first to diversify. The separation between policy-setting financial institutions and commercial ones has become increasingly clear. While many different types of financial institutions continue to coexist, commercial banks are still predominant among them.

Subsequently, a more diversified financial system took shape in response to the needs of the market economy. This system, with the People's Bank of China at the core, is made up mostly of banks, and also includes securities agencies and insurance companies. Greater diversity in financial institutions has fueled innovation in financial instruments and financing methods. Multiple types of credit are already available in China, and the variety of direct investment tools is expected to increase.

G. Wang, *A Study on Interest Rate Liberalization in China*, Research Series on the Chinese Dream and China's Development Path,
https://doi.org/10.1007/978-981-97-3644-7_2

Most notably, stocks have become the most important financial instrument in China's financial market.

Of course, as we continue to push financial reform forward and keep the country's financial market open to the rest of the world, the importance of innovation also becomes increasingly evident. Banks, the stock market and insurance companies are always introducing new products and services, offering consumers a vast array of options to choose from.

Since the policy of reform and opening up was adopted, China has literally built its financial market from scratch. In addition to the establishment of a diversified financial system, this period has also seen structural improvement of the financial market through the development of segments of the markets for currency, capital, foreign exchange and gold. While this evolution process is by no means unique on the whole, there are aspects to it that are distinctly Chinese. The most notable of them is the leadership role the government has played and continues to play in this process, which for that reason strongly reflects the country's unique economic system and environment.

Moreover, an overview of the way China's financial structure has evolved shows a persistent tendency to prioritize the growth and expansion of the total volume over structural optimization, which is often altogether overlooked. This has prevented the potential of the function of those financial instruments in China's economic tool box from being fully unleashed to serve the needs of a rapidly growing economy. Moreover, the development and reform of China's financial structure has mostly been superficial, barely ever touching its substratum. Despite increasing structural diversity on many dimensions, it leaves much to be desired in terms of functionality and efficiency. Further studies on the adjustment and optimization of China's financial structure are in order.

2.1.1 An Analytical Overview of China's Financial System

Since the policy of reform and opening up was adopted, the rapid development of economy has brought about the continuous expansion of trading volume in China. This chapter analyzes the developmental trend marked by the 2001–2013 annual volumes derived from their corresponding year's data, including the money supply and the balances of deposits and loans.

2.1.1.1 Changes and Trend of Money Supply in China

Money supply is an important financial indicator that reflects the operation of a country's macro-economy. It not only serves as an important reference for the central bank to formulate and implement monetary policy, but also reflects the supply and demand of social funds under certain economic conditions. Highlighted here are the analyses on the trends and the current situation of the three classifications of money

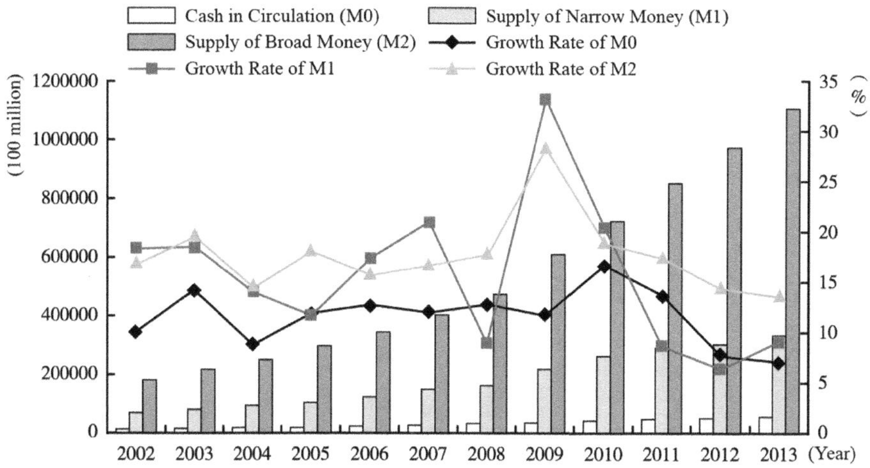

Fig. 2.1 2002–2013 growth rate of money supply in China (*Source* Wind Info)

supply, M0, M1 and M2. Figure 2.1 shows the changes in the amount of money supply and the corresponding annual growth rate for the three classifications from 2002 to 2013 in China.

A significant increase in money supply in all classifications during this period is notable, which is consistent with the rising trend of total economy in China, as the money supply required for economic growth continues to expand thus drives the overall increase of money supply. At the same time, we can see that the fluctuations of the year-on-year growth rate of money supply in different classifications are different in the same time period. In terms of the growth rate, the fluctuation of M0 is obviously smaller than that of M1 and M2; the fluctuation of M2 comes in between that of M0 and M1. However, M0, M1, M2 display sharp fluctuations between 2007 and 2010, for which the reason is that the financial crisis starting in 2007 affected the stability of money supply in China. As the central bank took a rigorous monetary policy in response to the crisis, the result was the intensified fluctuation in the money supply.

2.1.1.2 Changes and Trend of Deposits and Loans Offered by the Financial Institutions in China

Figure 2.2 shows the changes of amount and corresponding annual growth rates of deposits and loans of financial institutions from 2002 to 2013. The analysis suggests that the total amounts of deposits and loans associated with financial institutions are on the rise in China. In terms of the growth rate, before the financial crisis, the growth rate of deposits was higher than that of loans, and the fluctuation of deposits is lower than that of loans, consistent with the traditional high savings rate among the Chinese people. After the financial crisis, the growth rate of loans increased slightly higher than that of deposits, which was due to the inflation exacerbated by aggressive

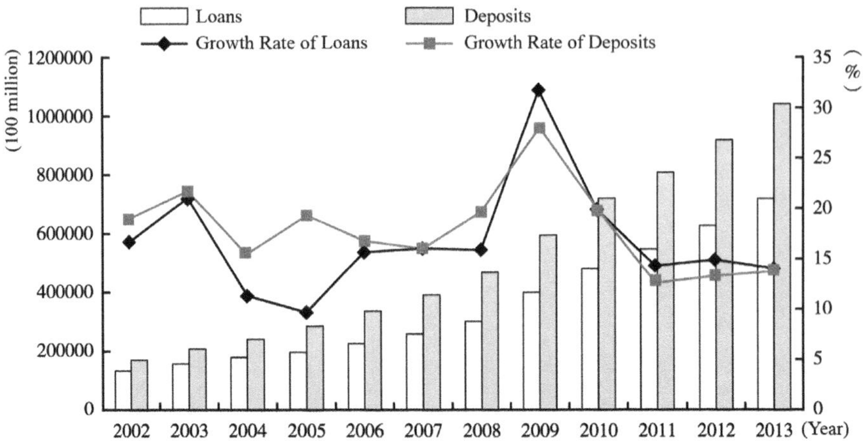

Fig. 2.2 Growth in various loans and deposits of China's financial institutions from 2002 to 2013 (*Source* Wind Info)

monetary policy. The result is that the customers were less interested in savings and sought after all sorts of high-yield loans. At the same time, after the financial crisis, both savings and lending saw diminishing fluctuations in growth rate.

2.1.1.3 Level of China's Economic Monetization

Monetization refers to that the total of goods, services, and the entire production process, including investment and distribution, are exchanged through currency in an economy; monetization ratio is generally represented by the ratio of broad money M2 to GDP. Since the financial development of developing countries is still in the early stage, non-monetary assets only account for a minor portion of the total financial assets, M2 / GDP is usually used as an indicator in analyzing the financial progress of developing countries.

McKinnon has also used this indicator to analyze the gap of financial development between developing and developed countries. Since the policy of reform and opening up was adopted, China's economy has experienced significantly accelerated monetization and become one of the countries with the fastest financial development in the world as shown in Fig. 2.3.

2.1.1.4 The Financial Development in China

The financial interrelations ratio (FIR), constructed by Goldsmith, is the ratio of the value of all financial assets to the value of all tangible assets (national wealth) in existence in a country. FIR can reflect the overall situation of the country's financial structure and the level and stage of financial development; it is a major indicator to

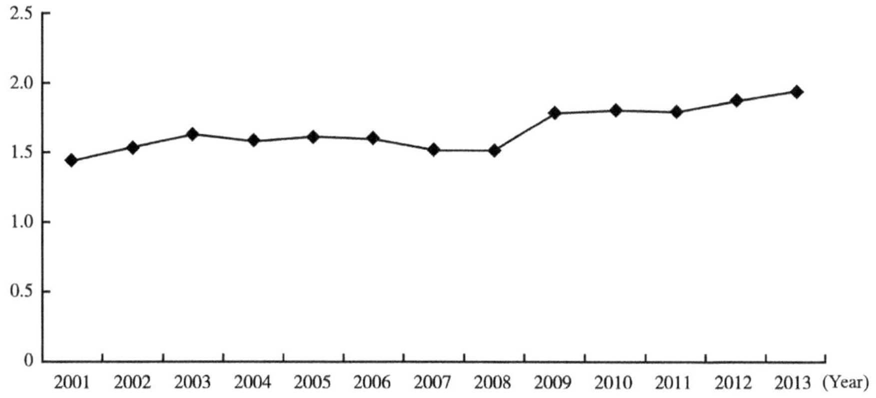

Fig. 2.3 2002–2013 Changes of the degrees of monetization in China's economy (*Source* Wind Info)

measure the level of a country's financial development or reform that it has reached. According to Goldsmith's findings, FIR can be defined as the ratio of the value of all financial assets to GDP during a given period.

In general, the higher the FIR, the higher the extent of separation between savings and investment, the larger the scale of the financial system and the stronger its capability to allocate resources; in turn, the lower FIR indicates the lower level of financial system development, smaller scale of the financial system, and lower capability in resource allocation.

According to the current development of financial system, China's financial assets can be divided into three categories: monetary financial assets, securities (including bonds and equity) and insurance-type financial assets. Since other types of financial assets are relatively small in scale and only account for a small proportion of all financial assets, they are not included in this study. The details are shown in Table 2.1.

Figure 2.4 shows that China's FIR increases significantly from 2002 to 2013, from 1.9 in 2002 to 2.85 in 2013. During this period, there was a dip in 2008, which was because the financial crisis had a huge impact on the Chinese stock market and resulted in a serious decline in negotiable market capitalization of the stock. In general, according to Goldsmith's financial structure theory, China's financial development advanced from the elementary level to a higher level between 2001 and 2013.

2.1.2 Analysis on the Structure of Financial Assets

The development of China's financial market brought about not only increasing numbers of financial instruments but also more diversified financial assets. The structure of financial assets is an integral part of the financial structure and, to a certain

Table 2.1 Statistics of China's financial assets (Unit: 100 million yuan)

Year	Currency Type (M2)	Securities		Insurance (Premium Income)	Total Financial Assets
		Stocks (Market Value)	Bonds (Escrow Balance)		
2002	185,006.97	12,484.56	28,333	3053.1	228,877.63
2003	221,222.82	13,178.52	37,118	3880.4	275,399.74
2004	253,207.7	11,688.64	51,625	4318.1	320,839.44
2005	298,755.67	10,630.52	72,595	4927.3	386,908.49
2006	345,577.91	25,003.64	92,452	5641	468,674.55
2007	403,401.3	93,064.35	123,339	7035	626,839.65
2008	475,166.6	45,213.9	151,102	9784.1	681,266.6
2009	610,224.52	151,258.65	175,295	11,137	947,915.17
2010	725,851.79	193,110.41	206,714	14,700	1,140,376.2
2011	851,590.9	164,921.3	223,959	14,300	1,254,771.2
2012	974,148.8	181,658.26	262,448	15,500	1,433,755.06
2013	1,106,524.98	199,579.54	299,522	17,200	1,622,826.52

Source Wind Info

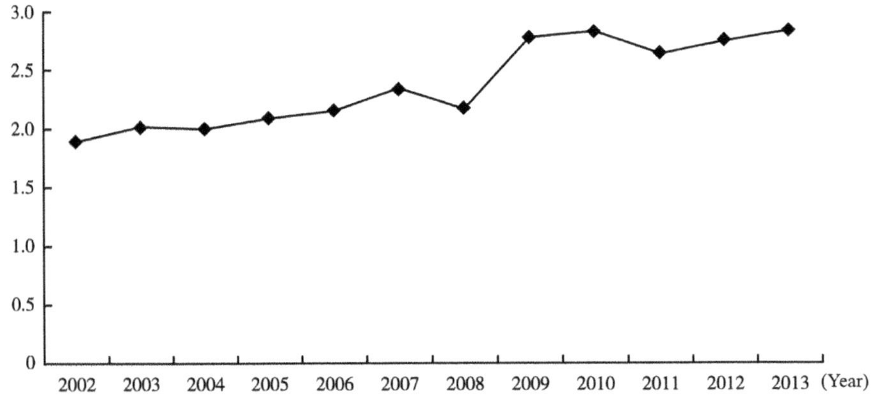

Fig. 2.4 2002–2013 Historical changes of China's FIR (*Source* Wind Info)

extent, can reflect its relationship to the economic growth of China. At present, China's financial assets, though of a great variety, can be grouped into the following categories: deposits and loans, stocks, bonds, insurance, financial derivatives and so on in financial institutions.

Although the financial asset actually covers more content, in view of the availability of data, this study mainly selects the data from a few given time periods with focus on currencies, bonds, stocks and insurance, etc. to discuss the amounts of China's financial assets and the specific internal structure of each category so as to understand the overall structure of China's financial assets. The specific data needed for the analysis are shown in Table 2.2.

Table 2.2 shows that the total amount of financial assets in China increased from about 24 trillion in 2002 to 162 trillion in 2013, an increase of nearly 6 times. The share of currencies in total financial assets decreased from 78% in 2002 to 68% in 2013. The proportion of bonds increased from 16% in 2002 to 18.45% in 2013, which is not remarkable; the proportion of premium income decreased from 1.29% to 1.06%, indicating that China's insurance asset is less valued in the entire financial asset; stocks jump from 5.26% to 12.30%, showing its increasing importance in financial assets.

2.1.3 Analysis on the Structure of Financial Institutions

At present, with the development of China's financial industry, a hybrid financial institutional system consisted of banking and non-bank financial institutions is gradually formed. The system features the collaboration among different types of financial institutions, such as regulatory, commercial and policy-setting institutions, and the combined operation of domestic and foreign financial institutions.

As of the end of 2013, the overall landscape of China's financial institutions is shown in Table 2.3, which displays the following traits of the current structure of China's financial institutions.

First, in terms of type, the varieties are relatively comprehensive. At present, China's financial institutions include banking institutions, securities agencies, insurance companies and other non-bank financial institutions. Various institutions required for economic and financial development are basically established, serving a relatively full range of financial functions. With relatively comprehensive industrial types, a solid foundation has been laid for a modern financial industry. At present, China's financial institutions are characterized by the existence of regulatory, commercial and policy-setting financial institutions, the co-existence of domestic-funded and foreign-funded financial institutions, and the dominance of banking institutions supplemented with non-bank financial institutions.

Second, banks are the dominant institution. In the structure of China's financial sector, the banking industry stands at the dominant position. Thus, the financial intermediary-led structure is prominent in the financial system. By the end of 2013, the financial assets of banking financial institutions accounted for 81% of the total financial assets, indicating that the entire system is a typical structure led by financial intermediaries.

Third, the state-owned financial institutions are of the oligopoly position in China's economy. This is a distinctive feature of Chinese financial structure. Among the country's financial institutions, state-owned commercial banks, policy-setting banks and state-controlled insurance companies have an absolute dominance in terms of asset structure or institutional network and staffing. Since the policy of reform and

Table 2.2 Changes in China's financial asset structure (Unit: 100 million yuan, %)

Types of financial assets		2002		2003		2004	
		Amount	Share	Amount	Share	Amount	Share
Currencies	M2	185,006.97	77.87	221,222.82	77.25	253,207.7	76.83
Bonds	Treasury bond	22,358.46	9.41	27,649.63	9.65	31,261.90	9.49
	Financial bond	12,416.93	5.23	15,523.30	5.42	17,740.87	5.38
	Corporate bond	602.30	0.25	867.30	0.30	1153.50	0.35
	Others	1652.34	0.70	4064.31	1.42	10,196.03	3.09
Stocks	Negotiable market capitalization	12,484.56	5.26	13,178.52	4.60	11,688.64	3.55
Insurances	Premium income	3053.1	1.29	3880.4	1.35	4318.1	1.31
Total		237,574.66	100.00	286,386.28	100.00	329,566.74	100.00
Currencies	M2	298,755.67	75.80	345,577.91	72.82	403,401.31	63.81
Bonds	Treasury bond	34,352.60	8.72	36,668.17	7.73	53,601.01	8.48
	Financial bond	21,637.04	5.49	25,759.28	5.43	32,560.70	5.15
	Corporate bond	1662.50	0.42	2297.50	0.48	3449.35	0.55
	Other	22,192.35	5.63	33,585.66	7.08	39,111.29	6.19
Stocks	Negotiable market capitalization	10,630.52	2.70	25,003.64	5.27	93,064.35	14.72
Insurances	Premium income	4927.3	1.25	5641	1.19	7035	1.11
Total		394,157.98	100.00	474,533.16	100.00	632,223.00	100.00
Type of financial assets		2008		2009		2010	
		Amount	Percentage	Amount	Percentage	Amount	Percentage
Currencies	M2	475,166.6	69.14	610,224.52	63.99	725,851.79	63.65
Bonds	Treasury bond	54,783.22	7.97	61,516.77	6.45	68,543.44	6.01
	Financial bond	41,329.34	6.01	50,326.46	5.28	57,694.84	5.06

(continued)

Table 2.2 (continued)

Types of financial assets		2002		2003		2004	
		Amount	Share	Amount	Share	Amount	Share
	Corporate bond	5272.25	0.77	9197.37	0.96	12,476.30	1.09
	Others	55,721.51	8.11	59,985.32	6.29	67,999.90	5.96
Stocks	Negotiable market capitalization	45,213.9	6.58	151,258.65	15.86	193,110.41	16.93
Insurances	Premium income	9784.1	1.42	11,137	1.17	14,700	1.29
Total		687,270.92	100.00	953,646.09	100.00	1,140,376.68	100.00
Type of financial assets		2011		2012		2013	
		Amount	Percentage	Amount	Percentage	Amount	Percentage
Currencies	M2	851,590.90	67.87	974,148.8	67.94	1,106,524.98	68.19
Bonds	Treasury bond	72,728.57	5.80	77,877.86	5.43	87,043.36	5.36
	Financial bond	72,874.24	5.81	90,280.96	6.30	102,914.63	6.34
	Corporate bond	15,995.54	1.27	24,757.13	1.73	30,325.09	1.87
	Others	62,360.20	4.97	69,532.41	4.85	79,238.94	4.88
Stocks	Negotiable market capitalization	164,921.3	13.14	181,658.26	12.67	199,579.54	12.30
Insurances	Premium income	14,300	1.14	15,500	1.08	17,200	1.06
Total		1,254,770.75	100.00	1,433,755.42	100.00	1,622,826.54	100.00

Source Wind Info

Table 2.3 Overview of China's financial institutions

Category			Amount (numbers)	Assets (100 million)	Assets Percentage (%)
Regulatory financial institutions			4		
Policy-setting financial institutions			3	113,723.11	6.88
Commercial financial institutions	Bank Type	State-owned commercial banks	5	627,133.81	37.93
		Joint-stock commercial banks	12	354,369.8	21.43
		Urban commercial banks	143	96,843.2	5.86
		Rural commercial banks	43	17,599.35	1.06
		Rural credit cooperatives	3056	80,752	4.88
		Postal saving banks	1	49,000	2.96
		Foreign-funded banks	37	25,805	1.56
	Non-bank Type	Securities companies	114	51,900	3.14
		Fund company	82	3000	0.18
		Insurance company	167	82,900	5.01
		Financial company	174	41,400	2.50
		Trust company	68	109,000	6.59
Total			3909	1,653,426.25	100.00

Source Wind Info and the websites of SFC, CBRC and other institutions

opening up was adopted, the share of the total assets of banking financial institutions has steadily decreased while the proportion of non-bank financial structure has gradually increased. With the development of joint-stock commercial banks, the proportion of state-owned financial institutions continues to decline. However, the state-owned commercial banks still account for considerable market share and occupy the oligopoly position, while the private-funded financial institutions are only in a complementary position. A dominant ownership structure will result in a singular financial risk structure; that is, the risk for the country/economy is highly concentrated.

Table 2.4 China's financial market structure in 2013 (Unit: 100 million yuan)

Money market	Interbank bond trading	598,047	Stock market	Total market capitalization	230,977.19
	Interbank borrowing	355,187		Negotiable market capitalization	199,579.54
Bond market	Interbank bond repurchases	1,519,757	Gold market	Transaction	32,133.844
	Issuance	80,057.92	Insurance market	Premium income	17,200

Source Wind Info

2.1.4 Analysis on the Structure of Financial Market

Financial market is the main venue where financial activities take place. The structure of financial market is also an integral part of the financial system. At present, China's financial market can be regarded as a compound entity, which includes not only the traditional money market and capital markets (including the bond market and stock market) but also the insurance market and gold market. The current size of each market is shown in Table 2.4.

It is clear that China already has a relatively well-developed financial market. However, the quantitative structure is unbalanced, indicating the traditional market is relatively developed but the financial derivatives market is underdeveloped, which is related to the limited liberation in China's financial development. At the same time, China's money market and capital market account for a relatively large proportion, indicating that the unbalanced structure of the financial market and the insubstantial liberation in market development.

2.1.5 Outlook of China's Financial System

The previous analyses show the following problems in China's financial structure.

First, China's financial structure and economic structure are out of balance. In the current financial system, the ownership structure, space structure and scale structure are more prominent. First, the ownership structure in the financial structure is disproportionate, as the state-owned component takes up a large proportion. The single ownership structure is not conducive to a healthy financial development among competitive institutions and easily lowers financial efficiency. Second, China's financial space structure is unbalanced, as the financial development sees capitals and resources pooling in the eastern region while significantly dwindling in the central and western regions. The unbalanced development between the urban and rural areas also causes the monotonous financial market, only with the traditional deposit and lending business, in rural areas. Finally, the underdevelopment of small and medium-sized financial institutions results in the centralization of financial institutions. The financial structure, which is dominated by state-owned large banks, leads to the highly concentrated financial business and the sluggish development of local small and medium-sized financial institutions as well as the non-bank financial institutions.

Second, the financial industry structure is not well proportioned. Although China's financial system has bid farewell to the dominance of the banking sector, seen the rise of other newly-developed financial industries, and formed an industrial system composed of banking, securities, insurance and trust, the internal structure of the financial industry is still unbalanced. Obviously, the banking sector is thriving and dwarfs other nonbank institutions. As of the end of 2013, the financial assets of China's banking financial institutions accounted for 81.53% of the total financial assets. Moreover, the state-owned banks, due to the lack of competitors, emphasize scales rather than efficiency and quality, while the credit businesses easily muster risks onto the banking industry. These deficiencies will inevitably cause discordance among China's financial industries and intensify the internal structural inconsistency, leading to an unsound financial industry structure.

Third, the financial market structure is not rational. China's current financial market has relatively comprehensive market types, including not only the traditional money market and capital market but also the gold market and insurance market. However, quantity doesn't guarantee quality. Even with a satisfactory variety, the market structure is unbalanced, which is embodied by the imbalance among the components. In another word, the capital markets pay more attention to stocks and securities but care less about corporate bonds. Even the stock market is concerned more about circulation than issuance. Such imbalance not only fails the operation of financial market but also thwarts investment and financing activities, undermining the stability of financial markets.

Fourth, the financial asset structure is not sound. With the development of financial innovation, China's financial asset boasts relatively rich varieties. However, the quantity and variety of financial assets are still insufficient to meet the huge market demand; for example, non-monetary financial assets only account for a small proportion; only a few financial innovative products are available with an irrational composition of financial instruments.

Looking forward, we expect to see the following development trends in China's financial structure.

In terms of volume, the annual growth rate of China's economy is set at about 7.5% in the next period of time because China's economy is shifting from high-speed growth to medium and high-speed growth. In addition, since the government is more cautious in using aggressive monetary policy to stimulate economic growth, China's money supply will show a steady upward trend and the growth rate will slow down. At the same time, due to the growing financial markets, especially in wealth management sector, individuals and institutions will prioritize other forms of investment over deposits in asset allocation. In the future, the growth rate of deposits should still be slightly lower than that of the loans.

In terms of financial asset structure, on the basis of the state policy that aims to speed up the construction of multi-level capital market, the enhanced innovation capability of China's shadow bank, the gradually standardized business model, and the deepening reform of bond and stock issuance system, the bond and stock assets will take up a significantly increased proportion in the financial asset structure, and the structures of bond asset and stock asset will be gradually improved.

In terms of financial institution structure, the bank-based structure will not go through a big change in the next few years. However, with the adjusted national policy and economic development, the asset size of banks will decrease while that of the non-bank financial institutions will steadily increase. At the same time, the internal structure of the bank will see the declining importance of large state-owned commercial banks, and the increasing importance of policy-setting banks, urban commercial banks that support of small and medium-sized businesses, rural commercial banks that are dedicated to serve agriculture modernization. What are reflected in the asset structure include the reduced asset scale of state-owned commercial banks and joint-stock commercial banks and the increased scale of the assets of the policy-setting banks, commercial banks and rural commercial banks.

In terms of the financial market structure, a substantial change is not expected in the near future. The money market and the capital market still remain dominant, to which the only change will be the structural adjustment (this also depends on the development of the corporate bond market). The scale of gold, insurance and other markets will continue to expand with the development of economy.

In terms of financial development, from 2001 to 2013, China's financial interrelations ratio showed a slow growing trend. If there is no major economic disruption (such as the 2008 financial crisis), this low growth rate will experience no significant change. China's financial interrelations ratio will steadily expand with the continuous development of financial markets.

2.2 Loan Interest Rate Liberalization's Effects on China's Corporate Sector

Despite rapid development in China's bond and stock markets, Chinese enterprises still rely on loans as their primary financing channel. Interest rate liberalization will significantly influence firms' investment and financing decisions. Over the years, China has introduced interest rate regulation policies to artificially hold down loan interest rates and promote investment-driven economic development.

2.2.1 Effects of Loan Interest Rates on the Investment and Financing Decisions of China's Corporate Sector

Theoretically, lower loan interest rates will stimulate investment, and vice versa, i.e., investment is fully elastic to change in the loan rate. The interest rate elasticity of investment is also subject to multiple factors such as economic cycle and environment. When the economy is in an upswing, loan interest rates will rise, but under the expectations for higher return, investment demand will further increase. With an easy monetary policy in place, the loan interest rate will decrease, and investment growth will outpace the loan interest rate hike. This points to the loan interest rate elasticity of investment, but other factors also influence investment. At the micro-level, economic entities consider cost and return before deciding to invest. As a financial cost, interest is a key component of firm cost. Therefore, the loan interest rate is only one determinant of investment, and there can be no correlation or a relationship contrary to general theories between investment and loan interest rate, as is often the case in transition economies. Loan interest rate elasticity of investment in China is extremely small, i.e., the interest rate has a minimal impact on investment in China. The loan interest rate is not correlated with total investment in fixed assets and the growth rate in loans issued by financial institutions.

The interest rate elasticity of investment has a lot to do with interest rate level. If the loan interest rate is low, i.e., access to capital is cheap, financing cost will make up a smaller share of a firm's total cost, and its change makes little difference to its total cost. Hence, firms may stay profitable by focusing on bigger-ticket costs such as production, labor, and overhead costs. At this moment, firms are less sensitive to loan interest rates. On the contrary, if the loan interest rate is high, i.e., access to capital is expensive, financing cost will account for a big share of a firm's total cost, and its change makes a big difference to a firm's total cost. In this case, firms find it harder to manage their total cost, and are much more sensitive to loan interest rates in deciding to invest.

Before the liberalization of the lower limit on loan interest rates, most studies believed that under the higher interest rate risks after loan interest rate liberalization, more competitive and creditworthy enterprises with good-quality assets will prevail in market competition through easier access to credit or bond issuance, which helps slash the cost of financing. On the contrary, less competitive and qualified firms face higher interest rates due to their risk premium. The higher cost of credit financing eats into their business margin, putting them in a disadvantaged competitive position.

2.2.2 Effects of Liberalizing the Lower Limit on Loan Interest Rates

On July 20, 2013, the People's Bank of China (PBoC), China's central bank, liberalized the lower limit on loan interest rates, allowing financial institutions to set their loan rates based on commercial principles. Theoretically, banks will be forced to cut loan rates in price competition with other banks, thus holding down loan rates. With the liberalization policy in place for nearly a year, neither did loan interest rate liberalization prompt financial institutions to slash loan rates, thus causing wild volatility in financial markets nor did it give a boost to non-financial corporations and provide SMEs with much-needed loans at affordable rates.

First, under China's current economic system and financial structure, liberalizing the lower limit on loan interest rates may benefit large enterprises and offer little help to SMEs. Theoretically, loan interest rates are related to the creditworthiness of enterprises and individuals and the due diligence cost of banks, and loan interest rate liberalization does not necessarily help large enterprises and hurt small businesses. In practice, however, this assumption may not hold. Backed by implicit credit guarantee from the government, large enterprises have more chances to obtain loans at a fair price; less creditworthy SMEs are less likely to receive credit at modest interest rates.

Before the policy was in place, the Central Bank set the lower limit on loans to be 70% of the benchmark loan interest rate. After the policy took effect, if the loan interest rate dropped to half the benchmark interest rate of 6.15% on one to three-year loans, i.e., down to 3.075%, total interest paid on the newly issued mid-and long-term loans worth 1.23 trillion yuan in the first half of 2013 can be reduced by 15.129 billion yuan. Instead of shared across the corporate sector as a whole, however, the benefits of this policy were limited to government-backed large enterprises, which accounted for less than 5% of total loans issued in China.

Before the lower limit on loan interest rates was deregulated, China's loan interest rates were already at modest levels, and the lower limit was reduced to 0.7 times the benchmark rate after a few rounds of downward adjustment. The interest rate on one-year loans was reduced to 6% X 0.7 = 4.2%. With the range of deposit interest rates raised to 3.25% ~ 3.3%, if the lower limit on loan interest rates was to be followed, the interest spread for banks would be a mere (4.2%-3.25%)-(4.2%-3.3%) = 0.95%-0.9%. Given this paper-thin margin, very few companies and projects would qualify for a loan interest rate at the lower limit, which could only be granted to extremely safe large enterprises and projects that would be potentially lucrative or bring other business opportunities in the long run. There is no further room for banks to offer more preferential loan interest rates.

Lastly, China's corporate sector increasingly relies on alternative modes of financing such as credit and trust finance and less on bank loans. Even with loan interest rates deregulated, banks may still keep their actual interest rates similar to previous levels by offering wealth management products. Banks already saw a decline in their loan business before loan interest rate liberalization. According to the PBoC's data, Renminbi loans in China leapt by 5.08 trillion yuan in the first half of 2013 or 221.7 billion yuan more than it did in the previous year, and made up 50.0% of aggregate financing to the real economy during the same period, down 12.4 percentage points to a record low. Meanwhile, net financing from corporate bonds hit a record high, with domestic bond and equity financing of non-financial corporations jointly making up 13.3%, up 0.8 percentage points year-on-year. Financing from undiscounted bank acceptance notes, entrusted loans, and trust loans to the real economy amounted to 2.86 trillion yuan, up 1.43 trillion yuan. Banks have found new sources of revenue from establishing trust funds, serving as financial product channels, offering acceptance notes, among other means.

2.2.3 Comments on the Liberalization of the Lower Limit on Loan Interest Rates

Being an important step of interest rate liberalization reforms, removing the lower limit on loan interest rates does little to change the overall financial structure. Through financial innovations, large and innovative banks had already minimized the policy impact before the deregulation. In this sense, removing the lower limit on loan interest rates was more a symbolic gesture of reform. Facts have proven that under China's current economic system and financial structure, liberalizing the lower limit on loan interest rates could hardly influence corporate financing behaviors in China in any significant way.

Yet in the long run, banks will face fiercer competition as China's financial system structure improves, i.e., bank loans as a mode of indirect financing will account for a smaller share in corporate financing, and credit and stocks-- especially those of the SME board-- will account for a rising share. At this moment, falling profit margins will prompt banks to adjust their business strategies and lower loan interest rates to broaden lending scope. Only at this moment will the cancellation of a lower limit on loan interest rate start to make a difference, allowing the corporate sector and especially SMEs to benefit in real earnest. That is to say, the issuance of such financial policies as interest rate liberalization must go hand-in-hand with adjustments in the economic system and financial structure. Well-functioning market economic and financial systems are essential for a sound financial policy to achieve its intended effects. Without a proper social background and financial environment, a financial policy could be counterproductive to growth and financial development without achieving its intended effects.

2.3 Loan Interest Rate Liberalization's Effects on China's Household Sector

Savings deposits are a primary form of financial assets in China. Lifting the upper limit on deposit interest rates, therefore, will have profound effects on household saving and consumption behaviors.

2.3.1 Current Status and Effects of Deposit Interest Rates

Over the years, China's household savings have been rising rapidly and inelastically to deposit interest rates. The reason is that deposit interest rates have both positive and negative effects on consumption and savings. When income is constant, deposit rates are negatively correlated with consumption and positively correlated with savings: a low savings interest rate policy may discourage savings and increase consumption. With a change in income taken into account, a low deposit interest rate policy will reduce depositors' interest income, thus dampening consumption as income is a source of consumption. The impact of deposit interest rates on consumption and savings depends on the intensity of the substitution effect and income effect. The substitution effect of deposit interest rate on consumption is insignificant, as proven by China's high savings rate despite a low deposit interest rate policy in place over the years. This can be explained by two factors: first, inadequate social security created high expectations for future consumption; second, households had very few alternatives to invest their savings other than depositing them in banks. These factors have pushed up the deposit growth rate even with a low interest rate in place. Further reducing interest rates did little to discourage household savings and stimulate consumption.

Economic reforms have made Chinese households feel more uncertain about future income and spending. Uncertainties in future income expectations primarily stemmed from a market-based employment system. After years of reforms, most employers recruit personnel on a non-permanent contract basis. Currently, China's "intra-system" employees including civil servants, military and police personnel, as well as permanent employees of public institutions and state-owned enterprises account for a much smaller share of the total workforce compared with the early times of the reform and opening-up program in the 1980s. Contract employees and business owners, who account for the vast majority of the workforce, feel uncertain about their future income expectations. There are a wide array of uncertainties about future spending, including elderly care, education, healthcare, and housing. Imperfections in these social systems have led people to worry about—and save for—future spending in these areas. Uncertain expectations are a key driver behind the sharp rise in China's household savings.

Over the years, indirect financing through banks has held sway in China, where households had few alternatives to invest their savings. In developed countries, however, the stock market offers an alternative for households to invest their savings. Established in 1990 in the reform era, China's stock market has existed for only over 20 years with a small volume and high risks for investors. The market capitalization of shares in China in various years was equivalent to only about 20% of total household savings deposits during the same period. If the numerous institutional and corporate investors are excluded, households account for an even smaller proportion of share trading in China.

China has kept deposit interest rates low to support economic development over the years. The flipside is that households earned little from their savings deposits. As a return on deposits, interest on deposits is closely watched by the household sector. Household savings deposits are inelastic to deposit interest rates because households consider a host of factors as far more important than interest rates. Yet with other factors being constant, depositors are fully—and even extremely—sensitive to deposit interest rates, as evidenced in financial disturbances that occurred in some small and medium-sized cities in the 1980s.[1] These financial disturbances occurred when the local branches of banks competed in attracting deposits by offering interest rates above the policy limit in explicit or disguised forms, which was unlawful. People took leave from their jobs and queued before their banks to withdraw their savings and deposit them elsewhere just for a tiny additional income on interest. Preventing the offering of high interest rates to attract deposits is a key target of China's tight interest rate control and the premise for implementing the low interest rate policy. It remains a key responsibility of China's financial regulators. Strong Treasury bond sales reflect sensitivity to interest rates. Like bank deposits, Treasury bonds are also a financial product backed by State credit. They are slightly less liquid but yield a bit higher than time deposits. With other factors being constant, the slightly higher yield has made Treasury bonds an extremely popular alternative to savings deposits. That is to say, without other factors taken into account, savings deposits are fully elastic to interest rates.

2.3.2 Effects of Deposit Interest Rates on Savings Deposits in China's Household Sector

The reform and opening-up program launched in 1978 has been followed by steady increases in China's household incomes. The marginal propensity to save varies across the high-income, middle-income, and low-income groups. The high-income group represented by business owners has an extremely low marginal propensity to save. Their income is most likely property-related, such as business income and return on assets. The nature of their incomes determines their extremely low marginal propensity to save. Most businesses are run on debt. Since business owners still need to finance from the capital market, they are not inclined to convert corporate income into personal income via dividend distribution or other means and deposit such

[1] An example is the "Patriotic Savings Deposit Month" incident in Xiangfan City, Hubei Province in 1989. In March 1989, the local branches of banks launched a "Patriotic Savings Deposit Month" campaign in Xiangfan City, Hubei Province. As of March 1, all major banks substantially raised deposit interest rates and bid up interest rates through auctions. In the first half of the month, the "big four" banks—including the Industrial and Commercial Bank of China (ICBC), the Agricultural Bank of China (AgBank), the Bank of China (BOC), and the China Construction Bank (CCB)—significantly raised deposit interest rates. Branches of the same bank offered different interest rates. Even the same branch of the same bank had different interest rates on savings deposits in the morning and in the afternoon of the same day. In Xiangfan, people took leave from their jobs to move their savings deposits from one bank branch to another, causing chaos in the financial business. By noon on March 15, overwhelmed banks had to close for business and were smashed by angry depositors.

income in banks. Property-related incomes primarily include incomes from financial assets and immovable properties.

Holders of significant financial assets tend not to be extremely risk-averse, and only those who are risk-averse would prefer savings deposits as a financial instrument. The high-income group prefers such financial assets as stocks to savings deposits and invests in housing properties usually on loans from banks with high mortgage ratios. The nature of property investment means that the high-income group with property investments will only have a smaller propensity to deposit savings in banks. The low-income group has the highest marginal propensity to save. For low-income people, most of their incomes are spent in the current period, and only a fraction of their income can be saved. This part of saved income, however, usually only meets their future needs of necessities and unexpected expenses. Low-income people are extremely risk-averse and have a very higher propensity to save. With low and unstable incomes, low-income people tend to opt for time deposits with lower interest rates.

The middle-income group's propensity to save is in between those of high-income and low-income groups. Middle-income people depend mainly on wages and less on property-generated income. They are relatively risk-averse on the while though some are much more so than others. On the one hand, middle-income people save part of their income in banks to meet their future needs of necessities and unexpected expenses. On the other hand, they choose to invest the remainder of their income, which is primarily salary income, in financial assets. Business owners in the middle-income group will choose to invest their income in business expansion. In a nutshell, household income is the most important determinant of household consumption. Irrespective of income levels, savings deposits are always subject to the effects of a low-interest rate policy, and part of the interest income will be converted into deposits and lent by banks to borrowers.

2.3.3 Under the Current Deposit Interest Rate Policy, the Following Alternative Instruments to Deposit Interest Rate Liberalization Can Be Found: Wealth Management Products

China's proactive monetary policy in coping with the global financial crisis of 2008 has fueled domestic inflation, causing deposit interest rates to stay below inflation. To protect their savings from depreciating, depositors started to look for investment opportunities. Through wealth management products, which earn higher profits for the banks and are not subject to interest rate regulation, banks invest household savings in financial markets. In what should otherwise be a proxy investment process, however, the "implicit guarantee" in China means that wealth management products also have an attribute of savings deposits, i.e., at least the principal should be protected. Market-based return on wealth management products has a substitute effect on depository interest, making wealth management products an alternative to deposit interest rate liberalization.

As an alternative to deposit rate liberalization, wealth management products (WMPs) have numerous positive effects on deposit interest rate liberalization, both in terms of their maturities and yield-based pricing. Yield rates of wealth management products based on competition and supply and demand provide a reference for market-based interest rate pricing. When inflation is high, wealth management products accelerate a shift away from savings deposits, thus hastening interest rate liberalization, and the pricing of wealth management products offers a more realistic reflection of capital price. Wealth management products are linked to currency markets in terms of both their design and product form. They are an innovation and breakthrough to China's current interest rate control and an embryonic form of market-based interest rates.

2.3.4 Conditions for Interest Rate Liberalization

As of July 20, 2013, the People's Bank of China (PBoC), China's central bank, removed the lower limit on loan interest rates for financial institutions, allowing them to independently determine loan interest rates based on commercial principles. This policy marks an acceleration in China's interest rate liberalization, which entered a critical phase. However, this policy announcement did not mention the adjustment of deposit interest rates, which would have more far-reaching implications for the economy as a whole. Based on the international experience, deposit interest rate liberalization requires more demanding conditions to achieve the intended goal and may trigger an economic crisis. For a financial system, the question is what conditions must be in place before deposit interest rate can be deregulated? In our view, the following conditions must be ready:

First, the banking sector must possess certain capabilities for financial innovation. After deposit interest rate liberalization, the banking sector will first face a reduction in profits as interest rate difference no longer generates sufficient revenues. To stay profitable, banks must develop new financial products or offer financial products free from the interest rate impact. They must be capable of financial product and service innovation to create more revenue sources. Aside from product and service innovation, banks must also develop internal risk control, management innovations, pricing power, and all-round strengths to stay competitive. It was also pointed out that deregulating deposit interest rates could force the banking sector into financial innovation. Yet financial innovation capacity cannot be fostered overnight. Before deposit interest rate liberalization, the banking sector must be fully prepared to cope with potential risks. Though China's state-owned and large joint-stock commercial banks are innovative enough to cope, small and medium-sized banks have yet to catch up and become more innovative by following differentiated paths.

Second, China must bring its capital account under strict control before liberalizing deposit interest rates. Normally, deposit interest rate liberalization will be followed by a sharp rise in deposit interest rates, which will heighten the risks of international capital flow. In the absence of deregulating interest rates, international hot money had struck China's financial markets many times, causing huge shocks that otherwise could have triggered a financial crisis were it not for sufficient precautions in place. Capital account control is a barrier against risks from the international capital flow. Hence, the imposition of strict capital control is a basic condition for deposit interest rate liberalization to be carried out smoothly.

The third condition is mechanisms must be in place to prevent vicious competition within the banking sector. After liberalization, interest rates will be determined independently by the banking sector, triggering a race to the bottom among banks to attract deposits. Without necessary administrative systems in place, such competition is likely to become vicious and trigger an adverse selection and moral hazards on the part of banks, causing market-based interest rates to rise and triggering a banking crisis. After liberalization, interest rates will cease to be a monetary instrument for government regulation and instead becomes a target of government regulation. At this moment, the government has to use other monetary instruments such as the reserve ratio requirement and open market operations to intervene in the market and regulate market-based interest rates to keep them within a reasonable band of volatility and keep financial crises at bay.

Last but not least, the macro-economic environment must be stable before deposit interest rates can be liberalized. Deposit interest rate liberalization must be carried out at an appropriate time to minimize the policy's shocks to the market. This requires a correct assessment of the macroeconomic environment. Policymakers should avoid attempting interest rate liberalization reforms when the economy overheats or is in recession. In an economic recession, there will be less demand for investment and capital, which presents challenges to bank operations. Interest rate deregulation at this moment will induce competition and increase the operational costs for the banking sector. When the economy overheats, deregulating deposit interest rates will unleash a huge demand for capital, causing interest rates to spike. Soaring operating costs will induce banks to pursue risky projects and fuel economic bubbles, which may burst and cause the economy to collapse.

Unlike deregulating the lower limit on loan interest rates, deregulating the upper limit on deposit interest rates will create tremendous shocks to China's existing financial system structure. The banking sector, which dominates China's financial system, will bear the brunt the most and suffer from nosediving profits, fiercer competition, and a serious deterioration in asset quality. Any shocks to China's tremendous banking sector will be felt by the whole sector as well. It should be noted that deregulating the upper limit on deposit interest rates helps address inefficiencies and wasteful use of financial resources in China's financial system. It also helps improve China's financial structure. For these reasons, deregulating the upper limit on deposit interest rates is risky but necessary and must be carried out extremely cautiously.

2.4 Deposit and Lending Interest Rate Liberalization's Effects on China's Banking Sector

Currently, China's banking sector is still focused on deposit and loan business and earns most of its profits from interest rate spread. Through interest rate spread, the liberalization of deposit and lending interest rates will profoundly influence banking sector profits and stability. For this reason, we will first discuss the negative effects of deposit and lending interest rate liberalization on China's banking sector.

2.4.1 Negative Effects of Deposit and Lending Interest Rate Liberalization on China's Banking Sector

The liberalization of deposit and lending interest rates will adversely impact banks' deposit business. A floating band of deposit interest rates is a natural result of China's interest rate liberalization reforms and is consistent with the requirements of financial market development. It will also have a tremendous impact on China's banking sector as a whole. Allowing deposit interest rates to float within a certain scope has already intensified deposit business competition in China's banking sector. A floating band of interest rates, once launched, will undermine the banking sector's bargaining power and make it more likely for deposit interest rates to float upwards. The banking sector's deposits primarily consist of deposits from companies, financial institutions, and individuals. Among them, floating deposit interest rates will affect the personal savings business much more than they affect the corporate savings business.

First, most corporate deposits are demand deposits or time deposits with a maturity of less than one year. Based on corporate customers' financial needs, the balance of savings deposits is subject to frequent and significant change. Moreover, corporate customers have far more business correlation with banks than do personal customers. Corporate customers are also stickier to a bank. Even if key corporate customers have the bargaining power to ask for a deposit interest rate markup within the regulatory range, the short maturities of their deposits and additional lending business opportunities they bring may help the bank minimize the adverse impact of such deposit rate markup.

Second, most personal savings deposits are of longer maturities, and due to China's financial regulatory requirements and inadequate social security, personal depositors have smaller risk appetites for financial products and attach more importance principal security. Since 2006, high-risk-appetite personal customers have withdrawn their savings deposits and invested them in high-risk wealth management products such as investment funds and trust products, and most personal financial assets still deposited in banks are demand deposits and low-risk wealth management products. Once a floating deposit interest rate system is in place, a large amount of funds already invested in low-risk wealth management products will be converted back to deposits through new bargaining opportunities. With tighter supervision in place, the banking sector will find it hard to cope with rising costs due to higher deposit interest rates by developing various forms of personal banking business.

Third, personal deposits, whose maturities are generally higher than those of corporate deposits, have been regarded by the banking sector as the foundation of their deposit business. Long-term loans and other high-interest-rate loans from the banking sector must be supported by savings deposits with long maturities. Due to historical reasons, the big four state-owned commercial banks represent a high market share of savings deposits, i.e., they possess a lion's share of lending resources in China. Interest rate liberalization, therefore, will prompt small and medium-sized banks to use new instruments to compete with the big four banks for savings deposits, thus intensifying overall competition in the savings deposit market.

As can be seen from the above analyses, floating deposit interest rates will primarily affect the market share of the banking sector and especially the big four state-owned commercial banks in the savings deposit business.

In the banking sector, about 95% of savings deposits are of maturities below one year; time and demand deposits account for about 60% and 40% of household and corporate deposits with maturities within one year, respectively. If the upper limit on bank deposit interest rates is removed first for long-term deposits as the first step and then for short-term deposits as the second step, the effects will appear gradually.

If the upper limit on the interest rates for long-term loans with maturities above one year is deregulated and subject to contractual deposit interest rates in the same period, we expect deposit interest rates to rise by 100 basis points. If 5% of bank deposits are long-term deposits, banks' cost of deposits will rise by about five basis points due to the deregulation of deposit interest rates with maturities above one year, which represents an increase in their total cost of deposit by less than 3%.

If the upper limits on both time and demand deposits with maturities below one year, which represents the vast majority of bank deposits, banks' cost of deposits will increase much more significantly. Currently, three-year principal-protected fixed-return wealth management products in China yield 100 to 150 basis points above the statutory interest rate for savings deposits with the same maturity. Following this difference, the cost of deposit may also increase by about 100 basis points after deregulating the upper limit on short-term deposit interest rates, which is equivalent to a rise in deposit interest cost by nearly 45%. In reality, some banks have recognized their cost of deposits in marketing expenses to downplay the rising cost of deposits. Deregulating the upper limit on interest rates, therefore, will cause some marketing expenses to be moved back to the cost of deposits so that overall marketing expenses will be smaller. Following a 20% change, interest rates on short-term deposits with maturities within one year are likely to increase by 80 basis points, representing an increase in the cost of deposit by 35%.

Hence, if the Central Bank only scraps the upper limit on interest rates for long-term loans with maturities above one year, the difference between deposit and lending interest rates for banks will narrow by about 40 basis points. Following the difference of 2.5 to 3 percentage points between deposit and lending interest rates for China's banking sector, deregulating the upper limit on long-term deposit interest rates will change this interest rate spread by about 15% for China's banking sector. Currently, net interest income accounts for about 85% of the net interest income of China's banking sector. If the Central Bank deregulates the upper limit on the deposit interest rates for China's banking loans with maturities within one year, the interest rate spread will narrow by 80 basis points due to the increasing cost of deposit. Following the current interest rate spread of 2.5–3 percentage points for China's banking sector, complete deregulation of interest rates is likely to slash the interest rate spread in China by 30% to 40%. In this case, China's banking sector will cope with the sharply shrinking interest rate spread by restructuring interest income and cost, so that the final effect can be 15% to 20% less severe, i.e., the interest rate spread may narrow by 15% to 25%. Meanwhile, banks will see their operating revenues fall by 13% to 20% due to a narrower interest rate spread.

As can be learned from the above analysis, deregulating the upper limit on interest rates for long-term deposits would leave the banking sector less affected. Yet once the Central Bank deregulates interest rates on short-term deposits with maturities within one year, which comprise the bulk of loans issued by China's banking sector, banking sector profitability will no doubt take a dive.

Interest rate spread is a key source of bank profits in the era of regulated interest rates. Banks' traditional profit models will be upended as interest rate liberalization transforms the way interest rates are determined, thus altering deposit and lending interest rate levels and the net interest spread. Moreover, the effects will also be seen in banks' balance sheet structure. Judging by international experience, the banking sector tends to seek higher profits from high-interest-rate loans to cope with the rising cost of deposits after interest rate liberalization.

Theoretically, banks may introduce more competitive interest rates, i.e., raising the cost of deposit, to absorb deposits after interest rate control is lifted. Also, fixed-rate deposits will account for a smaller share, and banks will increase the sensitivity of loan interest rates. By the same token, banks' exposure to risks from interest rate changes will also become in direct proportion to asset and liability sensitivity. As the competition among banks intensifies, interest rate liberalization will inevitably narrow the interest rate spread. However, this assumption is not supported by conclusions from an assessment of international data, especially those from developed countries, where the interest rate spread tended to increase in the long run.

As can be seen from all statistical reviews on interest rates, both incomes on loans and cost of deposit increased sharply due to generally higher interest rates. Research on historical data of international interest rate liberalization finds that interest rate liberalization may raise negative or low interest rates to positive and relatively high levels. Another effect of interest rate liberalization is a greater resiliency to rate change. Banks became more sensitive to changing market-based rates and more exposed to interest rate risks. Overall, actual interest rate spread did not keep narrowing as expected after interest rate liberalization as it was subject to the joint effect of multiple factors such as the levels of competition in financial markets, market sophistication, and financial regulation. Compared with developed countries, interest rate spread in developing countries tends to increase and stays above the average level of developed countries.

First, deposit and lending interest rate liberalization may reduce the interest rate spread in the initial stage, but in the long run, interest rates tend to increase back to their previous levels. Banking sector competition is likely to intensify in the early stage of interest rate deregulation. While banks raise rates to attract deposits, they are unable to restructure their lending portfolio by issuing loans to borrowers at higher lending rates. A potential increase in loan interest rates would be limited. As banks broaden the scope of the financial business, deepen financial innovations, and explore new sources of capital in a later stage of interest rate liberalization, they cannot find new sources of capital just by lowering loan interest rates. Instead, they start to profit from excess returns on loans, thus widening the interest rate spread.

Second, interest rate competition will stabilize in the long run, and non-price competition will hold sway. The non-price competition will raise banks' operating costs and dent their profit margin. Banks will transfer costs to borrowers to profit from interest rate spread. For banks, a broader interest rate spread serves their interests.

Lastly, banks are intrinsically monopolistic in financial markets in the developing countries and regions, where interest rate spread is the main source of their profit and has little room for further increase even after interest rate liberalization as demand for capital is less elastic to interest rates, leaving banks unable to lend more even with a smaller interest rate spread.

Interest rate liberalization may optimize banks' balance sheet structure by beefing up the share of their lending business and thus partially offset their waning attraction to depositors. A shift in the maturity structure of debts and savings will increase the cost of capital for banks, prompting them to prioritize higher-interest-rate lending business to stay profitable. First, in the early stage after interest rate liberalization, loans will make up a greater share in banks' balance sheets while the share of deposits remains stable. Judging by the historical data of the United States, the ratio of bank deposits to total bank liabilities kept decreasing in the 1970s before starting to rise in the 1980s through interest rate liberalization. That is to say, deregulating interest rates would make the banking sector more competitive—as competitive as capital markets—in attracting deposits, whose stable source of cash deposits reduced banks' liquidity risks.

Second, banks' deposit structure shifted from a low-cost to a high-cost one. With or without interest rate deregulation, financial intermediation via banks is destined to wane. After the 1990s, the United States saw another decrease of deposits as a share of interest-bearing liabilities due to mixed operations, diversified investment and financing avenues, and the falling propensity of households to save, forcing banks to borrow large sums of capital at higher costs.

Third, pricier loans are more attractive to banks. From banks' point of view, when loan interest rates rise, large enterprises will raise more capital from direct financing and borrow less from banks, forcing them to turn to new borrowers such as SMEs. From customers' point of view, pricier loans will increase their risk appetite, resulting in huge capital flows into riskier businesses such as real estate. The implication is that financial institutions start to compete for deposits and offer indirect financing to riskier sectors, which will increase banks' business risks and lead to deteriorating asset quality in the financial industry as a whole.

In addition, interest rate liberalization will influence net interest rate spread. Banks' net interest spread and deposit and loan interest spread are similar concepts. While the deposit and lending interest rate spread is the difference between the cost of capital and return on capital while the net interest rate spread reflects the effect of using capital. The net interest rate spread can be big or small because it does not account for the fact that interest-bearing assets and interest-bearing liabilities may comprise different instruments at different scales, which results in its differences with deposit and lending interest rate spread. The extent to which interest rate liberalization affects banks' deposit and lending interest rate spread is correlated with a change in the net interest rate spread. As can be learned from data analysis, the net interest rate spread and deposit and lending interest rate spread follow different trends.

When a central bank takes steps to lift the upper and lower limits on deposit and lending interest rates, the banking sector may decide the pricing of its deposit and loan business on its own, and the central bank, through its open market operations, may influence the benchmark interest rate and thus market pricing. In the early stage of interest rate liberalization, price competition will dominate in the banking sector. As liberalization deepens, banks will foster core competencies in serving differentiated customers, products and services, along with improving risk-based pricing capabilities. The banking sector will see a quickening pace of product innovation, falling interest revenue, and rising non-interest incomes. Interest rate liberalization essentially means that the banking sector should be given the right to determine interest rates independently. Pricing management is of global importance and overall guidance for banks and a key factor in developing competitive advantage. As the differentiated competition takes hold, market mechanisms and self-regulation start to play a dominant role in the central bank interest rate policy transmission and financial market order, which require greater pricing capabilities on the part of financial institutions.

The risk of adverse selection arises from interest rate liberalization due to information asymmetry, and causes banks to price loan rates with a risk-based markup. If banks decide to raise rates, higher interest rates will discourage investment in more stable but low-return projects and encourage investment in riskier projects with a higher return. The result is riskier projects crowding out low-risk ones, giving rise to the risk of adverse selection and causing banks' expected yield rates to be lower than their actual loan interest rates.

After interest rate liberalization, banks will transform their business concepts and balance sheet, pricing, and risk management, giving rise to interbank competition that makes it more likely for a crisis to loom large. Small and medium-sized banks face greater risks due to their gaps with large banks in terms of management performance, technology, talent, and risk identification and mitigation.

2.4.2 Positive Effects of Deposit and Lending Interest Rate Liberalization on the Banking Sector

Despite risks to the banking sector's profit model and operating environment, deposit and lending interest rate liberalization will also influence the banking sector in some positive ways.

First, the deposit and lending interest rate market will give China's banking sector more autonomy essential to building up core competencies. In the era of tightly regulated interest rates, banks had to strictly follow the Central Bank's uniform standards on lending interest rates irrespective of a customer's asset scale, business status, and credibility. In such a circumstance, the price of capital cannot reflect the banking sector's business costs and risks, causing the banking sector to overlook internal management and risk control. As the backbone of the indirect financing market, the banking sector will experience distortions in its financial resource allocation mechanism, directing most credit capital to large and medium-sized SOEs.

With progress in deposit and lending interest rate liberalization, banks became independent market entities in real earnest and possessed greater interest rate pricing power. Such independence allows banks to adjust the price of capital flexibly in light of their customers' creditworthiness and business operations, development prospect, as well as their operating characteristics and target profitability, and market interest rates. Without a doubt, the banking sector is given much greater autonomy in selecting customers and matching risk with return.

Interest rate liberalization will also transform the way banks compete. In the past, banks focused on relational customers as they could only provide homogeneous products under strict interest rate control and relied on non-price competition such as service quality and marketing. The shift from non-price to price competition will lead to fiercer competition. Price competition allows banks to engage in differentiated competition by providing customers at various levels with products of different pricing. This requires banks to set up market-based mechanisms, follow a market-oriented approach, and create a team of professionals for pricing in a scientific and reasonable way. When banks acquire these capabilities in real earnest, they naturally become more competitive.

Second, deposit and lending interest rate liberalization will induce financial innovation in the banking sector. Under the interest rate control, banks could not set interest rates on their own and are not motivated to develop financial products as new products come with new interest rate pricing. Most banks could only provide products with similar functions and prices and lacked competitiveness. Relaxing interest rate control will give banks greater autonomy and encourage them to configure financial products of different sorts based on interest rate as a variable. Before interest rate liberalization started in the US, banks had already invented negotiable large-sum negotiable certificates of deposit (CDs) to bypass interest rate regulation and attract deposits. Amid interest rate liberalization, new financial products emerged, including negotiable order of withdrawal (NOW) and currency market deposit accounts. Interest rate liberalization goes hand in hand with financial innovation. To some extent, financial innovation in the banking sector will quicken the pace of interest rate liberalization.

Unregulated deposit and lending interest rates will expose banks to huge interest rate risks, the mitigation of which requires continuous and effective financial innovation.

Third, deposit and lending interest rate liberalization may effectively weaken the adverse effects of shadow banking and broaden profit sources for the banking sector. Regarding the relationship between interest rate liberalization and shadow banking, Edward S. Shaw said that the "OTC market has to face competition from organized financial sector deepening" and "each country has the best way to integrate its OTC market with organized finance."[2] "OTC market" is today's shadow banking.

In China, shadow banking in the broad sense refers to lending institutions outside the formal financial system and free from regulatory supervision. Under interest rate control, the formal financial system is barred from setting interest rate pricing independently and cannot lend to SMEs at a risk premium rate, giving rise to credit rationing that diverts capital to less risky large and medium-sized SOEs. Despite credit rationing, cash demand from SMEs will not shrink and is instead satisfied by shadow banking. Many underground banks are run in China's Jiangsu and Zhejiang provinces home to numerous SMEs and flourishing private finance. Financing demand from SMEs—often to cover unexpected expenses—can be well addressed by the underground banks. By promising lucrative returns to depositors, such underground banks became hugely popular in Jiangsu and Zhejiang. Yet the high return goes with great potential risks as underground banks are exposed to unknown risks and cannot guarantee the security of deposits. The existence of underground banks may also cause macro-regulatory policies to lose effect.

With deposit and lending interest rates liberalized, banks will have more autonomy to determine the price of capital based on customers' risk profile, and such flexibility will allow them to serve SMEs. Compared with underground banks, the formal banking sector wields more financial resources and offers more diverse and professional services. With the barrier of interest rate control removed, SMEs will prefer to borrow from formal banks.

As can be seen from the above analyses, deposit and lending interest rate liberalization does more harm to the banking sector than it helps. Such a conclusion may also be drawn from international experience: interest rate liberalization in other countries was all accompanied by bank closures and restructuring. Yet the adverse effects are mostly short-term and technical while the positive effects tend to be long-term and institutional. In the long run, interest rate liberalization reforms will improve the banking sector's business and institutional environment and enhance banks' core competencies. It is fair to say that while improving China's financial structure, deposit and lending interest rate liberalization will also help address the lack of competitiveness in China's hefty banking sector.

[2] Quoted from *Financial Deepening in Economic Development* by Edward S. Shaw.

2.5 Deposit and Lending Interest Rate Liberalization's Effects on Monetary Policy Effectiveness

An understanding of how monetary policy regulates the economy through interest rates is essential to unraveling deposit and lending interest rate liberalization's effects on monetary policy effectiveness. Central banks regulate investment and consumption by adjusting interest rates to achieve broader goals of economic regulation.

2.5.1 Interest Rate and Monetary Policy Transmission Mechanisms

When making each investment, the corporate sector and the household sector will consider the cost of capital for investment. Normally, the corporate sector does not have sufficient capital to invest, and when investment opportunities arise, seeks to borrow from banks. The corporate sector must pay interest on loans as a cost while profiting from an investment made with credit capital. When the return on capital is above the loan interest rate, the corporate sector will find it profitable to invest with loans and decide to do so, and such investment decisions will influence a country's economic performance.

On the contrary, when investment capital yields below loan interest rate, the corporate sector will make losses on investments made with loans and decide not to invest with borrowed funds at all, and such decisions will also influence a country's economic performance. When investment return is below loan interest rate, the corporate sector will consider downsizing its balance sheet by paying off loans, and fewer investments would cause economic growth to slow. When a central bank enforces a monetary policy such as increasing the money supply and inducing interest rates to fall, the corporate sector will face a smaller cost of loans that makes it potentially profitable to invest with borrowed funds. In this case, the corporate sector will consider financing for investment, and more investments will boost economic and job growth.

Monetary policy may also regulate household consumption through interest rates. To maximize utility, consumers will consider the future level of consumption when deciding to spend in the current period. They may, based on changes in the economic environment, decide to spend more in the current period and less in a future period, and vice versa, which is referred to as consumers' intertemporal substitution behavior. An important variable influencing consumers' such decisions is the deposit interest rate. The reason is that the deposit interest rate is the opportunity cost of a consumer's decision to spend in the current period.

If a consumer decides not to spend in the current period, he may deposit his money in a bank and earn interest income that can be used for consumption in the next period. Higher deposit interest rate means higher opportunity cost of consumption in the current period and greater motivation for consumers to spend less in the current period, and vice versa. Then, the central bank may use a variety of monetary policies to regulate interest rates to achieve the goal of regulating consumption and thus influencing economic performance.

For instance, the central bank may raise interest rates via monetary policy, thus raising the opportunity cost for consumers to spend in the current period. Consumers seeking to maximize their self-interest will consider spending less and saving more in the current period for future consumption. Of course, current deposit interest rates cannot fully determine consumers' inter-temporal substitution behavior, which is also subject to their consumption preference. Moreover, the central bank may influence consumers' intertemporal substitution behavior via loan rates. The booming consumer credit industry allows consumers to spend with borrowed funds via such means as credit cards, i.e., consumption with borrowed funds exceeds income in the current period, and the opportunity cost is the loan interest that consumers must pay, which is similar to deposit interest that consumers may receive if they elect to deposit their savings. The level of loan interest rates also influences consumers' decision to spend with borrowed funds, and the higher loan interest rates, the higher opportunity cost for consumption with borrowed funds in the current period, and the less motivated consumers will be to apply for a loan, and vice versa.

Monetary policy may also regulate the inflow of foreign capital through the adjustment of interest rates. Interest rates are also a key consideration for foreign investors to decide which country to invest in. When Country A offers higher deposit interest rates, foreign investors will flock to invest in Country A to profit from the interest-rate margin with, of course, exchange rate risk taken into account. Without considering exchange rate risk, the central bank may adjust deposit interest rates with a variety of monetary policies to raise interest rates above international levels by a certain degree to be able to attract foreign capital, the inflow of which will influence domestic capital markets with spillover effects on overall economic performance.

2.5.2 *Deposit and Lending Interest Rate Liberalization's Effects on Monetary Policy*

Deposit and lending interest rate liberalization will influence monetary policy effectiveness through its effects on the definition and measurement of money, money supply, and monetary policy transmission.

2.5.2.1 Deposit and Lending Interest Rate Liberalization Challenges the Definition and Measurement of Money

First, interest rate liberalization will spur financial innovation, thus making the definition of money nebulous. Greater interest rate volatility and risks resulting from interest rate liberalization will fuel financial innovation.[3] Before the emergence of financial innovation, both narrow money and broad money were clearly defined and not difficult to measure. Financial innovation, however, has increased the substitutability of financial assets and changed the liquidity of various financial assets, thus disrupting the original boundaries in the definition of M1, M2, and M3, which is based on liquidity. Hence, the definition of money becomes nebulous. In narrow money, NOW (negotiable order of withdrawal) account, automatic transfer service and other new instruments are not in the originally defined scope of money. Since these new instruments can be used to issue cheques and transfer cash, i.e., ready purchasing power, it is inappropriate to classify them as M1, but neither is it appropriate to put them into M2 category, whose balance is mostly the balance of deposits for investment. Their boundary with M2 and M3 is nebulous. For another instance, deposit and lending interest rate liberalization will prompt banks to pay more attention to SME consumers and offer them a wide range of services to stay competitive. In this case, credit cards will become used more widely to promote consumer credit. At this moment, money is neither in one's pocket nor account; it is only a form of committed liability. In a nutshell, interest rate liberalization will induce all sorts of financial innovation, making it elusive to give money a clear and constant definition.

Second, deposit and lending interest rate liberalization makes it hard to define money. Since money supply at various levels is defined according to the liquidity of financial assets, change in liquidity or emergence of new financial assets in response to changing interest rates will greatly influence the scope and accuracy of the original definition of money. On the one hand, interest rate liberalization will trigger tremendous changes in the liquidity of assets. For instance, traditional financial instruments can be sold or redeemed in a short period at a low operating cost and loss, but with the steady progress of interest rate liberalization, the emergence of new instruments will make liquidity a less relevant indicator. On the other hand, liquidity is difficult to redefine. With emergency financial instruments, banks may reduce their reserve funds, which calls for liquidity to be redefined to ensure monetary policy effectiveness. For instance, the UK revised its definition of money for multiple rounds in 1970–1984, and identified eight aggregate indicators, including M0, M1, M2, M3, Sterling M3, Domestic Credit Expansion (DCE), PSL, and PSL2. The US revised its definition of money seven times in 1971–1984 and used such money aggregate indicators as M1, M2, M3, and Debt5. Each aggregate indicator was assigned increasingly broad and detailed implications. Yet the revised definitions of money failed to keep pace with innovation, and it took time to adopt a revised definition. As a result, the definition of money kept lagging behind financial developments. Deposit and lending interest rate liberalization will cause the liquidity of financial assets to be unstable, making their supply a bad intermediate target of monetary policy.

Third, deposit and lending interest rate liberalization makes it more difficult to measure money supply. On the one hand, international capital flow will grow after

[3] Prof. Li Yang and Prof. Huang Jinlao noted that interest rate liberalization will surpercharge interest rate derivative business.

deposit and lending interest rate liberalization. International financial market integration will prompt enterprises and their affiliates to adjust the balance of their current assets according to changing interest and exchange rates, thus disrupting the stability of money demand and aggregate credit. For instance, some international banks swap domestic and international liabilities from time to time. In principle, overseas deposits should be recognized in cash reserves, but in fact, central banks do not have such information. Judging by the central bank's monetary policy implementation, it is necessary to monitor such items as overseas deposits and emergency positions. Yet these items are usually not included in monetary aggregates and elude surveillance. On the other hand, interest rate liberalization will intensify banking competition, especially over off-balance-sheet businesses. Those businesses offered by commercial banks are not recognized in their balance sheets and include guarantee services and business activities that charge commissions and service fees. Some of such businesses are not reported to the central bank or are not required to be fully reported. As deposit and lending interest rate liberalization deepens, information available to the central bank will become even less complete due to these two factors, making many aggregates harder to be measured timely and precisely.

Since 1993, China started to disclose money supply to the public and since 1996, started to use money supply M1 and M2 as monetary policy targets, which marks the first step of China's use of intermediate monetary policy targets. The money supply is indisputably an intermediate target of China's monetary policy.

2.5.2.2 Deposit and Lending Interest Rate Liberalization Has Weakened the Central Bank's Control of the Money Supply.

First, it is hard to determine the extent to which exchange rate variations have affected money supply since the substitutability between money and debt is unstable. On the one hand, demand for narrow money is highly elastic to change in interest rate; meanwhile, interest rate variations have smaller effects on broad money, and the correlation between them is smaller. When controlling the M3 growth rate, central banks such as the US Federal Reserve, the Bank of France, and the Bank of Japan will closely follow the structural change between money and bonds. Comparatively speaking, it is easier to control the supply of narrow money but more difficult to reach a reasonable target of the broad money supply. On the other hand, the substitutability between financial assets in the currency market and long-term bonds in capital markets indicates a change in the maturity structure of interest rates. Once short-term interest rates increase and expected interest rates stay at a certain level, the rise in short-term interest rates will effectively lead to a rise in long-term interest rates. When the central bank fails to exert effective control over capital markets, its monetary policy becomes less potent. In particular, the increased international capital flow will undermine the central bank's monetary policy autonomy and effectiveness. Hot money may cause wild swings in a country's short-term interest rates. When international capital flows into the long-term bond market, long-term interest rate variations are transmitted internationally, thus affecting monetary authorities' choice of short-term interest rates and ultimately the central banks' choice of the money supply.

Second, deposit and lending interest rate liberalization may cause the money multiplier to be unpredictable. The money multiplier is expressed as: $K = (1 + R_{c)}/(R_c + R_d + R_e + R_t \times t)$, where, R_c (currency ratio) $= C/D_t$, C is currency held by the public, D_t is demand deposit; $t = D_t/D$ is time deposits; R_d and R_e are the statutory reserve ratios for demand and time deposits, respectively, and R_t is the ratio between excess reserves and demand deposit. Among them, R_d and R_t are controlled by the central bank, and R_c, $R_{e,}$ and t are subject to external factors. Generally, the money multiplier is inversely proportional to currency ratio R_c, statutory reserve ratio R_d and R_e, and excess reserve ratio R_t. Hence, when deposit and lending interest rate liberalization affects R_c, $R_{e,}$ and t, the money multiplier will change accordingly.

Third, deposit and lending interest rate liberalization affects the influence of monetary policy instruments as it erodes the potency of the statutory reserve ratio. First, the scope of statutory reserve ratio (SRR) becomes smaller as interest rate liberalization prompts financial institutions to attach greater importance to liquidity and create more liquid financing instruments. A striking manifestation is the increasingly important role of financing securitization, which drew huge sums of capital from banks to non-depository financial institutions to bypass the reserve ratio requirement. Furthermore, financial institutions have experienced a changing debt structure. In contrast to the shrinking share of deposits in their liabilities, commercial banks have seen a steady increase in short-term borrowed funds such as interbank lending, repurchase agreements, and Eurodollar, as well as other longer-term liabilities such as financial bonds. This has reduced their actual submission of the statutory reserve funds. As mentioned before, China's statutory reserve ratio will decrease, and rising interest rates will nudge commercial banks to seek better financing opportunities and create all sorts of brand-new liabilities to evade the submission of statutory reserve funds. Many commercial banks have used subsidiaries and affiliates free from the statutory reserve ratio as vehicles to transfer funds and evade the submission of reserve funds. With a higher availability of excess reserves, banks become less dependent on statutory reserves. Normally, increasing and reducing statutory deposit reserves may shrink or expand money creation from banks, provided that the excess reserves remain unchanged. With interest rate liberalization giving a boost to financial market development, the highly sophisticated currency market offers more avenues for banks to acquire excess reserves. When a bank wishes to lend but is short on capital, it may finance from the currency market without relying on the central bank. Commercial banks' lesser dependence on the statutory reserve ratio means less relevance of the statutory reserve ratio.

Second, relending policy will also become less potent. When open market businesses are not ready, the central bank may adjust credit and money supply rediscount and relending rates as the most flexible and effective way of adjustment. Due to underdeveloped discount services in China, financial institutions rely on central bank relending for credit activities. The central bank's relending rate may, to some extent, adjust the direction and volume of capital flow in the economy, which has been proven in reality. Under the conditions of interest rate liberalization, market-based interest rates are a key determinant of capital flow, and the effects of relending interest rate will diminish.

Third, open-market operations will become reinforced. In regulating base money, China's central bank already relies on open-market operations as its primary policy. In interest rate liberalization, the establishment of benchmark interest rates is vitally important. In China, benchmark interest rates are bank interest rates and set the minimum Treasury bond rates. After interest rate liberalization, rising or fluctuating bank interest rates should not serve as benchmark interest rates to avoid adverse effects on Treasury bond issuance.

2.5.2.3 Deposit and Lending Interest Rate Liberalization Will Greatly Influence China's Monetary Policy Transmission Mechanism.

First, deposit and lending interest rate liberalization will transform the stable relationship between the intermediate and final targets of monetary policy, making it more difficult for the central bank to control the money supply. Interest rate liberalization will allow the public and financial institutions to meet their demand for capital through derived credit extension, making actual money growth more difficult to assess for the central bank.

Second, deposit and lending interest rate liberalization will transform the substance of monetary policy targets. As mentioned before, money needs to be redefined amid the changing concept of the money supply. Meanwhile, the changing relationship between interest rate and macroeconomic variables presents greater difficulties to interest rate control.

Third, interest rate liberalization will transform the correlation between the operational and intermediate targets of monetary policy. Technological progress in information collection, storage, and transmission has expedited—and will continue to expedite—interest rate liberalization. With the growing importance of cash management, the central bank becomes less efficient in regulating money and credit growth through money supply. Hence, some believe that under the condition of interest rate liberalization, the central bank must shift from aggregate control to indirect interest rate control and rely more on price mechanisms to maximize monetary policy effectiveness. Deposit and lending interest rate liberalization is accompanied by profound changes in the monetary policy transmission mechanism. With floating-rate bonds and hedging financial instruments in broad use, monetary policies may become less potent in influencing savings and investment decisions as long-term investments such as real estate and infrastructure are less sensitive to interest rate volatility. Restrained by credit rationing, monetary policies can hardly achieve their targets of tightening or relaxing credit, and total spending has to be influenced by interest rate variations.

2.5.3 *Choice of Benchmark Interest Rates After Deposit and Lending Interest Rate Liberalization*

After liberalizing deposit and lending interest rates, we must determine the benchmark interest rates as guidance for market-based interest rates. Judging by international experience, countries having completed interest rate liberalization tend to follow currency market interest rates as benchmark interest rates, which normally include: (i) Interbank lending rate: Taking the US and Japan as representative countries, the US adopts the federal funds rate, i.e., the overnight lending rate, Japan follows interbank interest rates as benchmark interest rates; (ii) Short-term Treasury bond rates: the US also adopts three-month Treasury bond rate as benchmark interest rate; (iii) Treasury bond repurchase rate: used as a benchmark interest rate by the UK, Germany, France, and Spain.

In China's case, most scholars have concluded that currency market interest rates should be followed as benchmark interest rates. Among them, Zhang Xiaohui (2011) noted that SHIBOR's (Shanghai Interbank Offered Rate) benchmark position in China's currency market has been established with improving quotation quality and broadening the scope of application. Guo Jianwei (2009) found that interest rate liberalization reforms would correlate financial institutions' asset and liability business with SHIBOR, thus fostering a new monetary policy transmission avenue, and verified that SHIBOR could improve the effectiveness of indirect interest rate by helping to achieve the final targets of monetary policies through deposit and lending interest rates. Based on a systematic analysis of the interest rate structure and characteristics of China's currency market in light of interest rate liberalization and currency market development, Zhang Lijuan (2010) investigated the choice of benchmark interest rates for the interbank money with the options of interbank lending rate and bond repurchase rate and identified problems for the interbank lending rate to be followed as a benchmark interest rate. By testing SHIBOR's benchmark attributes (independence, zero risk, correlation, stability, and authoritativeness), Feng Zongxian, Guo Jianwei and Huo Tianxiang (2009) found market-based benchmark interest rates to be superior to official benchmark interest rates through qualitative analysis. With a further quantitative comparison of the three market-based interest rates, they found that SHIBOR meets the most criteria for a benchmark interest rate. According to international benchmark interest rate standards, Shi Guang and Gao Ke (2012) performed a theoretical and empirical analysis to test SHIBOR's effectiveness as China's currency market benchmark rate, and found that SHIBOR met the basic criteria for—but lacked effectiveness as—a benchmark interest rate. Referencing FFR and LIBOR's quantitative attributes, Wang Zhidong (2012) employed such models as EGARCH and Granger to test the candidate benchmark interest rates for the currency market, and found the seven-day interbank repurchase interest rate as the best-performing benchmark interest rate in the current currency market. In summary, more scholars are in favor of SHIBOR as a currency market benchmark rate and call for enhancing SHIBOR's guidance for the pricing of other financial products in its role as a benchmark rate. In our view, SHIBOR is well-developed in China with a broad scope of applications; it can significantly influence certain economic variables and is suitable to be a currency market benchmark interest rate.

2.6 Deposit and Lending Interest Rate Liberalization's Effects on Financial Structure

2.6.1 Necessity of Interest Rate Liberalization and Reform Process

Amid economic and financial market development, the case for China to liberalize its interest rates becomes stronger than ever.

First, interest rate liberalization reforms are an initiative compatible with the market-based economic system. Under China's current financial management system, lending rates are mostly controlled by the Central Bank. The formulation of standards by one institution without sufficient market feedback is likely to cause interest rates to be incompatible with the current economic environment, resulting in inefficient use of capital. All banks and financial institutions, which currently have the right to floating interest rates, should be granted real autonomy in setting interest rates. A market-based economic system must serve the goal of optimizing resource allocation. Interest rate liberalization is conducive to capital allocation across various sectors of the economy according to return on capital. Market-based interest rates will effectively raise capital to support China's industrial transition, maximize profits, and allocate resources efficiently.

Second, interest rate liberalization reforms are conducive to macroeconomic regulation. Amid economic development, macroeconomic regulation depends more on value leverage and market mechanisms. China's traditional interest rate control has hamstrung the price lever's effect on resource allocation. Inelastic interest rates cannot keep pace with a changing market and cannot properly guide investment. They also prevent the State from effectively regulating the money supply in macroeconomic regulation to meet expected targets. Interest rate liberalization, however, builds a market-based transmission mechanism for private investment and consumption, enabling the central bank to effectively conduct macroeconomic regulation through interest rate variations to influence commercial banks' behaviors and pricing power, bringing into full play the role of interest rates as economic levers.

Third, interest rate liberalization helps improve financial markets and bring China's market-based economy in line with international practices. It allows China to develop synchronously with other economies. More frequent international exchanges and fiercer competition since China's WTO entry entailed changes to China's previous interest rate control. Only by following internationally recognized market rules will China stay competitive in finance. China's market-based economy remains nascent and financial markets imperfect. In this context, interest rate liberalization is conducive to forming cross-border, diversified, and full-fledged financial markets efficient at distribution and investment. In such financial markets, financial institutions may avoid operational risks through a variety of transaction modes such as scattered asset portfolios and avoid investment risks via a broad range of risk avoidance instruments. Foreign-funded banks and enterprises operating in China will be able to finance from international financial markets at substantially lower costs of financing. Chinese enterprises, on the other hand, may also borrow from foreign-funded banks.

Since the release of the *Decisions on Financial System Reforms* at the 14th CPC National Congress in 1993, China has carried out financial interest rate liberalization following the approach of "taking the first step of reform for foreign currencies before the home currency, loan interest rate before deposit interest rate, long maturities before short maturities, and large-sum transactions before small-sum ones." By 2004, China achieved the goals of fully deregulating interest rates on deposits and loans denominated in foreign currencies and "lower limit on loan interest rates and upper limit on deposit interest rate" for Renminbi-denominated loans and deposits. Subsequently, the Central Bank shifted its priority to the development of a market-based interest rate system to create a basic environment for fully market-based deposit and loan rates. Currently, China has established a market-based interest system with SHIBOR rate as pricing basis and supplemented by Treasury bond rate and interest rate swap. On July 20, 2013, the complete deregulation of loan interest rates for financial institutions marks a critical step forward in China's interest rate liberalization. Table 2.5 describes the detailed process of China's interest rate liberalization. Going forward, China's interest rate liberalization reforms will enter the most critical and risky stage: deposit interest rate liberalization. At this juncture, we should first take stock of the effects of interest rate liberalization in the past and forecast future pathways for deposit rate liberalization.

2.6.2 Status of Deposit and Lending Interest Rates in China's Interest Rate System

In determining the status of deposit and lending interest rates in China's interest system, we must first look at the composition of China's interest rate system. China's interest rate system can be divided into official and market interest rates, and official interest rates include: (i) Relending rate, i.e., interest rate for the Central Bank's relending to financial institutions; (ii) Rediscount rate, i.e., interest rate for rediscounting discounted notes held by financial institutions at the central bank; (iii) Deposit reserve rate, i.e., interest rate paid by the Central Bank on the statutory reserves deposited by financial institutions; (iv) Excess deposit reserve rate, i.e., the interest rate paid by the Central Bank on the part of reserves deposited by financial institutions above the statutory deposit reserve; (v) Statutory deposit and loan rates for financial institutions. Meanwhile, the Central Bank also controls the floating band of deposit interest rates.

Table 2.5 China's Interest Rate Liberalization Reform Process

Liberalizing interest rates for currency market and bond market	In January 1996, China established a nationally unified interbank lending market; In June 1996, the Central Bank stipulated that the interbank rate should be determined independently between the lender and the borrower according to supply and demand of capital; In June 1997, China established the national interbank bond market, and the Central Bank decided to deregulate interbank bond repurchase rate and spot trading price; In 1998, China adopted market-based pricing for policy financial bonds and Treasury bonds through public tendering
Taking steps to deregulate domestic foreign currency deposit and lending interest rates;	In September 2000, the Central Bank announced the deregulation of foreign currency loan interest rates and large-sum foreign currency deposit interest rates; in November 2003, the Central Bank set an upper limit on small-sum foreign currency deposit interest rates In November 2004, the Central Bank deregulated interest rates for small-sum foreign currency deposits with maturities above one year

(continued)

Table 2.5 (continued)

Deregulating interest rates on Renminbi loans	In January 1987, the Central Bank allowed commercial banks to raise loan interest rates to 1.2 times the statutory benchmark interest rate on working capital loans; In January 2004, the Central Bank raised the upper limit on loan interest rates for commercial banks and city credit cooperatives to 1.7 times the benchmark loan interest rate, raised the upper limit on loan interest rates for rural credit cooperatives to 2 times the benchmark loan interest rate, and kept the lower limit on loan interest rates for financial institutions at 0.9 times the loan benchmark interest rate; In October 2004, the Central Bank removed the upper limit on Renminbi loan interest rates for financial institutions, kept the lower limit at 0.9 points the benchmark loan interest rate, and raised the upper limit on loan interest rates for city and rural credit cooperatives to 2.3 times the loan benchmark rate; In 2006, the Central Bank cut the lower limit on commercial interest rates on personal housing mortgage loans to 0.85 times the benchmark interest rate; In October 2008, the Central Bank cut the lower limit on commercial interest rates on personal housing mortgage loans to 0.7 times the benchmark interest rate; In June and July 2012, the Central Bank took two steps to adjust the lower limit on loan interest rates to 0.7 times the benchmark loan interest rate; In July 2013, the Central Bank deregulated loan interest rate control, removed lower limits on loan interest rates except for personal housing mortgage loans, deregulated discounted interest rate control, and ceased to set an upper limit on loan interest rates for rural credit cooperatives On October 25, 2013, the Central Bank announced the launch of Loan Prime Rate (LPR) with nine quoting banks in the first group

(continued)

Table 2.5 (continued)

Liberalizing Renminbi deposit interest rates	In October 1999, the Central Bank approved the offering of market-priced negotiable certificate of deposit (CD) business by financial institutions, expanded the scope of CD holders, and took steps to widen the floating band of deposit interest rates for financial institutions; In October 2004, the Central Bank set an upper limit on Renminbi deposit interest rates and deregulated the lower limit; In March 2005, the Central Bank deregulated interbank deposit interest rates for financial institutions, and granted commercial banks pricing power for six types of deposits excluding time and demand deposits; In June 2012, the Central Bank allowed financial institutions to raise Renminbi deposit interest rates with an upper limit 1.1 times the benchmark deposit interest rates

Taking credit risks into account, market interest rates include: (i) interbank lending rate, which refers to the interest rate on collateral-free credit lending between financial institutions in the interbank market; (ii) interbank Treasury bond repurchase rate, which refers to short-term lending interest rates between financial institutions with Treasury bonds as collateral in the interbank market; (iii) exchange-based Treasury bond repurchase rate, which refers to the short-term lending rate for financial institutions with Treasury bonds as collateral in the securities exchange market; (iv) central bank note rate, which refers to interest rates on various notes issued by the central bank; (v) Treasury bond rate, which refers to interest rates on Treasury bonds of various maturities issued by the Ministry of Finance; (vi) Corporate bond rate, which refers to interest rates on various bonds issued by firms in the bond market.

Interest rate liberalization is by no means targeted at market interest rates, which are determined by supply and demand. Instead, interest rate liberalization is mainly targeted at officially regulated interest rates, and the interest rate liberalization reforms are normally targeted at the statutory deposit and lending interest rates of financial institutions. First, the relending, rediscounting, deposit reserve, and excess deposit reserve rates are lending rates between the Central Bank and financial institutions (primarily commercial banks) and can be fully controlled by the Central Bank. Deposit and lending interest rates are lending interest rates between financial institutions and lenders, and the Central Bank cannot monitor each deposit and loan transaction.

Second, among all official interest rates, deposit and lending interest rates for financial institutions exert direct effects on every sector of economic life. Relending rate, rediscounting rate, deposit reserve rate, and excess deposit reserve rate only reflect the lending relationship between financial institutions and the Central Bank, but deposit and lending interest rates for financial institutions are related to both investment and financing decisions of the corporate sector and household sector savings, consumption and investment, as well as asset and liability businesses of the banking sector.

Third, deposit and lending interest rates are the foundation for various market interest rates. All central banks must guide and regulate interest rate markets with or without interest rate liberalization to prevent excess volatility in market interest rates and major deviations in the cost of capital and ensure the effective implementation of its monetary policies. Before deposit and lending interest rate deregulation, deposit and lending interest rates serve as such fundamental and guidance interest rates in China.

For these reasons, deposit and lending interest rates are fundamental to China's interest rate system. Deregulating deposit and lending interest rates, therefore, will inevitably cause tremendous shocks to the existing interest rate system. This is why China should liberalize its interest rates in a cautious, steady, and step-by-step manner.

2.6.3 Deposit and Lending Interest Rate Liberalization's Overall Effects on China's Financial Structure

Previous sections analyzed the effects of liberalizing loan interest rates on the corporate sector, deposit interest rates on the household sector, deposit and lending interest rates on the banking sector, and deposit and lending interest rates on monetary policy. From such analyses, we may discern the effects of deposit and lending interest rates on various sectors of China's economy. In this section, we will explain how a succession of interest rate liberalization initiatives adopted by China has structurally influenced China's financial system.

For financial institutions, deposit and lending interest rate liberalization reforms are putting an end to their profiteering from interest rate spreads, forcing them to develop innovative financial products and services. Meanwhile, interest rate liberalization reforms are testing financial institutions' risk management competence. Based on international experience, interest rate liberalization is likely to trigger a wave of mergers and acquisitions in China's financial industry. Since the start of interest rate liberalization, banking financial institutions will offer highly differentiated deposit and lending interest rates for different sorts of depositors and borrowers and are expected to face a higher nonperformance loan (NPL) ratio unless they strive to improve their risk management capabilities. Interest rate volatility arising from interest rate liberalization will force financial institutions to step up interest rate risk management. More frequent capital flows made possible by interest rate liberalization will force financial institutions to ramp up liquidity risk management. Differences in these capabilities will slowly lead to a divergence in financial institutions. Those that are well run and can reduce operational and administrative costs will see their market share expand swiftly; those that are run poorly and struggle to keep up with the change will have to close loss-making outlets, downsize operations, experience shrinking revenues, and even go out of business.

For the financial market, deposit and lending interest rate liberalization is unleashing more opportunities to direct finance. Interest rate liberalization will allow households to invest in direct finance, thus ploughing more funds into financial markets. It will also increase the diversity of financial instruments, and help form complete, multitiered financial markets consisted of interbank lending, foreign exchange, securities, and gold markets. Interest rate liberalization is transforming the distorted supply and demand of capital and promoting reasonably priced financial instruments. Financial markets have seen an emergence of financial instruments with highly differentiated credit ratings and a sharp increase in high-risk and high-return financial instruments. Innovative financial instruments such as subordinated bonds, financial derivatives, and structural financial instruments will offer financial markets more risk management alternatives to meet customers' investment and risk management needs. Wilder interest rate volatility will give rise to interest rate derivatives such as interest rate futures, options, and swaps to help all financial market participants to avoid interest rate risks. On top of interest spread income, banking financial institutions will offer more paid services and innovative interest rate wealth management products to meet the customers' wealth management needs.

As far as financial security is concerned, interest rate liberalization reforms will bring both challenges and opportunities. Without sufficient preparations, interest rate liberalization may threaten financial security when the macroeconomic environment is not stable. After interest rate liberalization is completed, interest rates could be sharply higher than in the pre-reform era, causing an inflow of excess foreign capital, home currency appreciation, and inflation. If a country is overwhelmed by foreign capital inflows and forced to depreciate its currency, its external debt will become costlier to serve, leading its financial institutions to fail and thus triggering a financial crisis. With mature financial markets and regulatory systems in place, however, well-timed interest rate liberalization reforms will lead to benign interactions between financial markets, institutions and regulatory systems, which in turn will advance reforms in other areas and help form a sound financial system.

In the context of financial internationalization, interest rate liberalization reforms will make China's financial system more resilient against shocks from hot money. Under such reforms, financial asset prices in China will be more aligned with international financial asset prices, allowing China's financial markets to attract more international investment funds. Interest rate liberalization will also narrow the interest rate spread between domestic and international financial assets, propel the reforms of the exchange rate mechanism, and expedite the internationalization of Renminbi as a currency for international trade, investment, and reserves. A less resilient financial system, however, will expose financial markets to shocks from hot money inflow and outflow, overburden the exchange rate system to the brink of collapse, and even trigger a financial crisis, as Latin American countries have learned to their cost.

References

Guo Jianwei: "Interest Rate Pricing Practice for Financial Institutions with Shibor as Benchmark", *China Finance*, Vol.21, 2009.

Wang Zhidong: "Empirical Study on the Choice of Benchmark Interest Rate for China's Monetary market", *Review of Investment Studies*, Vol.1, 2012.

Zhang Xiaohui" "Elevating Shibor's Position as Benchmark Interest Rate for Monetary market", *China Finance*, Vol.12, 2011.

Chapter 3
China's Return on Capital and Real Interest Rates in Relation to Investment

Since the adoption of the policy on reform and opening up in 1978, investment has played a direct and important role in China's rapid economic growth. Chinese scholars extensively debated the sustainability of China's investment-driven growth model. From the perspective of labor migration, some studies identified high investment and high return on capital (ROC) as China's intrinsic economic growth phenomena. On the basis of calculating return on capital, this chapter will verify the relationship between investment and return on capital minus interest rate referencing Knut Wicksell's theory to empirically support the conclusions of such theory and test the relationship between investment and interest rate. Most existing studies on return on capital have been carried out from global and regional perspectives, and some studies have identified the efficiency loss arising from factor price distortions. From a sectoral perspective, this chapter will focus on observing return on capital in resource sectors and further identify whether differences in return on capital in those sectors will influence monetary policy. Based on the theoretical research and calculation result in this chapter, our conclusion is that China's current investment-driven development model is facing a turning point. To deepen the results of industrial development, China must reform the existing stock and iron out uneven return on capital across sectors. In the final section of this chapter, we will discuss China's strategies for urbanization and globalization under the broader goal of further unleashing potential economic output.

G. Wang, *A Study on Interest Rate Liberalization in China*, Research Series on the Chinese Dream and China's Development Path,
https://doi.org/10.1007/978-981-97-3644-7_3

3.1 Brief Review of Literature

Over the past three decades of reform and opening up, China's economy has maintained rapid growth with GDP annual growth rate averaging 9.83%.[1] Investment has played a decisive role in shoring up growth, contributing an average of 39.78% to China's economic growth since 1978. After the Asian Financial Crisis of 1997, investment contributed an average of as much as 49.97%—and more than 60% in some years—to China's economic growth.[2] This phenomenon naturally aroused controversies over the sustainability of China's economic model. According to the neoclassical growth theory, capital deepening will lead to a smaller return on capital, which ultimately converges to a constant value, i.e., economic growth is convergent.

The most straightforward method for determining investment sustainability is to measure return on capital. In May 2006, the World Bank's China Office reported an increase in the return on equity (ROE) of Chinese enterprises since 1998 in the *China Quarterly Update* (World Bank China Office, 2006). As analyzed in the World Bank's two other research reports on the relationship between savings and investment in China (Kuijs, 2005, 2006), corporate savings (retained earnings) comprised a major—and growing—share of total savings in China, and retained earnings made up the primary source of funds for corporate investment driven by steadily rising return on capital. As an inference, the limited external financing (bank loans) meant that banks' risk exposure was smaller than expected. In the section of policy recommendations, the authors kindly reminded policymakers that economic development and demographic shift would lead to a decrease in the savings rate, and that the government should spend less to subsidize corporate investment and more on social programs and shift its policy focus away from encouraging labor-intensive industries. These reports by the World Bank have received a great deal of attention from academia and the industry. After the Asian Financial Crisis, China's capital formation rate plateaued at around 50%, and the non-performing loans (NPL) ratio of China's banking sector remained high even after the technical NPL carve-out.[3] In such a context, one might wonder whether the conclusions of those reports reflected the reality or distorted the facts to seek public attention or contained a hidden agenda. In any case, those reports touched upon an important topic and sparked intense debates.

Dr. Shan Weijian (Shan, 2006; Shan Weijian, 2006a, 2006b) was the first to rebuke, describing the World Bank's reports as "illusory." He cited many facts to support his rebuttal: first, China's banking sector NPL ratio was too high to be justified by the alleged high return on capital; second, Dr. Shan Weijian also noted that Kuijs' calculation would overestimate return on capital by not deducting income tax, investment income, and subsidy income; third, as far as the trend of return on capital is

[1] Data is from the NBS and calculated by taking the geometric mean of GDP fixed-based index, and data period is between 1978 and 2012.

[2] Data is from the NBS, and investment contribution rate was 63.30% and 87.58% in 2003 and 2009, respectively.

[3] According to the 2006 Annual Report of the China Banking Regulatory Commission (CBRC), China's banking sector NPL ratio was 17.9%, 13.2% and 8.9% from 2003 to 2005, respectively.

concerned, China faced a "biflation" (rising costs of raw materials coexisted with falling prices of finished goods). How come return on capital rose in the face of those adversities? Hofman & Kuijs (2006) responded to Shan Weijian's doubts, primarily relating to the first and third points, without delving into details about return on capital.

Given the importance of this issue, academic discussions on how to correctly estimate return on capital became vibrant. A typical study is Bai Chong'en et al. (Bai et al., 2006), who followed the factor approach of national income accounting based on macroeconomic data to calculate corporate return on capital by subtracting tax income from numerator in the ratio between capital income (total income minus labor compensation) and capital stock. By using macroeconomic data, this method avoids the problems of omission, understatement and repetitive calculation associated with microeconomic data. With the above method, Bai Chong'en et al. estimated China's return on capital to stay at the level of around 20% after 1998 before starting to rise since 2001 instead of 1999. The exclusion of tax income led to a decline in return on capital by about 10%. With microeconomic data, Lu Feng et al. (2007) calculated seven types of return on capital in China. Before calculation, they fully discussed the potential impact of tax, investment and subsidy incomes mentioned by Shan Weijian, and the final results of calculation suggested an increase in return on net fixed assets to 13.4%, up from 2.2% in 1998. These clear-cut conclusions, however, did little to dampen academic interest in the calculation of return on capital. With a microeconomic approach, Shan Haojie and Shi Bo (2008) estimated return on industrial capital in China and reached consistent conclusions with Lu Feng et al. (2007). They also applied the same method in regional estimation and reached a conclusion on the convergence of interprovincial return on capital. Following a macroeconomic approach, Fang Wenquan (2012) re-estimated China's return on capital, stressing that capital heterogeneity and the effect of year led to an overstatement of depreciation rate and an understatement of capital stock, thus causing return on capital to be overestimated.[4] Despite different results, the above estimates agreed on the following trend: China's return on capital tended to increase after 2000.

Estimating return on capital is only the first step of research. The key is to explain the coexistence between China's high return on capital and high investment to further determine whether this model is sustainable. In his book *China's Miracle*, Justin Yifu Lin et al. (2002) took stock of China's general reform experience: He pointed out that most post-reform countries failed in their catch-up strategies because they did not bring their comparative advantage into play (irrespective of

---

[4] Appealingly, this paper brought forth a discussion on "economic growth and wealth accumulation" from the topic of depreciation rate, referring to it as a "vanishing Eiffel Tower." This proposition has the following connotations: In the same year when the Paris World Expo ended, Eiffel Tower's costs of construction and operation were recovered. After a century, its residual value became zero, or in other words, Eiffel Tower vanished from the account book and could be dismantled and rebuilt to generate a higher present value of assets and GDP. Yet the fact is that after re-painted many times, Eiffel Tower continued to play its role in capital production. In China's case, mandatory capital loss and replacement, though uplifting GDP and return on capital, contributed little to wealth accumulation.

their social systems; reform should be intended to change the institutional environment to effectuate comparative advantage. After removing the adverse institutional factor that constrained the production possibility frontier, China's biggest comparative advantage turned out to be labor resources. Under a standard Solow model, Cai Fang (2005) revealed how exogenous population growth (demographic shift) would affect economic growth and explained the underlying high investment and high return phenomena: When the working-age population as a share of a country's total population increases, the savings rate/investment rate will increase, and the capital-to-labor ratio will move to the right; when various factors in the economy are fully substitutable, the level of capital equipment for the new workforce will remain constant; a relatively low initial capital stock means higher return on capital. In discussing this high-growth model, Cai Fang (2005) underscored the importance of a well-functioning mechanism to induce a high savings rate compatible with the working-age population, which shares a consistent intrinsic logic with the priority on incremental reforms to "invigorate micro-level operation mechanisms" elaborated by Justin Yifu Lin (2002).

Li Yang and Yin Jianfeng (2005) investigated China's high-investment phenomenon from the perspective of labor migration. By introducing the factor of labor migration into Frank P. Ramsey's neoclassical growth model, they induced a leap in the convergence path of the phase diagram in Ramsey's model. In the model, the expected value of new-type labor productivity is greater than 1, which is a core, delicate and insightful design. Not only does it explain the phenomenon of rising return on capital, but it also unravels China's high savings and high investment puzzle in the transition stage. New-type labor productivity greater than 1 is related to the "learning by doing" effect during labor migration, and its scope may also be extended to include the spillover effect of foreign direct investment (FDI). Through an extensive survey, Jiang Xiaojuan and Li Rui (2002) uncovered that most multinational companies had adopted advanced technologies from their parent companies that were otherwise not available domestically in China, and that multinational companies also contributed to human resource development in China. Zhang Yu and Jiang Dianchun (2008) found that foreign direct investment (FDI) created positive spillover effects by inducing industrial agglomeration. With a panel autoregression model, Chen Peixin (2013) explained the benign interactions among productivity, return on capital, and economic growth. These studies have reinforced from various facets the conclusion that labor migration had undergirded China's economic growth. It is fair to say that "continuous labor migration has served as a core mechanism underpinning China's economic growth over the past two decades, and the high savings rate and high investment rate over the years have both resulted from and contributed to labor migration."[5]

Labor migration affects economic growth primarily on the supply side. To avoid excess volatility in the economy, aggregate demand management—especially interest rate policy—plays a pivotal role in macroeconomic regulation. In its research report

[5] Li Yang, Yin Jianfeng: "High Savings, High Investment and China's Economic Growth during Labor Migration", *Economic Research Journal*, Vol.2, 2005, p. 15.

Determinants of Corporate Investment in China (IMF, 2012), the International Monetary Fund (IMF) noted that investment overheating in China might harm China's banking system, lead to an increase in fiscal deficit, and trigger trade frictions, and that investment could be cooled down only with an interest rate hike, exchange rate appreciation, and financial deepening. Although this report did not elicit any heated debate as did the World Bank's report in 2006, it received great attention from the People's Bank of China (PBoC): considering China's weighted lending rate of 7% to 8% from 2011 to the first half of 2012, the IMF's assertion that interest rates in China were too low naturally had to be treated seriously to determine whether it was a valid or false claim. This is also one of our considerations in deciding to draft this paper. Discussions on the investment impact of interest rates generally fall into the Keynesian school and the Swedish school. According to the Keynesian school, as the cost of investment capital, interest rates have a direct reverse effect on investment and may also generate an indirect reverse effect by influencing firms' replacement cost and balance sheet. According to the Swedish school, interest rates are not the sole determinant of investment and must be examined in conjunction with the natural rate of interest (return on capital). When the natural rate of interest is above loan interest rate, both investment and production will expand until the two rates become equal; a reverse trend will occur only when loan interest rate is above the natural rate of interest.[6] The Keynesian school adopts the stock analysis method,[7] under which investment does not generate any direct impact on interest rates and may only influence interest rates through the "back door" of income. The biggest advantage of the Swedish school is that the effects between investment and interest rates are interactive, i.e., investment change will induce change in return on capital, which has a direct impact on the difference between the two interest rates. But the biggest disadvantage of the Swedish school lies in its ineptitude to account for the flow volume.

In light of China's practice of interest rate policy, numerous studies have shown that interest rates have a minimal impact on investment: Yao Lingzhen and Wang Shuhao's (2003) regression analysis showed a negative correlation between the two, but the goodness of fit was extremely low. Following the same approach, Zeng Linghua and Wang Chaojun (2003) reached consistent conclusions, but attributed the insignificant interest rate impact to a lag effect of central bank regulation. Using the panel method, Song Fangxiu (2008) performed an empirical analysis of listed manufacturing companies, and found the transmission mechanism of interest rate impact on investment to be impeded. She referred to such impediment as the soft constraint of interest rates, which is subject to the direct impact of the relative size and

[6] Knut Wicksel (2007). See Wicksell's statements in Chapter 8.

[7] The Keynesian school is not completely focused on the analysis of stock, and 1S curve shows a relationship of flow. John Hicks pointed out this drawback: "These two curves should not be drawn in the same diagram since one is about flow and the other is about stock. It is extremely unreasonable to put them on the same diagram since they involve fundamentally different time dimensions J." Hicks, *Towards a More General Theory*, appeared in S. C. Tsiang and M. Kohn eds., *Finance Constraints, Expectation and Macroeconomics*, The Oxford Lniversity Press, 1988, pp. 3–4.

transferability of interest cost. Zhou Ying (2009) tested the mechanism under which interest rates affected investment through the balance sheet, and found interest rates to be negatively correlated with firms' net worth, which was positively correlated with investment. However, the direct test result of the relationship between interest rate and investment is that the two are negatively correlated, i.e., even if interest rates could affect investment through the balance sheet, such an impact is feeble. In addition, studies following the Swedish school have made some progress. Through a regression analysis, Shen Kunrong and Wang Jian (2000) reached the following conclusion, i.e., China's real interest rates basically ceased to exert any impact on economic growth rate after 1990 (even if an impact had existed, it was against the theoretical pattern), and the difference between return on capital and market interest rates (i.e., interest rate spread) is an important variable that might incentivize corporate investment. With a dynamic model of real interest rate gaps, Shi Zhuxian et al. (2006) performed a test and uncovered that when the real interest rate was above the long-term natural rate of interest, investment would be pent-up and inhibiting economic growth; when the real interest rate equaled or was below the natural rate of interest, investment would create a positive effect on economic growth.

This chapter reviews literature at considerable length in the interest of the following objectives: (i) demonstrate from an empirical perspective that difference between the return on capital and interest rate is a driver of investment growth, and thus indirectly prove that China's economic growth in the three-decade reform era has been underpinned by labor migration as its core mechanism; (ii) since growth derived from labor migration, the opportunity window for demographic dividends[8] will close sooner or later, which is why China's policy agenda now calls for "unleashing reform dividends." Price distortions of key factor resources and monopolies in certain sectors have long been blamed for their damaging effects on the economy. Based on the relationship between investment and interest rates, we will determine whether a sector's development meets the principle of efficiency and thus identify reform priorities; (iii) if the widely criticized ownership and sector discrimination facing the financial industry stems from the pursuit of a higher return on capital and is not arbitrarily imposed by the financial system itself, reforms should be first targeted at the real-economy sectors. Regarding this topic, we will test how sectoral differences of return on capital affect monetary policy. The remainder of this chapter is structured as follows: First, we will measure overall industrial and sector-specific real return on capital, respectively, and explain the sectoral difference of return on capital; second, we will calculate real interest rates and test how the difference between the real return on capital and real interest rates affects investment; third, we will discuss whether the sectoral difference of return on capital will influence monetary policy regulation; lastly, we will draw conclusions and put forth policy recommendations on China's economic development priorities going forward.

---

[8] Cai Fang elaborated on the consistency among the three concepts of demographic transition, demographic dividends, and labor migration. Refer to Cai Fang's "Demographic Transition, Demographic Dividends and the Lewis Turning Point", *Economic Research Journal*, Vol.4, 2010.

3.2 Estimation of China's Return on Capital and Analysis of Sectoral Difference

3.2.1 Estimation Method, Data Source and Treatment Explanation

3.2.1.1 Estimation Method

The rate of return on capital ("return on capital" for short) refers to the ratio between the amount of return on capital and the amount of capital employed to create such return. This ratio can be expressed by the following equation: Return on capital = Amount of return on capital/capital stock. In the literature review section, we have already explained the methods of estimation, including those at the macro and micro levels based on factor income. Since sectoral differences are to be examined in this section, it is more appropriate to use the microscopic method. We have fully referenced Lu Feng et al.'s (2007) calculation method, which estimates seven indicators of return on capital from various perspectives. Given our focus on the ability of capital to yield return, we have included social return and aggregate return on capital into the numerator. The denominator is equity capital, which is equivalent to the net value of fixed assets defined in calculation. In the four years from 2003 to 2006, the two had very close values (their average ratio was 0.95) and shared a consistent trend (correlation coefficient is as high as 0.99). We decided to use the former only because the former had more complete data. Given the need to calculate the real return on capital, we have followed Lu Feng et al.'s (2007) method regarding the price factor with a depreciation rate of 10%.

3.2.1.2 Data Source and Treatment Explanation

Data source and treatment involve three issues:

First, sector merger. According to the NBS classification of industrial sectors, there are 39 Class I sectors. In the real world, some industrial sectors such as petroleum extraction and petroleum refining and processing have formed a vertically integrated system with potential internal transfer pricing. As such, we have merged those sectors. We have also merged sectors with similar product attributes or processing technologies for the convenience of calculation and observation of final results. Please refer to Table 3.1 for the specific method of merger.

Second, the time span and frequency of data. Our data starts from 1999, when China's monetary policy shifted from direct to indirect regulation. Also in this year, deflation occurred in China, suggesting a shift of the market economy from the seller's market to the buyer's market. Data frequency is quarterly data since the standard definition of return on capital is normally the return from capital operation in a year. Thus, we initially perform an annualized treatment of quarterly return

Table 3.1 Method for sector merger

Name of sector after merger	Original sectors included	Codes of original sectors
Coal mining and washing	Coal mining and washing	06 (not merged)
Petroleum extraction and petrochemical refining	Petroleum and natural gas extraction, petroleum processing, coking and nuclear fuel processing	07, 25
Metal and non-metal ore mining and dressing	Ferrous metal ore mining and dressing, nonferrous metal ore mining and dressing, non-metal ore mining and dressing, other mining	08–11
Processing of agricultural and sideline foods	Processing of agricultural and sideline foods	13 (not merged)
Food and beverage manufacturing	Manufacture of foods, manufacture of beverages	14, 15
Manufacture of tobacco	Manufacture of tobacco	16 (not merged)
Manufacture of textile, footwear, caps, and leather	Manufacture of textiles, manufacture of textile, apparel, footwear, and caps, and manufacture of leather, fur, feather and related products	17–19
Processing of timber and manufacture of furniture	Processing of timber, manufacture of wood, bamboo, rattan, palm, and straw products, and manufacture of furniture	20, 21
Papermaking, printing and manufacture of articles for culture and education activity	Papermaking and paper products, printing and recorded media, manufacture of articles for culture, education and sport activities	22–24
Manufacture of chemical raw materials and chemical fibers	Manufacture of chemical raw materials, and manufacture of chemical fibers	26, 28
Manufacture of medicines	Manufacture of medicines	27 (not merged)
Manufacture of rubber and plastics	Manufacture of rubber and manufacture of plastics	29, 30
Metal and non-metal smelting and manufacture	Manufacture of non-metallic mineral products, smelting and pressing of ferrous metals, smelting and pressing of non-ferrous metals, and manufacture of metal products	31–34
Manufacture of general-purpose machinery	Manufacture of general-purpose machinery	35 (not merged)
Manufacture of special purpose machinery	Manufacture of special purpose machinery	36 (not merged)
Manufacture of transport equipment	Manufacture of transport equipment	37 (not merged)

(continued)

Table 3.1 (continued)

Name of sector after merger	Original sectors included	Codes of original sectors
Manufacture of electrical machinery and equipment	Manufacture of electrical machinery and equipment	39 (not merged)
Manufacture of communication equipment, computers and measuring instruments	Manufacture of communication equipment, computers and other electronic equipment, and manufacture of measuring instruments and machinery for cultural activity and office work	40, 41
Production and distribution of electric power and heat power	Production and distribution of electric power and heat power	44 (not merged)
Production and distribution of gas	Production and distribution of gas	45 (not merged)
Production and distribution of tap water	Production and distribution of tap water	46 (not merged)

on capital, i.e., multiplying such data by 4. In addition, the NBS only provides the cumulative values for February, May, August, and November in four years from 2007 to 2010, which have been specifically processed. Return on capital calculated for January and February approximately denotes return on capital for the first quarter and is multiplied by 6 as an annualized treatment. Return on capital from March to May, from June to August, and from September to November approximately denotes return on capital for the second, third and fourth quarters and is multiplied by 4 as an annualized treatment.

Third, data sources and the quarterly adjustment of data. Data in this paper is from CEIC, China Applied Statistical Data, and Wind information. NBS sectoral statistics are subject to adjustment in certain years, and each database adopts inconsistent data criteria. Some databases have no record of sectoral data. We have searched various databases to supplement data for all sectors. For data with the same statistical criteria, cross-verification can be performed across databases. Having verified the above data, our data cut-off date is the end of 2012. After the initial treatment of data, we found that firm profit and taxation were highly seasonal in nature, so we used X-11 addition to make a seasonal adjustment of the estimated return on capital.

3.2.2 Estimation Results and Brief Explanation

Figure 3.1 shows change in China's return on industrial capital estimated with the above method. As can be learned from Fig. 3.1, China's return on industrial capital

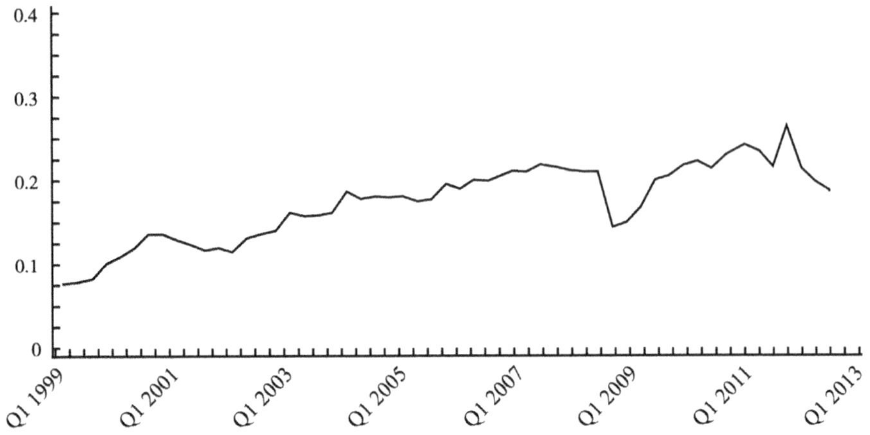

Fig. 3.1 China's return on industrial capital, 1999–2012

has been steadily on the rise since 1999, which verifies Li Yang and Yin Jianfeng's (2005) theoretical argument that the continuous migration of labor force is a key driver behind increasing return on capital. In addition, our quarterly data after taking annualized average is roughly consistent with the results estimated by Lu Feng et al. (2007), which indicates our methodological correctness throughout the whole process of application.

On the curve of rising return on capital, two timeframes warrant attention. The first timeframe is from the second to the fourth quarter of 2008, when China's return on capital took a dive as the global financial crisis rampaged through the real economy and crimped the external demand. This slump is a sobering reminder that China's high return on capital during the transition process was largely achieved through external demand, i.e., rapid economic growth stemmed from the dividends of globalization. Second, China's return on industrial capital also tumbled in 2012. According to Cai Fang's research,[9] 2013 marks a turning point of China's diminishing demographic dividends. The steep decline in return on capital since 2012 as shown in the figure is surprisingly consistent with the conclusions of theoretical research.

Figure 3.2 shows sector-specific return on capital. From the chart, we may arrive at the following conclusions: first, return on capital in each sector is roughly consistent with the overall trend. In 2012, in particular, almost all sectors reported falling return on capital (except for manufacture of tobacco and the production and distribution of heat), which seems to lend further credence to the long-term turning point; the fact that not all sectors experienced a slump in 2008 indicates that not all sectors were affected by external demand.

[9] Cai Fang: "2013 Marks a Turning Point of China's Vainishing Demographic Dividends", *21st Century Business Herald*, April 12, 2012. Web address: http://www.21cbh.com/HTML/2012-4-2/30MDY5XzQxMDI30Q.html. Last visited date: November 28, 2013.

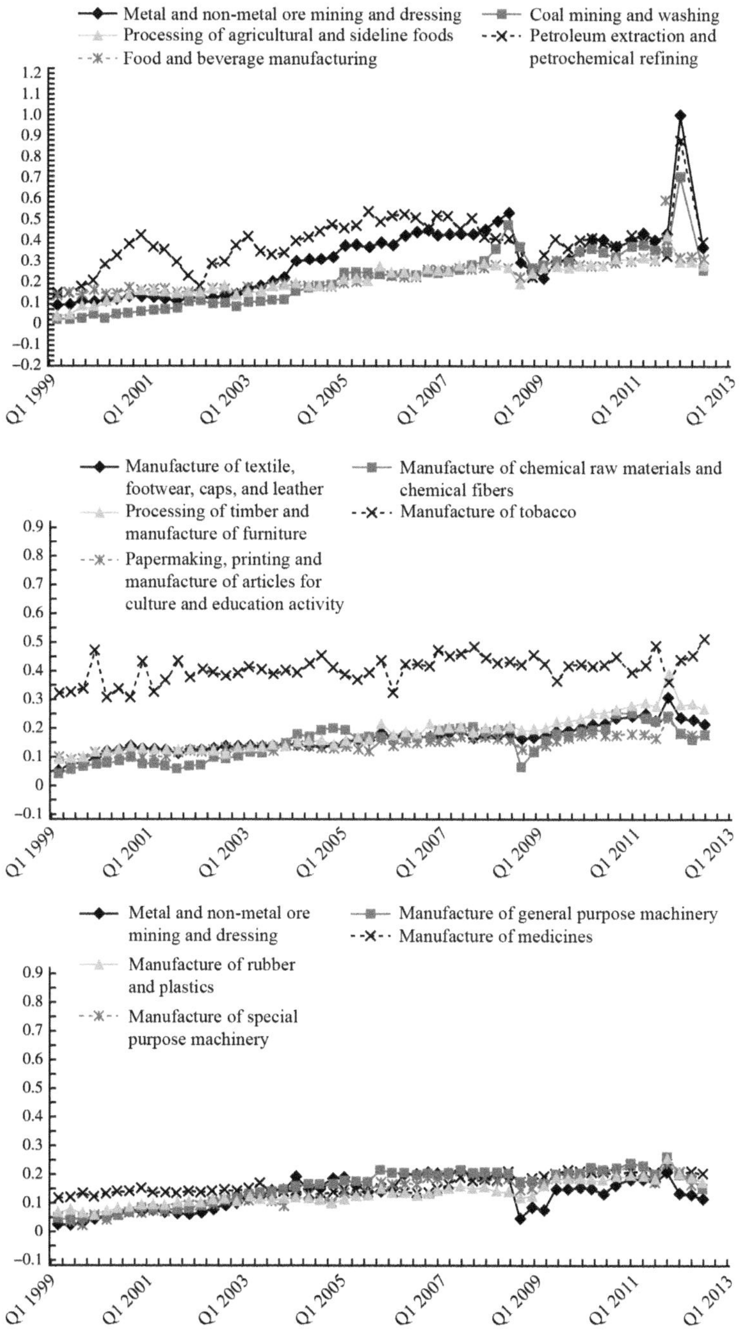

Fig. 3.2 Sector-specific returns on capital, 1999–2012

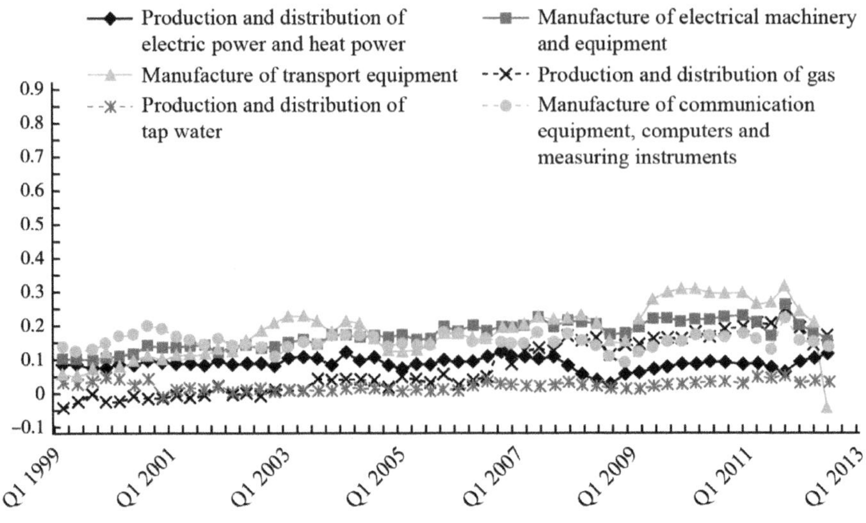

Fig. 3.2 (continued)

Second, petroleum extraction, petrochemical refining, and mining and processing of ferrous and non-ferrous metal ores reported far higher return on capital than other sectors did. Excess returns on capital in these sectors are possibly due to monopoly.

Third, there was a great deal of volatility in the return on capital in the above-mentioned two sectors plus coal mining and dressing, and all these three sectors are resource sectors, reflecting their integration with international market prices. Moreover, these three sectors deviated from the general trend of gradually rising return on capital in other sectors, indicating that their returns on capital were unrelated to labor migration.

Fourth, manufacture of tobacco saw a stable return on capital at around 40% over the years, which is obviously a result of sectoral monopoly.

Fifth, some labor-intensive sectors (such as manufacture of textiles, footwear, hats and leather and manufacture of general purpose equipment) saw a relatively significant increase in their return on capital while some capital and technology-intensive sectors (i.e., manufacture of communication equipment, computers and measuring instruments, manufacture of medicines, and manufacture of electrical machinery and equipment) reported slow increases in their returns on capital, which was high in the early stage. A possible explanation is that the rising return on capital in labor-intensive sectors was helped by labor migration while the relatively high return on capital in capital and technology-intensive sectors in the early stage could be attributed to the seller's market and showed no more evident increases as the seller's market turned into a buyer's market.

Sixth, three sectors reported modest returns on capital, including production and distribution of electric power and heat power, production and distribution of gas, and production and distribution of water. A possible reason is the public goods attribute of those sectors, where a state controlling stake ensures affordable pricing for the public. Despite modest returns, labor compensation is rather high in the production and distribution of electric power and heat power, which relates to the issue of fair income distribution.

To more clearly compare the differences in return on capital across sectors, we have taken the average of each sector's quarterly data to compare such sectoral differences. Figure 3.3 is a vivid reflection of the calculation results. As shown in the chart, manufacture of tobacco, petroleum extraction and petrochemical refining, and metal and non-metal ore mining and dressing boasted significantly higher returns on capital than other sectors; the three sectors of production and distribution of electric power and heat power, production and distribution of gas, and production and distribution of water reported much lower returns on capital than other sectors. The remaining 15 sectors recorded similar returns on capital in the range between 14 and 20%. This result is very close to the view of average sectoral profitability and implies that structural problems in the economy mainly exist in resource and public sectors.

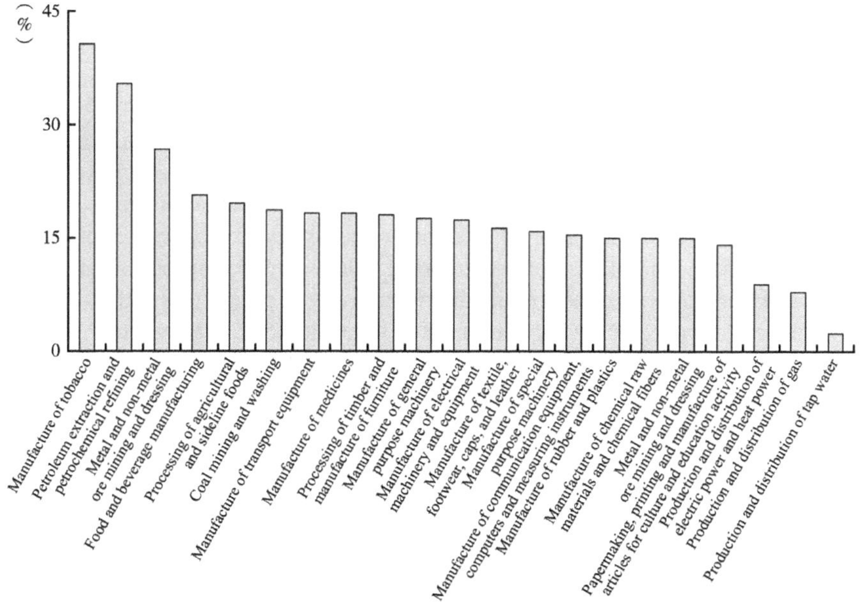

Fig. 3.3 Sectoral difference of return on capital

3.2.3 *Analysis of Sectoral Differences*

Some sectors (manufacture of tobacco, petroleum extraction and petrochemical refining, metal and non-metal ore mining and dressing, and production and distribution of electric power and heat power) significantly deviated from the average sectoral return on capital. Most of such sectors are state-controlled and monopolized. Liu Xiaoxuan (2003) demonstrated that since the state ownership and heft of SOEs were associated with a government monopoly of the market, even a high industry concentration would lead to negative business performance, but such negative effects of state ownership should be partially offset by market barriers generating excess monopolistic returns. Yu Liangchun and Zhang Wei (2010) estimated the intensity of monopoly and efficiency loss in four typical sectors of administrative monopoly, including electric power, telecom, petroleum, and railway sectors. They uncovered that administrative monopoly led to huge efficiency losses at the microscopic, sectoral and macroscopic levels. With a panel model and regression model, we will test whether monopoly has led to high returns on capital in these sectors.

3.2.3.1 Analysis Based on Panel Data

Sector-specific estimation shows an evident trend in the return on capital data, making it necessary to consider the time effect in the panel model specification. Regarding sectoral differences, manufacture of tobacco, petroleum extraction and petrochemical refining, metal and non-metal ore mining and dressing sectors reported significantly higher returns on capital than other sectors; production and distribution of electric power and heat power, production and distribution of gas, production and distribution of water sectors posted much smaller returns on capital than other sectors. Considering the individual effect, we assume that those sectoral differences of return on capital derive from the market share of state-owned enterprises (SOEs). In addition, the panel model should also consider the control variable of capital stock per capita, whose sign is expected to be negative, i.e., with rising capital stock per capita, return on capital will decrease, reflecting the law of diminishing return on capital.

Based on the above analysis, we specify the following time and entity fixed effects model:

$$r_{it} = c + \gamma_t + c_1 k + c_i soepro_{it}. \tag{3.1}$$

In Eq. (3.1), *ROC* denotes return on capital; c is intercept term; γ_t is time effect; k is the logarithm of the net value of fixed assets per capita; c_1 is the coefficient of the logarithm of the net value of fixed assets per capita; $soepro_{it}$ is sales revenue of SOEs as a share of total sectoral sales revenue and sales revenue of medium and large enterprises as a share of total sectoral sales revenue; c_i is its coefficient.

Return on capital data is calculated based on the above equation; the net value of fixed assets per capita is calculated by dividing the net value of fixed assets by the average number of workforce in the sector with data from Wind information; sales revenue data of state-owned and state-controlled enterprises is from CEInet. Since the quarterly data of the net value of fixed assets is available until 2007, we have employed annual data for calculation instead, and the annual data of return on capital is obtained by taking a simple average of quarterly data.

Before calculating, we need to perform a unit root test of the equation to avoid spurious regression. As shown in the trend of return on capital in Fig. 3.2, we may determine that the test regression equation should include constant and trend terms. Table 3.2 provides the test results of five test methods. The result of LLC method and PP-Fisher method is that the unit root test is passed, but other methods have led to opposite results. Despite inconsistencies in the test results, we still referenced the above equation for calculation. The following section will provide a linear regression model result with market share as the explanatory variable.

Calculation shows that the equation's goodness of fit is 0.8579 and the adjusted goodness of fit is 0.8349; F statistic is 37.3569; F statistic's P-value is 0.0000. The above results indicate a generally good fit of the equation. The econometric software provides the coefficient of time effect, and the coefficients of various years depict an upward trend of return on capital. Table 3.3 shows the constant term and the common coefficient, i.e., the net value of fixed assets per capita and the coefficient of sector-specific SOE sales revenue as a share of the sectoral total. The constant term has passed T-test, reflecting the general level of return on capital; the coefficient of the net value of fixed assets per capita is negative, reflecting the law of diminishing marginal return on capital, but the statistic did not pass T-test; among the sectoral coefficients reflecting the impact of SOEs' market share on return on capital, petroleum extraction and petrochemical refining, metal and non-metal ore mining and dressing, manufacture of tobacco, manufacture of foods and beverages, manufacture of medicines, and manufacture of transport equipment have passed T-test with positive coefficients, indicating that SOEs' excess market shares had created sectoral access thresholds that pushed up return on capital. The first the three sectors had the highest coefficients, and their monopolistic and high-return attributes are consistent with people's general impressions. The two sectors of production and distribution of gas and production and distribution of water have also passed T-test,

Table 3.2 Unit root test results of panel model for the sectoral difference of return on capital (including constant and trend terms)

Testing method	Statistic	P-value	Number of cross-sections	Number of samples
LLC—T-test	−1.7728	0.0381	63	671
Breitung—T-test	6.7091	1.0000	63	608
IPS—W-test	4.6086	1.0000	63	671
ADF—Fisher chi-square test	72.504	1.0000	63	671
PP—Fisher chi-square test	150.346	0.0686	63	734

but their coefficients are negative, indicating that SOEs had served public interest after dominating those sectors.

3.2.3.2 Analysis Based on a Simple Regression Model

The above panel model generally reflects the impact of SOEs' market share on return on capital. From a monopoly perspective, however, the typical analytical method is to perform an analysis of the market share of the top four firms (*CR*4) and the top eight firms (*CR*8). Since data of top eight firms (*CR*8) is not available every year, we employed a unique sequence,[10] and the sectoral data of return on capital was obtained by taking a simple average. Figure 3.4 shows the relationship between sectoral return on capital and the market share of top eight firms, from which we may notice a consistent relationship of change between the two. After excluding such sectors as production and distribution of electric power and heat power, production and distribution of gas, and production and distribution of tap water, we examined correlation between sectoral return on capital and market share of top eight firms, and found the coefficient of correlation between the two to be 0.8249.

More rigorous calculation was completed with the regression model. By the same token, we need to include the net value of fixed assets per capita as a control variable and hence create the following model:

$$r_i = c + c_1 k_i + c_2 CR8_i \tag{3.2}$$

Table 3.4 provides the regression results, and the equation's goodness of fit is 0.3580, and *F* statistic has passed the test. The constant term, the net value of fixed assets per capita and *CR8* have passed *T-test*; the coefficient of the net value of fixed assets per capita is negative, indicating a decrease in return on capital amid rising capital stock per capita and reflecting the law of diminishing returns; the coefficient of *CR8* is positive, indicating an increase in return on capital amid rising market concentration and reflecting the role of monopoly in raising return on capital.

[10] Data source: Chen Zhiguang: "Monopoly or Efficiency: an Empirical Study on China's Manufacturing Industry", *Management World*, Vol.12, 2004; Du Chuanzhong "Analysis on the Correlation between China's Industrial Concentration and Profitability", *Economic Review*, Vol.10, 2002. We performed a comparison of data between the two papers, and found a decrease of an average 1.81 percentage points in CR8 indicator with data from the former relative to data from the latter. Since the former employs more recent data, we have adopted the former as our data source. Although the former has incomplete data, the missing sectors are coal mining and washing, petroleum extraction and petrochemical refining, metal and non-metal ore mining and dressing, production and distribution of electric power and heat power, production and distribution of gas, and production and distribution of tap water. With SOEs advancing and private enterprises retreating in key sectors, we believe that CR8 will not decrease and have supplemented the missing data with data from the latter paper.

Table 3.3 Panel regression results of sectoral differences in return on capital

Constant term, common coefficient and sector	Coefficient	Standard deviation	*T* Statistic	*P* value
Constant term	0.3461**	0.1746	1.9823	0.0488
Net value of fixed assets per capita	−0.0168	0.0158	−1.0629	0.2891
Coal mining and washing	0.0086	0.0270	0.3173	0.7514
Petroleum extraction and petrochemical refining	0.2970***	0.0451	6.5882	0.0000
Metal and non-metal ore mining and dressing	0.2110***	0.0531	3.9749	0.0001
Processing of agricultural and sideline foods	0.1474	0.1131	1.3032	0.1940
Food and beverage manufacturing	0.1401*	0.0786	1.7834	0.0761
Manufacture of tobacco	0.2833***	0.0333	8.5168	0.0000
Manufacture of textiles, apparel, footwear, caps and leather	0.0413	0.1663	0.2482	0.8042
Processing of timber and manufacture of furniture	0.1006	0.2292	0.4389	0.6612
Papermaking, printing and manufacture of articles for culture and education activity	0.0045	0.1099	0.0407	0.9676
Manufacture of chemical raw materials and chemical fibers	0.0335	0.0713	0.4697	0.6391
Manufacture of medicines	0.0889*	0.0528	1.6849	0.0936
Manufacture of rubber and plastics	−0.0077	0.1628	−0.0473	0.9623
Metal and non-metal smelting and manufacture	0.0407	0.0605	0.6734	0.5015
Manufacture of general-purpose machinery	0.0661	0.0680	0.9719	0.3323
Manufacture of special purpose machinery	−0.0075	0.0523	−0.1435	0.8860
Manufacture of transport equipment	0.0745**	0.0365	2.0436	0.0423
Manufacture of electrical machinery and equipment	0.1653	0.1317	1.2547	0.2111
Manufacture of communication equipment, computers and measuring instruments	0.1257	0.0856	1.4688	0.1435
Production and distribution of electric power and heat power	−0.0165	0.0523	−0.3147	0.7533

(continued)

Table 3.3 (continued)

Constant term, common coefficient and sector	Coefficient	Standard deviation	*T* Statistic	*P* value
Production and distribution of gas	−0.1095**	0.0513	−2.1360	0.0339
Production and distribution of tap water	−0.1305***	0.0432	−3.0199	0.0029

Note *, ** and *** respectively denote significance at 10%, 5% and 1% significance levels

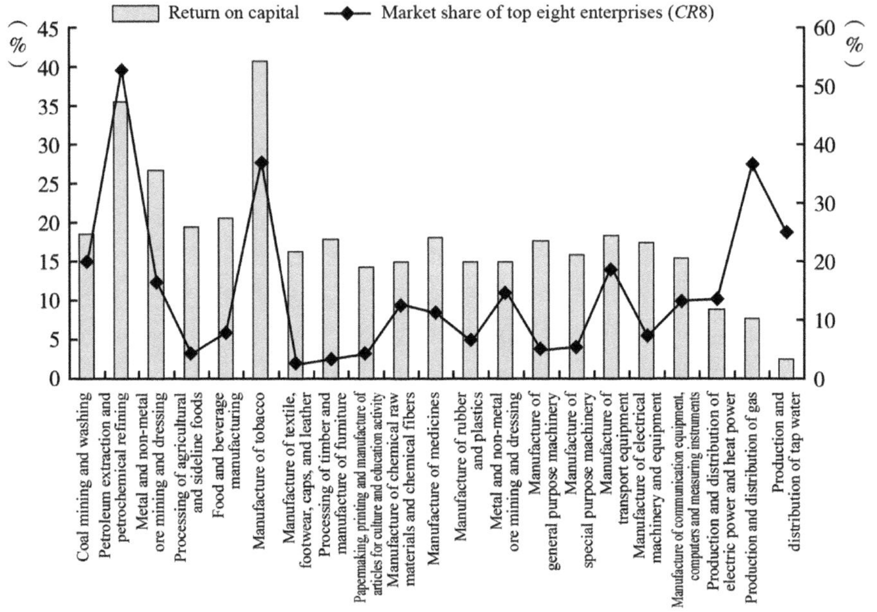

Fig. 3.4 Relationship between return on capital and the market share of top eight firms

Table 3.4 Linear regression results of return on capital

Variable	Coefficient	Standard deviation		*T* Statistic	*P* value
Constant term	0.8757**	0.3237		2.7050	0.0145
Net value of fixed assets per capita	−0.0658**	0.0289		−2.2798	0.0350
Market share of top eight firms	0.5365***	0.1694		3.1677	0.0053
R^2	0.3580	Adjusted R2	0.2866	*p* test value of *F* value	0.0185

Note *, ** and *** respectively denote significance at 10%, 5% and 1% levels

3.3 Test of the Relationship Among China's Return on Capital, Real Interest Rates and Relationship with Investment

3.3.1 Measurement of Real Interest Rate

The above estimation of return on capital has excluded the price factor. In this section, we will examine the relationship among the three after obtaining the real interest rate by excluding price factor from the interest rate. Considering the relationship between real interest rate and investment, it is more appropriate to use real loan interest rate. We need to first obtain the one-year weighted average loan interest rate before performing a price adjustment. Since the PBoC only has data for one-year weighted loan interest rate after 2005, we need to estimate data before 2005 based on the one-year benchmark loan interest rate. We found that when inflation was high, the weighted interest rate was above the benchmark rate by a greater margin, and that the increase was subject to a lag effect after inflation had decreased. Following this pattern, we estimated the increase of the one-year weighted interest rate relative to the benchmark rate before calculating the one-year weighted interest rate. After completing the above calculation, we should also perform a price adjustment of such interest rate. Using month-on-month CPI data, we estimated quarter-on-quarter data before calculating the annual price inflation rate assuming the same degree of inflation (we did not directly use year-on-year CPI data due to different base points for comparison). After adjusting the weighted average interest rate for price, we also need to perform a seasonal adjustment because return on capital is also adjusted for price. Figure 3.5 is the estimated real interest rate and the real interest rate after seasonal adjustment.

3.3.2 Test of Correlation Among the Three

According to Knut Wicksell's accumulation process theory, when the natural rate of interest on capital (similar to return on capital) is above monetary (loan) interest rate, firms will obtain excess profits and expand their business operations, thus incurring additional investments and loans. Hence, we expect that the difference between expected return on capital and real loan interest rate is positively correlated with investment. According to the standard theory of economics textbooks, interest rate enters the IS curve as an investment cost, and the increase in real loan interest rate leads to a decrease in investment. Hence, we expect that a negative correlation exists between the two.

Table 3.5 provides the test results of how the difference between return on capital and real interest rate is correlated with investment, as well as the correlation between real interest rate and investment, respectively, and tests those two relationships with

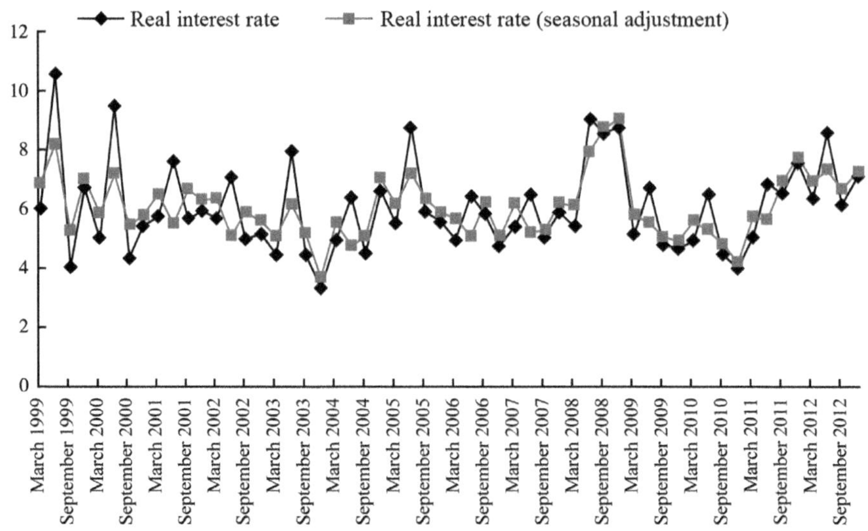

Fig. 3.5 Real loan interest rates and seasonally adjusted real interest rate

a one phase lag of investment. As far as industrial sectors are concerned, we found that the difference between return on capital and real interest rate was highly positively correlated with investment no matter under contemporaneous or one-phase investment lag conditions; correlation between real interest rate and investment is extremely low no matter under contemporaneous or one-phase investment lag conditions (correlation coefficient is less than 5%), and the sign under the contemporaneous condition is opposite to the theoretical expectation. Therefore, we believe that Wicksell's theory better explains China's high investment rate while interest rate as the cost of capital has an extremely weak restrictive effect on investment. Based on analyses in the literature, we are convinced that China's high investment rate over the past more than a decade stemmed from endogenous growth amid rising return on capital in the process of labor migration. The strategy to reduce investment by raising interest rates, therefore, would be futile. In *Interest and Price*, Wicksell stressed that "the above statements are predicated upon the assumption of unchanged market conditions" in demonstrating the movement of loan interest rates towards the natural rate of interest. Wicksell went on to emphasize that: "The natural rate of interest is not a fixed or unchangeable rate.... Normally, it is subject to the efficiency of production, the existing amount of fixed and active capital, as well as the supplies of labor and land."[11] China's story over the past decade reflects the second part of Wicksell's statement.

On a sector-specific basis, there is no obvious correlation between investment and real interest rate in all sectors no matter on a contemporaneous or one-phase investment lag basis, which is consistent with the assessment for overall industrial

[11] Knut Wicksell: *Interest and Prices*, The Commercial Press, 2007. p. 86.

Table 3.5 Test of correlation between return on capital and investment

Name of sector	Correlation of the difference between return on capital and real interest rate with investment	Correlation between real interest rate and investment	Correlation of the difference between return on capital and real interest rate with investment (one-phase investment lag)	Correlation between real interest rate and investment (one-phase investment lag)
Overall level of all industrial sectors	0.7284	0.0419	0.7600	−0.0065
Coal mining and washing	0.1267	0.1801	0.2322	0.0682
Petroleum extraction and petrochemical refining	−0.3215	0.1838	−0.1626	0.0578
Metal and non-metal ore mining and dressing	−0.1185	0.1636	−0.0169	0.0854
Processing of agricultural and sideline foods	0.6135	0.1640	0.6055	0.0781
Food and beverage manufacturing	0.7392	0.1506	0.7323	0.0682
Manufacture of tobacco	0.0592	0.1119	0.0725	0.0022
Manufacture of textile, footwear, caps, and leather	0.6876	0.1680	0.7238	0.0660
Processing of timber and manufacture of furniture	0.7181	0.1697	0.6903	0.0811
Papermaking, printing and manufacture of articles for culture and education activity	0.4004	0.1954	0.4630	0.1151
Manufacture of chemical raw materials and chemical fibers	0.0876	0.1923	0.1563	0.1186
Manufacture of medicines	0.6187	0.1498	0.7053	0.0611

(continued)

Table 3.5 (continued)

Name of sector	Correlation of the difference between return on capital and real interest rate with investment	Correlation between real interest rate and investment	Correlation of the difference between return on capital and real interest rate with investment (one-phase investment lag)	Correlation between real interest rate and investment (one-phase investment lag)
Manufacture of rubber and plastics	0.6271	0.1421	0.6693	0.0538
Metal and non-metal smelting and manufacture	−0.3123	0.1770	−0.1947	0.0930
Manufacture of general-purpose machinery	0.3127	0.1596	0.4114	0.1030
Manufacture of special purpose machinery	0.4619	0.1719	0.5565	0.1214
Manufacture of transport equipment	0.2947	0.1660	0.6013	0.1050
Manufacture of electrical machinery and equipment	0.3156	0.1469	0.4103	0.0738
Manufacture of communication equipment, computers and measuring instruments	−0.0577	0.1744	0.0265	0.0517
Production and distribution of electric power and heat power	−0.2846	0.1299	−0.1834	0.0386
Production and distribution of gas	0.6836	0.1351	0.6710	0.0175
Production and distribution of tap water	0.2520	0.0981	0.2728	0.0359

sectors. The following characteristics can be found from the correlation of the difference between return on capital and real interest rate with investment. First, for most competitive sectors, the difference between sectoral return on capital and real interest rate has a relatively high degree of contemporaneous correlation with investment. Such sectors include, for instance, processing of agricultural and sideline foods, manufacture of textiles, footwear, hats and leather, and timber processing and manufacture of furniture. In some sectors such as manufacture of special-purpose equipment and manufacture of transport equipment, even if contemporaneous correlation is not high, correlation between the two will still increase sharply with a one-phase lag. Second, most sectors where the difference between return on capital and real interest rate is not highly correlated with investment are monopolistic sectors such as manufacture of tobacco, petroleum extraction and petrochemical refining, and production and distribution of electric power and heat power. In many of those sectors, the correlation coefficient is negative, i.e., an increase in return on capital would lead to less investment (or less investment will lead to a higher return on capital). This indicates that the high return on capital in such sectors derives from monopoly and not from efficiency improvement due to labor migration.

3.3.3 Granger Causality Test of Relationship Among the Three

The above correlation only demonstrates the positive or negative correlation between the two while the existence of causality between the two still needs to be proven with a Granger causality test. The premise for performing their Granger causality test is that variables should satisfy stationarity condition. We have performed a stationarity test for the time sequence of the difference between return on capital and real interest rate for the overall production industry and 21 sectors. Results suggest that manufacture of special-purpose equipment and manufacture of transport equipment failed to the pass the test while all other sectors have passed the stationarity test. Results of stationarity test for investment are as follows: papermaking, printing and manufacture of articles for culture and education activity, manufacture of chemical raw materials and chemical fibers, manufacture of transport equipment, production and distribution of gas, production and distribution of tap water failed to pass the test, and all other sectors have passed the test. Real interest rate has also passed the stationarity test. For the purpose of sector comparison, we have performed the Granger causality test for all sectors although some sectors do not have the conditions for the Granger causality test.

Table 3.6 is the Granger test results for the correlation of the difference between return on capital and real interest rate with investment. For the production industry as a whole, under a one-phase lag, the difference between return on capital and real interest rate is the Granger cause of investment, and investment is also the Granger cause of the difference between return on capital and real interest rate; under a two-phase lag, the difference between return on capital and real interest rate ceases to be the Granger cause for investment, but investment remains the Granger cause of the difference between return on capital and real interest rate. The above results suggest that mutual causality exists between investment and return on capital in a relatively short time span, reflecting that under this endogenous growth pattern, return on investment sustains for a relatively long-time span but has a diminishing trend.

Sector-wise, most sectors that meet the above overall pattern are competitive sectors such as processing of agricultural and sideline foods, manufacture of rubber and plastic products, and papermaking, printing and manufacture of articles for culture and education activity. In addition, the difference between return on capital and real interest rate with a two-phase lag would still induce investment growth in some labor-intensive sectors, such as manufacture of foods and beverages, manufacture of textile, apparel, footwear, caps and leather, and processing of timber and manufacture of furniture, which are more indicative of the impact of labor migration on return on capital in these sectors. Most sectors where the difference between return on capital and real interest rate has no causality with investment are monopolistic sectors such as petroleum extraction and petrochemical refining, manufacture of tobacco, and production and distribution of electric power and heat power. In addition, some competitive sectors—such as manufacture of communication equipment, computers and measuring instruments—are inconsistent with the above pattern possibly due to the existence of hefty foreign investment in this sector: through internal transfer pricing, foreign investors repatriate profits from China, thus blurring the causality between the two.

Table 3.7 is the Granger causality test results of real interest rate versus investment. There is no causality between real interest rate and investment no matter for the overall production industry and individual sectors with a one-phase or two-phase lag. The Granger causality test in this section is consistent with the results of the above correlation test, which once again suggests that sectoral return on capital rather than interest rate is the most important factor of investment.

3.4 Sectoral Difference of Return on Capital and Monetary Policy Regulation

In the above section, we analyzed the sectoral difference of return on capital and examined its relationship with investment. The question is whether such sectoral difference will pose any challenge to monetary policy regulation. For instance, are some firms insensitive to monetary regulation by investing with their own funds as claimed by the IMF (2012) report? Is there any monopolistic sector with guaranteed high return on credit capital even in times of a credit crunch? Since the asymmetrical effect of "flight to quality" (Bernanke et al., 1996) has been extensively examined

Table 3.6 Granger causality test results of the correlation of the difference between return on capital and real interest rate with investment

Name of sector	Difference between return on capital and real interest rate is not the Granger cause of investment (one-phase lag)	Investment is not the Granger cause of the difference between return on capital and real interest rate (one-phase lag)	Difference between return on capital and real interest rate is not the Granger cause of investment (two-phase lag)	Investment is not the Granger cause of the difference between return on capital and real interest rate (two-phase lag)
Overall production industry	0.0040	0.0001	0.9063	0.0001
Coal mining and washing	0.2826	0.0209	0.0206	0.0337
Petroleum extraction and petrochemical refining	0.5116	0.8984	0.3400	0.1749
Metal and non-metal ore mining and dressing	0.6414	0.7631	0.8433	0.8286
Processing of agricultural and sideline foods	0.0807	0.0019	0.1426	0.0326
Food and beverage manufacturing	0.0047	0.0001	0.0406	0.0019
Manufacture of tobacco	0.6649	0.3286	0.6949	0.4997
Manufacture of textile, apparel, footwear, caps and leather	0.0107	0.0011	0.0761	0.0661
Processing of timber and manufacture of furniture	0.0486	0.0011	0.0729	0.0258
Papermaking, printing and manufacture of articles for culture and education activity	0.1167	0.0022	0.1979	0.0166

(continued)

Table 3.6 (continued)

Name of sector	Difference between return on capital and real interest rate is not the Granger cause of investment (one-phase lag)	Investment is not the Granger cause of the difference between return on capital and real interest rate (one-phase lag)	Difference between return on capital and real interest rate is not the Granger cause of investment (two-phase lag)	Investment is not the Granger cause of the difference between return on capital and real interest rate (two-phase lag)
Manufacture of chemical raw materials and chemical fibers	0.4916	0.2686	0.9856	0.1774
Manufacture of medicines	0.0026	0.0001	0.1897	0.0148
Manufacture of rubber and plastics	0.0340	0.0012	0.1666	0.0108
Metal and non-metal smelting and manufacture	0.9885	0.9540	0.9311	0.2426
Manufacture of general purpose machinery	0.4788	0.1727	0.2329	0.3209
Manufacture of special purpose machinery	0.1627	0.0521	0.4563	0.2194
Manufacture of transport equipment	0.1245	0.6545	0.5792	0.4909
Manufacture of electrical machinery and equipment	0.3857	0.0849	0.4989	0.1885
Manufacture of communication equipment, computers and measuring instruments	0.6293	0.6086	0.7686	0.2217
Production and distribution of electric power and heat power	0.5250	0.0344	0.5662	0.0213

(continued)

Table 3.6 (continued)

Name of sector	Difference between return on capital and real interest rate is not the Granger cause of investment (one-phase lag)	Investment is not the Granger cause of the difference between return on capital and real interest rate (one-phase lag)	Difference between return on capital and real interest rate is not the Granger cause of investment (two-phase lag)	Investment is not the Granger cause of the difference between return on capital and real interest rate (two-phase lag)
Production and distribution of gas	0.0125	0.0040	0.0704	0.1246
Production and distribution of tap water	0.3434	0.0007	0.8821	0.0004

in numerous studies, we expect that sectors with high return on capital (or monopolistic sectors) are insensitive to monetary policy regulation. After estimating sectoral effects of monetary policy, we took a deeper look at the causes of such effects.

3.4.1 Measurement of Monetary Policy's Sectoral Effects

3.4.1.1 Methodology and Data Explanations

Our approach for empirical study in this section is as follows: First, panel data is employed to analyze each sector's elasticity to monetary policy, and the size of elasticity denotes the level of the sector's sensitivity to monetary regulation; second, the variance analysis method is employed to analyze whether significant differences exist in those elasticity coefficients. In this section, we select money supply as the proxy variable of monetary policy because China's monetary policy regulation has focused on quantitative instruments over the years and the above analysis has also shown a lack of sensitivity of investment in various sectors to interest rates, and it depends mainly on the difference between return on capital and real interest rate. Hence, monetary policy analysis should shift its focus from capital price to capital availability. Specifically, our modeling approach is as follows:

According to the Cobb–Douglas production function $Q_{j,t} = A_{j,t}K_{j,t}^{\alpha}L_{j,t}^{\beta}$, a sector's output is subject to the effects of capital, labor and unexplainable factors. In the above equation, K and L respectively denote capital and labor, and α and β respectively denote capital and labor contributions. A is usually explained as technical factor. In this chapter, A is explained as monetary factor because we believe that monetary policy will affect output in annual and monthly data, i.e., short-term money is not neutral. The specific form of equation is as follows:

$$\ln Q_{j,t} = c_0 + c_{1,j}\ln M_t + c_{2,j}\ln K_{j,t} + c_{3,j}\ln L_{j,t} \tag{3.3}$$

Table 3.7 Granger causality test results of real interest rate versus investment

Name of sector	Real interest rate is not the Granger cause of investment (one-phase lag)	Investment is not the Granger cause of real interest rate (one-phase lag)	Real interest rate is not the Granger cause of investment (two-phase lag)	Investment is not the Granger cause of real interest rate (two-phase lag)
Overall production industry	0.7224	0.7594	0.6312	0.5499
Coal mining and washing	0.9697	0.7212	0.9367	0.9829
Petroleum extraction and petrochemical refining	0.8655	0.6923	0.9879	0.9906
Metal and non-metal ore mining and dressing	0.9311	0.6837	0.8045	0.9919
Processing of agricultural and sideline foods	0.8590	0.6660	0.7650	0.9923
Food and beverage manufacturing	0.8815	0.7504	0.8029	0.9757
Manufacture of tobacco	0.8171	0.7515	0.9860	0.7973
Manufacture of textile, apparel, footwear, caps and leather	0.7069	0.4663	0.6166	0.9509
Processing of timber and manufacture of furniture	0.7905	0.6266	0.8077	0.9854
Papermaking, printing and manufacture of articles for culture and education activity	0.9327	0.5766	0.8671	0.9909
Manufacture of chemical raw materials and chemical fibers	0.9111	0.6349	0.8738	0.9952
Manufacture of medicines	0.8618	0.6911	0.7299	0.9988

(continued)

Table 3.7 (continued)

Name of sector	Real interest rate is not the Granger cause of investment (one-phase lag)	Investment is not the Granger cause of real interest rate (one-phase lag)	Real interest rate is not the Granger cause of investment (two-phase lag)	Investment is not the Granger cause of real interest rate (two-phase lag)
Manufacture of rubber and plastics	0.7176	0.6189	0.6997	0.9891
Metal and non-metal smelting and manufacture	0.8606	0.7017	0.8464	0.9997
Manufacture of general purpose machinery	0.8157	0.6846	0.7609	0.9875
Manufacture of special purpose machinery	0.8884	0.5971	0.7598	0.9798
Manufacture of transport equipment	0.8573	0.6887	0.7867	0.9931
Manufacture of electrical machinery and equipment	0.6029	0.6709	0.6142	0.9708
Manufacture of communication equipment, computers and measuring instruments	0.4563	0.5459	0.5871	0.9641
Production and distribution of electric power and heat power	0.9464	0.8934	0.9130	0.8898
Production and distribution of gas	0.7012	0.8425	0.8729	0.9420
Production and distribution of tap water	0.9478	0.9481	0.7947	0.9224

In Eq. (3.3), Q denotes aggregate industrial output value. Although the industrial value-added indicator is adopted in most studies, we have decided to use aggregate industrial output value since NBS data is updated till 2007. M denotes money supply M2, K is the average balance of net fixed assets, and L is the annual average workforce of the sector. Except that money supply is from the PBoC's website, other data is from the China Statistical Data Application System.

3.4.1.2 Empirical Test Result

Before estimating the model, we need to first perform a stationarity test. Based on the variable sequence, the test should include the constant term and the trend term. Table 3.8 provides the test results. Despite the inconsistency between LLC test and Breitung of the common unit root, the equation's three tests of individual difference and individual root all suggest that the calculation sequence is stationary.

Table 3.9 uses the reaction coefficients of various sectors to money supply estimated with the panel model. Judging by the estimated results, 14 out of 21 industrial sectors have passed the T-test of coefficients, and these sectors account for a large share of China's production industry (in 2010, these 14 sectors made up 64.66% of China's aggregate industrial output value), indicating that change in money supply had universally influenced industrial sectors.

Table 3.10 provides the distribution of the reaction coefficients of sectors that have passed the test to money supply. We found that the elasticity coefficients of petroleum extraction and petrochemical refining, manufacture of tobacco, and production and distribution of gas are very small, which is consistent with our priori impression that monopolistic sectors are insensitive to monetary regulation. However, the elasticity coefficient of metal and non-metal ore mining and dressing is relatively high, which is consistent with the result that the sales revenues of SOEs in this sector as a share of sectoral total contributed to return on capital by a smaller margin. The high return on capital in the sector is probably due to the sector's attribute as a resource sector. The elasticity coefficient of production and distribution of electric power and heat power is negative, i.e., the tighter money supply is, the higher aggregate industrial output value would be. This may indicate that the sector is more closely linked with the real economy as tight money supply corresponds to an overheated real economy. In addition, some labor-intensive sectors (such as manufacture of textile, apparel, footwear, hats and leather, processing of timber and manufacture of furniture, and

Table 3.8 Unit root *t*-test result of the panel model of monetary policy's sectoral effects (including constant term and trend term)

Testing method	Statistic	*P* value	Number of cross sections	Number of samples
LLC—T-test	−9.63899	0.0000	64	690
Breit–ng—T-test	5.46709	1.0000	64	626
-PS—W-test	−2.12878	0.0166	64	690
ADF-Fisher Chi-square test	177.643	0.0024	64	690
PP-Fisher Chi-square test	287.293	0.0000	64	702

Table 3.9 Reaction coefficients of sectors to money supply and *t*-test

Sector	Coefficient	Standard deviation	*T* Statistic	*P* value
Coal mining and washing	5.4875***	0.8090	6.7831	0.0000
Petroleum extraction and petrochemical refining	1.8177**	0.7347	2.4741	0.0145
Metal and non-metal ore mining and dressing	4.8390***	0.3954	12.2383	0.0000
Processing of agricultural and sideline foods	2.9490***	0.5378	5.4833	0.0000
Food and beverage manufacturing	2.3165**	0.9410	2.4618	0.0150
Manufacture of tobacco	2.2662***	0.8079	2.8052	0.0057
Manufacture of textile, footwear, caps, and leather	1.0391	0.9743	1.0665	0.2879
Processing of timber and manufacture of furniture	0.7125	0.9885	0.7207	0.4722
Papermaking, printing and manufacture of articles for culture and education activity	1.9862	1.3869	1.4321	0.1542
Manufacture of chemical raw materials and chemical fibers	5.6379***	1.5623	3.6087	0.0004
Manufacture of medicines	0.9029	2.2047	0.4095	0.6827
Manufacture of rubber and plastics	1.2212	1.1796	1.0353	0.3022
Metal and non-metal smelting and manufacture	6.3025***	0.9222	6.8339	0.0000
Manufacture of general purpose machinery	4.1975***	0.5703	7.3602	0.0000
Manufacture of special purpose machinery	6.0946***	1.2070	5.0494	0.0000
Manufacture of transport equipment	4.2679***	0.8601	4.9619	0.0000
Manufacture of electrical machinery and equipment	1.5498*	0.8428	1.8389	0.0680
Manufacture of communication equipment, computers and measuring instruments	−1.2027	1.1424	−1.0528	0.2942
Production and distribution of electric power and heat power	−6.4654***	1.5665	−4.1272	0.0001
Production and distribution of gas	2.0947**	0.9785	2.1409	0.0339
Production and distribution of tap water	−0.6508	1.1808	−0.5511	0.5824

Note *, ** and *** respectively denote significance at 10%, 5% and 1% levels

Table 3.10 Regional distribution of the reaction coefficients of various sectors to money supply

Range of M2's coefficient	Number of sectors	Name of sector
(-7, 1)	1	Production and distribution of electric power and heat power
[1, 2)	2	Petroleum extraction and petrochemical refining, and manufacture of electrical machinery and equipment
[2, 3)	4	Processing of agricultural and sideline foods, manufacture of foods and beverages, manufacture of tobacco, and production and distribution of gas
[3, 5)	3	Metal and non-metal ore mining and dressing, manufacture of general purpose machinery, and manufacture of transport equipment
[5, 7)	4	Coal mining and washing, manufacture of chemical raw materials and chemical fibers, metal and non-metal smelting and manufacture, manufacture of special purpose machinery

manufacture of rubber and plastics) failed to pass the T-test despite having extremely low elasticity coefficients, and it is likely related to the export dependence features of the sectors. Increase in their output value is subject to the number of external orders and thus may not be sensitive to money supply.

3.4.1.3 Analysis of Variance

We perform a one-way analysis of variance (one-way ANOVA) to investigate whether significant differences exist in the above five ranges of elasticity coefficients. As its basic principle, the analysis of variance identifies the source of sample variance sum by comparing the explanatory powers of intra-group variance, inter-group variance and the overall sample variance sum. According to the test results provided in Table 3.11, the average inter-group variance is 133.7026, which is far greater than the average intra-group variance of 1.1399. At 5% significance level, F statistic's value is 263.9081 and rejects the null hypothesis. This indicates that the reaction coefficients of different sectors to money supply are not equal, and that sectoral differences have posed a challenge to monetary policy regulation.

3.4.2 Analysis of Causes Behind the Sectoral Effects of Monetary Policy

In the above section, we have employed the panel model to estimate the reaction elasticity of each sector to money supply, and the subsequent variance analysis indicates significant sectoral effects in monetary policy regulation. Here, we will analyze

Table 3.11 Variance analysis of the reaction coefficients to money supply

	Range of estimated values	Number of observations	Mean value	Variance
Grouping of the reaction coefficients of various sectors to money supply	(-7, 1)		-6.4654	–
	[], 2)	2	1.6838	0.0359
	[], 3)	4	2.4066	0.1398
	[], 5)	3	4.4348	0.1238
	[], 7)	4	5.8806	0.1457
Analysis of variance	Source of variance	Degree of freedom	Sum of variances	Average variance
	Inter-group	4	133.7026	33.4257
	Intra-group	9	1.1399	0.1267
	F Statistic	263.9081	*F*-tested *P* value	0.0000

the causes behind such sectoral effects. According to some facts about investment provided by the IMF (2012) report and our analysis of the causes behind sectoral differences of return on investment, we consider the following variables and expect that the following relationships exist. First, return on capital: higher return on capital means a smaller reaction elasticity coefficient since a high return on capital suggests stronger credit repayment capacity. In addition, the facts provided by the IMF (2012) suggest that most of those sectors invest with their own funds and are less affected by monetary policy regulation.

Second, capital intensity: our analysis has revealed the capital-intensive attribute of monopolistic sectors. Taking the first variable into account, we may conclude that a higher net worth of fixed assets per capita corresponds to a smaller elasticity, i.e., the coefficient is negative.

Third, the degree of export reliance: this variable is expressed by exports as a share of a firm's total sales revenue. More export-oriented firms are more dependent on external demand. If multinational companies receive working capital from their parent companies in times of need or banks recognize the future cash flow from firms' sales orders, the sector will be less affected by monetary regulation, and we expect its sign to be negative.

Fourth, trade credit: we denote inter-firm credit by asset turnover rate, deeming inter-firm credit as a supplement to bank credit. Firms with faster asset turnover, therefore, are less affected by monetary policy. However, Joseph E. Stiglitz and Bruce Greenwald (2005) also noted that both could suffer in a severe credit crunch, i.e., more inter-firm credit would expose firms to greater monetary policy impacts. The following research examines asset turnover rate without expecting its sign. The turnover rate includes three sub-indicators: total asset turnover rate, current asset turnover rate, and accounts receivable turnover rate. To avoid the problem of collinearity, each indicator is entered into the model for calculation individually.

Fifth, ownership attribute. This variable is denoted by the sales revenue of SOEs as a share of total sectoral sales revenue. As noted in the IMF (2012) report, more

SOEs would invest with their own funds. That is to say, sectors with SOEs accounting for a higher share of sales revenue are less affected by monetary policy. We expect the sign of such sectors to be negative.

Seven out of the above 21 sectors failed to pass T-test, but the reason for their failure to pass is probably due to their export dependence. Since the level of export dependence is taken into account in the following equation, we include those sectors into our samples, but the two sectors with negative coefficients have been excluded. To avoid the problem collinearity between explanatory variables, a correlation test is performed before regression analysis. Table 3.12 provides the calculation results of correlation between explanatory variables, from which the following traits can be discerned. First, most indicators have a low correlation and are free from the problem of collinearity; second, return on capital is inversely proportional to the level of export dependence, i.e., it seems that more export-dependent sectors have a smaller rate of return; third, there is a strong positive correlation between total assets turnover rate and current assets turnover rate, but the problem of collinearity is precluded since the two indicators are entered into the model individually.

In the specific regression analysis, we included the variables individually. We first considered the effects of return on capital and net fixed assets per capita on the reaction elasticity to money supply before individually including export sales revenue as a share of total revenue, asset turnover rate and the sales revenue of SOEs as a share of total sectoral sales revenue. When asset turnover rate was included, only one indicator could be included at a time. Table 3.13 provides the calculation results of the six models. As can be seen from the table, with the inclusion of more variables, the model's goodness of fit gradually increases, and the equation's overall F test statistic also increases gradually. This suggests that a multi-factor explanation of each sector's elasticity to money supply is more reliable.

Among the five types of indicators affecting the elasticity of money supply, return on capital has passed the significance test, suggesting that profitability is a key determinant of banks' decision to issue loans. That the sectors with high return on capital are less affected by monetary policy also indicates the existence of the "flight to quality" phenomenon in the monetary policy effect. The coefficient of net fixed assets per capita, which denotes capital intensity, is negative, indicating that sectors with high capital intensity are less affected by money supply. A possible reason is that most sectors with a high degree of capital intensity invest with their own funds and are thus less affected by monetary policy. The coefficient of export sales revenue as a share of total sales revenue, which denotes the level of export dependence, is negative, indicating that more export-dependent sectors are less affected by money supply. A possible reason is the make-to-order business mode of export-oriented sectors, whose manufacturing is tied to external demand and less affected by the domestic environment.

The coefficients of all the above three indicators passed the significance test, and none of the three indicators for measuring asset turnover rate passed the test. This implies that inter-firm credit had no impact on bank credit (no matter the substitution effect or complementary effect), reflecting China's reality of bank-dominated financial system. SOE assets as a share of total firm assets, which represents ownership

Table 3.12 Correlation between explanatory variables

Variable definition	Profitability	Capital intensity	Level of export dependence	Asset turnover rate			Ownership attribute
Variable	Return on capital	Average fixed assets per capita	Export sales revenue as a share of total sales revenue	Total assets Turnover ratio	Current asset turnover rate	Account receivables turnover rate	Sales revenue of SOEs as a share of total sectoral sales revenue
Return on capital	1.0000						
Net fixed assets per capita	0.2632	1.0000					
Export sales revenue as a share of total sales revenue	−0.4445	−0.0090	1.0000				
Total asset turnover rate	−0.1946	−0.1571	−0.6185	1.0000			
Current asset turnover rate	0.2109	0.2481	−0.7073	0.6384	1.0000		
Account receivables turnover rate	−0.0657	0.3459	0.0472	0.0992	0.4906	1.0000	
Sales revenue of SOEs as a share of total sectoral sales revenue	0.0467	0.5837	0.4369	−0.4100	0.1046	0.7355	1.0000

attribute, failed to pass the significance test, which may explain that return on capital instead of ownership nature was a key consideration in banks' decisions to issue loans.

Table 3.13 Factor analysis of each sector's elasticity to money supply

	Model 1	Model 2	Model 3	Model 4	Model 5	Model 6
Constant term	−0.0617	22.5636**	22.3959*	28.0195*	32.3928**	32.5401**
Return on capital	−0.0195	−0.0574	−0.0579	−0.1171*	−0.1138*	−0.1143*
Average fixed assets per capita	0.2833	−1.4072*	−1.397072	−2.0381*	−2.3908*	−2.3514*
Export sales revenue as a share of total sales revenue	–	−0.1443***	−0.1448***	−0.1399***	−0.1327***	−0.1275***
Total asset turnover rate	–	–	0.0629	1.5505	–	–
Current asset turnover rate	–	–	–	–	0.5288	–
Account receivables turnover rate	–	–	–	–	–	0.0608
Assets of SOEs as a share of total assets	–	–	–	0.0414	0.0406	0.0348
R^2	0.0069	0.5560	0.5560	0.6030	0.6031	0.5987
Adjusted R^2	−0.1172	0.4672	0.4292	0.4502	0.4505	0.4443
F statistic	0.0556	6.2609	4.3831	3.9484	3.9514	3.8791
F-tested P value	0.9461	0.0057	0.0166	0.0213	0.0212	0.0226

Note *, ** and *** respectively denote significance at 10%, 5% and 1% levels

3.5 Research Conclusions

This chapter first estimated return on capital in China's industrial sectors, then performed a correlation and causality test between return on capital and investment, and finally examined the reasons behind sectoral differences of return on capital and the challenges to monetary policy. After extensive data estimation and empirical tests, we have arrived at the following conclusions:

First, return on industrial capital in China has been on the rise since 1999 with two big dips. One occurred in 2008, and the other occurred in the period from the second half of 2011 to the first half of 2012. The first dip can be attributed to external demand. The second dip may have stemmed from supply because according to Cai Fang (2012), China's "demographic dividend window" had closed in 2013. According to our causality test, investment had a significantly positive correlation and causality with the difference between return on capital and the real interest rate. However, neither the correlation nor causality test between investment and real interest rate is significant, which validates Li Yang and Yin Jianfeng's (2005) view that high investment and high growth are endogenous results of labor migration; on the other hand, it also indicates the futility of attempting to curb investment by raising interest rates.

Second, the estimated results of sector-specific return on capital have revealed the following traits: most sectors had similar returns on capital, which is consistent with the average profit theory. Manufacture of tobacco, petroleum extraction and petrochemical refining, and metal and non-metal ore mining and dressing boasted significantly higher returns on capital than other sectors, which implies that monopoly would lead to high returns on capital. The three sectors of production and distribution of electric power and heat power, production and distribution of gas, and production and distribution of water reported much lower returns on capital than other sectors. Despite monopolistic traits, these sectors appear to provide more public-interest services. It is also widely recognized that labor compensation is high for these sectors despite modest returns on capital. We have dissected the causes of such sectoral differences. On the premise of controlling the net fixed assets per capita, the panel data suggests that sales revenues from SOEs as a share of total sales revenues have a significant impact on five sectors excluding electric power. This indicates that administrative monopoly—and not just monopoly—has led to high returns on capital. This conclusion is validated by our linear regression using the market share indicator of the top eight firms ($CR8$).

Third, we performed a sector-specific test of the relationship between investment and return on capital with the following results: relationship of investment with the difference between return on capital and real interest rate in most competitive sectors is consistent with the results of both correlation and causality tests for the overall production industry. However, there is no significant correlation between investment and real interest rate, indicating that high investment in most sectors was also an endogenous growth result of labor migration. Except that production and distribution of gas demonstrated the above features, investment showed no causal relationship with the difference between return on capital and real interest rate in the rest five monopolistic sectors, and the correlation is also very low. Furthermore, one phenomenon warrants attention: coefficients of correlation of investment with the difference between return on capital and real interest rate are negative for the three sectors of petroleum extraction and petrochemical refining, metal and non-metal ore mining and dressing, and production and distribution of electric power and heat power. That is to say, an increase in return on capital will lead to a decrease in investment (or less investment will lead to a higher return on investment), i.e., high return on capital in these sectors is driven by monopoly rather than efficiency improvement stemming from labor migration, which evidently has a distortive effect on the real economy.

Fourth, we tested whether such sectoral difference would pose a challenge to the monetary policy. We first calculated the elasticity of each sector to money supply, and the variance analysis showed significant differences in the elasticity coefficient, suggesting significant sectoral effects of monetary regulation. Then, we performed a regression analysis of the causes behind such sectoral effects and found that: more export-dependent sectors were less affected by monetary regulation due to their make-to-order business model. Closely linked with external demand, these sectors were less affected by the domestic environment; sectors with higher returns on capital were less affected by monetary regulation, which is indicative of the "flight to quality" phenomenon in the monetary policy effect. Monopolistic sectors with ultrahigh returns on investment not only have a distorted effect on the real economy's development, but also sharply reduce the effect of monetary regulation; sectors with higher net balance of fixed assets per capita were less affected by monetary regulation probably because capital-intensive sectors were more likely to invest with their own funds. State assets as a share of total sector assets, which denotes the ownership attribute, did not pass the significance test probably because the four major state-owned commercial banks and joint-stock banks had paid more attention to profit performance in their lending process under the internal and external constraints of the board of directors, the board of supervisors and investors after listed on the stock market. As shown in the above analysis, undesirable phenomena in monetary regulation have largely stemmed from the distortive effects at the real-economy level.

3.6 Policy Recommendations

The tests, analyses and conclusions in this paper offer an explanation of China's industrialization process over the past decade. Despite the commendable episodes in history, the steep decline in return on capital in China in 2012 is worrisome. The reason is that demographic research indicates that China's "demographic dividend window" has already closed, and the demographic variable is the most stable variable in economic forecasting. Moreover, some signs in China's economic performance also imply a downward trend of China's GDP growth. Any stimulus policy to shore up the flagging economy would most likely cause inflation. At the critical juncture of economic turning point, this chapter puts forth the following three policy recommendations on China's economic development.

First, continue to explore industrial development potentials. Numerous studies suggest that administrative monopoly would not only lead to efficiency loss in a sector, but also affect overall economic performance as well. Keenly aware of such problem, top decision-makers have sent the following clear messages in relevant decisions of the Third Plenary Session of the 18th CPC Central Committee: "We should allow the market to play a decisive role in resource allocation, strive to remove market barriers, and increase the efficiency and fairness of resource allocation." Relevant studies (Shao Ting, 2010) provided the estimated benefits of reform. If financial resources are allocated to private enterprises with a higher return on capital, China's GDP growth would be two to eight percentage points higher than the current rate. However, our research suggests that China's financial system is free from ownership discrimination, and that the behaviors of financial institutions are driven by a pursuit of high returns on capital. The prioritization of reforms thus comes into question. We believe that the reform of administrative monopoly in the factor market[12] should have priority over interest rate liberalization in the financial system. In other words, it is imperative for China to launch an inventory reform to reverse factor distortion for a future "Pareto improvement" even at the expense of an immediate "Pareto retrogression" in the short run.

Second, we should make great efforts to advance urbanization and improve the relevant fiscal and financial systems. Observed from the perspective of people's demand for housing, travel and education or the perspective of industrial evolution, urbanization is indisputably the engine of China's future economic growth. However, the exorbitant local debt (though indebtedness is free from major risks on a national scale) and high market interest rates are contradictory to the relatively relaxed monetary environment, reflecting an intense investment impulse and local governments and the heterization of financial ecosystem. At the financial level, we should allow local governments to broaden financing channels for urban development via a multitude of methods such as bonds to apply transparent information mechanisms and reverse "misinformed project evaluation by financing platforms and runaway interest rate hikes." Once the spending responsibilities related to bond issuance are clarified, the government should create a system of compatible fiscal capabilities, administrative powers, and spending responsibilities at the fiscal level. While easing corporate tax burden, the business tax to VAT reform has dented local government budgetary revenues, and the imposition of new local taxes should be researched and implemented.

Third, we should pursue the "going global" strategy following the trend of globalization. China's rapid economic growth since the reform and opening up in 1978 has been made possible by the dividends of both demographics and globalization. Yet the export-oriented globalization can be summarized as "employment of a country's domestic low-end production factors to meet the needs of foreign markets." This model also suggests that China remains at the low end of the global value chain, and that with the loss of China's labor resource advantage, less developed countries in East Asia will emerge as new labor-intensive manufacturing hubs. Changing the reality does not necessarily require an occupation of the high ends of the global value chain via indigenous innovation. The powers of capital are limitless. The essence of the "going global" strategy is to encourage home-grown enterprises to snap up innovative foreign firms cash-strapped in a financial crisis and thus occupy the high ground of the global value chain. Accordingly, the most important aspect is financial

[12] While administrative monopoly should be retained in sectors with natural monopoly attributes such as electric power and petroleum, competition mechanism should be introduced in downstream sectors such as power transmission and distribution.

system development - including the development of a stable and resilient exchange rate system that allows home-grown multinational corporations to better manage exchange rate risks and use their home currency—Renminbi—in cross-border settlements, and develop indigenous financial markets with sufficient breadth and depth to realize Renminbi's value storage function.

References

Bai, C, C. Hsieh, and Y. Qian, "The Return to Capital in China", *NBER Working Paper* No. 12755, 2006.

Bernanke, B. S., M. Gentler and S. Gilchrist: "The Financial Accelerator and the Flight to Quality", *Review of Economics and Statistics,* 78(1), 1996, pp. 1–15.

Cai Fang: "Demographic Transition, Demographic Dividends and Economic Growth Sustainability", appeared on *China Financial Forum 2005*, Social Sciences Academic Press (China), 2004

CCER China Economic Observation and Research Group: "Estimation of Return on Capital in China (1978–2006): Micro-Basis for New Round of Investment Growth and Economic Prosperity", *China Economic Quarterly*, Vol.3, 2007.

Fang Wenquan: "How High Is China's Return on Capital? Re-Estimation of Macroscopic Data from an Annual Capital Perspective", *China Economic Quarterly*, Vol.2, 2012.

Hofman, B., and L. Kuijs: "China's Prosperity Driven by Firm Profitability", *The Wall Street Journal (Chinese Edition)*, October 12, 2006.

IMF: "Determinants of Corporate Investment in China: Evidence from Cross-Country Firm Level Data", *IMF Working Paper*, 2012.

Stiglitz, J., and Bruce Greenwald: *Towards a New Paradigms in Monetary Economics*, CITIC Press, 2005.

Jiang Xiaojuan, Li Rui: "FDI's Contributions to China's Industrial Growth and Technology Progress", *China Industrial Economics*, Vol.7, 2002.

Justin Yifu Lin, Cai Fang, Li Zhou: *China's Miracle: Development Strategies and Economic Reforms (Supplemented Edition)*, Shanghai People's Publishing House, 2002.

Knut Wicksell: *Interest and Prices*, The Commercial Press, 2007.

Kuijs, L.: "How will China's Saving-investment Balance Evolve?", *World Bank Policy Research Working Paper* 3958, 2006.

Kuijs, L.: "Investment and Saving in China", *World Bank China Office Research Working Paper* No. 1, 2005.

Li Yang, Yin Jianfeng: "High Savings and High Investment in Labor Migration and China's Economic Growth", *Economic Research Journal*, Vol.2, 2005.

Liu Xiaoxuan: "Ownership Structure and Market Structure of China's Transition Economies", *Economic Research Journal*, Vol.1, 2003.

Shan Weijian: "China's Low-Profit Growth Model", *The Wall Street Journal (Chinese Edition)*, November 24, 2006.

Shan Weijian: "Profit Puzzle of Chinese Enterprises", *Far Eastern Economic Review*, September 6, 2006.

Shan, W.: "The World Bank as China Delusions", *The Wall Street Journal Asia,* Sep. 1st, 2006.

Shao Ting: "Financial Misallocation, Ownership Structure and Return on Capital: A Study on Chinese Industrial Enterprises, 1997–2007", *Journal of Financial Research*, Vol.9, 2010.

Shen Kunrong, Wang Jian: "Real Interest Rates and China's Economic Growth", *Economic Research Journal*, Vol.8, 2000.

Shi Zhuxian, Deng Chuang, Liu Junsheng, Shi Qinghua: "Relationship between China's Natural Interest Rate and Economic Growth and Inflation", *The Journal of World Economy*, Vol.4, 2006.

Song Fangxiu: "Effectiveness of China's Interest Rate Mechanism and Effects of Interest Rate Regulation", *Economic Perspectives*, Vol.2, 2008.

The World Bank's China Representative Office: *China Quarterly Update*, Report on the Second Quarter, 2006.

Yao Lingzhen, Wang Shuhao: "Interest Rate Policy and Investment in the Absence of Market Mechanisms", *Journal of Quantitative & Technical Economics*, Vol.11, 2003.

Yu Liangchun, Zhang Wei: "Study on the Intensity and Efficiency Loss of Sectoral Administrative Monopoly in China", *Economic Research Journal*, Vol.3, 2010.

Zeng Linghua, Wang Chaojun: "Income Elasticity and Interest Rate Elasticity of China's Money Demand and the Interest Elasticity of Investment", *The Theory and Practice of Finance and Economics*, Vol.4, 2003.

Zhang Yu, Jiang Dianchun: "FDI, Industrial Agglomeration and Industrial Technology Progress", *Journal of Finance and Economics*, Vol.1, 2008.

Zhou Ying: "Interest Rate Variation, Firm Net Worth and Firm Investment", Master's Dissertation at Zhejiang University, 2009.

Chapter 4
Household Savings Impact of Interest Rate Liberalization from the Perspective of Bank WMPs

This chapter collects information about bank wealth management products (WMPs) in China from 2006 to 2012, classifies such information into annual panel data of 31 provinces, and examines the household savings impact of bank WMP yield after controlling of some important variables. Our empirical results indicate a significantly negative correlation between WMP yield and household savings, and the negative correlation is more significant for products with shorter maturities. Based on the reality that WMPs follow the currency market as pricing reference, we may draw the following conclusion: China's current interest rate liberalization has been steadily advanced in the form of WMPs through the vehicle of the currency market. Empirical results also demonstrate the following relationship: household incomes have a significantly positive effect on household savings; the gross dependency ratio (GDR) has a slightly positive effect on household savings; consumption on "housing, travel and education" as a share of total household consumption (i.e., a more advanced consumption structure) has a significantly negative effect on household savings.

4.1 Brief Review of Literature

The Third Plenary Session of the 18th CPC Central Committee has called for letting the market play a "decisive" role in resource allocation. As far as the financial system is concerned, letting the market play a decisive role means bringing the price mechanism of interest rates into full play, i.e., interest rate liberalization reforms should be carried out to achieve fully market-based interest rates. Apart from the concise connotation of "letting the market play a decisive role in allocating resources", interest rate liberalization has broader effects and implications for easing the financial repression and enhancing financial services in less developed regions; narrowing the interest rate spread to force financial intermediaries to become more efficient and thus raising the efficiency of finance in serving the real economy; prompting market players to

G. Wang, *A Study on Interest Rate Liberalization in China*, Research Series on the Chinese Dream and China's Development Path,
https://doi.org/10.1007/978-981-97-3644-7_4

increase their price sensitivity to interest rates, which helps improve the monetary policy transmission mechanism; and so on.

China's interest rate liberalization reforms started in 1996. The People's Bank of China (PBoC), China's central bank, took steps to advance interest rate liberalization reforms under the approach of "taking the first step of reform for foreign currencies before the home currency, loan interest rate before deposit interest rate, long maturities before short maturities and large sum transactions before small-sum ones." As stated in the *Circular on Further Advancing Interest Rate Liberalization Reforms* released on July 20, 2013, the PBoC decided to remove the 0.7 times lower limit on loan interest rates for financial institutions, remove the 2.3 times upper limit on loan interest rates for rural credit cooperatives (RCCs), and remove discount rate control. Since then, deposit interest rate liberalization has remained the only unfinished task in China's interest rate liberalization reforms. It is also the last priority and difficulty in the reforms.

No further action had been taken to deregulate the upper limit of deposit interest rates because academics and decision makers worried about a potential transfer of deposits seeking higher interest rates, as well as financial system fragility resulting from a narrowing interest rate spread for banks. By investigating China's household savings deposit from 1990 to 1999, Wu Jian (2000) took note of a downward trend in savings deposit growth since 1994. In 1999, the balance of household savings deposits experienced negative growth. He also mentioned that household savings deposits were rather sensitive to the seven interest rate cuts after 1997, and the depository funds primarily flowed into the primary stock markets. Based on an analysis of the Central Bank's seven interest rate cuts, Wang Xiaoya et al. (2000) also arrived at a conclusion that the stock market had a substitutive effect on savings deposits. However, their study differentiated between savings in the broad sense and savings in the narrow sense, noting that the aggregate amount of savings deposits were insensitive to nominal and real interest rates, but rate cuts had a significant impact on the structure of savings, resulting in higher household liquidity.

An opposite conclusion is that household savings deposits in China are not sensitive to interest rate change, which is supported more extensively in the literature. Based on an empirical analysis of the determinants of household savings deposits in China from 1978 to 1998, Li Yan (1999) found that income growth and income level had greater effects on savings deposits than interest rate; nominal interest rate had a weak negative effect, and the real interest rate had an insignificantly positive effect. In an empirical study on China's household savings from 1982 to 2000, Xu Dongjiang (2002) almost reached the same conclusion as Li Yan's (1999), offering the following explanation on the negative coefficient of the nominal interest rate: "an increase in the nominal interest rate means an inflationary expectation that drives people to spend more and save less." Wang Jinbin and Yu Chunhai (2007) performed an empirical analysis of the determinants of time deposits per capita, and found that income was a more important determinant of time deposits per capita than real interest rate.

Apart from research on how interest rates influence savings deposits through simple money demand equations, some macroscopic and structural factors have also been brought into examination and empirical research. For instance, Li Yan (1999) identified "underdeveloped capital markets" as a "key barrier to the interest rate effects on household savings." That is to say, a dearth of investable financial products would lead to forced savings. Qi Tianxiang (2000) believed that uncertainties in the transition era would increase household motivations for precautionary saving and cause household savings to be insensitive to interest rates change. By introducing the concept of "target savings level" to reflect the precautionary savings motivation, Nabar's (2011) empirical finding suggested that when real interest rate was falling, Chinese households found it harder to reach their target savings level and thus tended to increase deposits. Macroscopic research focused on population burden. After controlling such variables as GDP per capita,[1] Wang Dewen et al. (2004) observed the effects of child support ratio and elderly support ratio on savings rate, and the coefficient of empirical results is negative, i.e., China's high savings rate benefited from a low demographic burden. Zhang Ming's (2007) literature review focused on international studies on the savings rate effects of demographic transition and social security system. International research suggests that rapid economic growth and demographic transition have contributed to China's high savings rate. Aziz and Li (2006) believed that aside from the precautionary saving motivation, a more important contributor to the low consumption rate (thus the high savings rate) was the falling share of household income in China's national income. Wang Guogang (2010) ascribed China's falling consumption rate to structural reasons, i.e., tepid growth in housing, travel and educational consumption had weighed on consumption rate (high savings rate).

All the above literature research conclusions suggest that savings rate in China is not sensitive to interest rate, thus no need to worry about the risk of narrowing interest spread for financial intermediation after interest rate liberalization. In the first decade of the twenty-first century, academics have sufficiently demonstrated interest rate liberalization theories, and conditions for deposit interest rate liberalization seemed ready. However, a disruptive change has transformed the market landscape and the environment in which bank intermediation operates. This important change is the boom of bank wealth management product (WMP) market, which has a substitutive effect on savings deposits and has intensified competition between banks as financial intermediaries. Apart from avoiding loan-to-deposit ratio assessment, easing the capital constraint, among other innovation factors, the flourishing of the bank WMP market has mainly been driven by interest rate liberalization. As extensively shown in the literature, the WMP market is becoming a test ground for China's gradualist interest rate liberalization reforms.

Yuan Zengting et al. (2010) noted that since 2004, bank WMPs have been characterized by a shortening average contract period, showing signs of evolving towards currency market funds. Based on her analysis of the yields of credit WMPs, Zhu Hongmei (2012) found that short-term credit products were significantly influenced by the interbank lending rate. Sheng Fangfu (2013) tested the causality and co-integration relationship between short-term WMP yields and SHIBOR short-maturity

[1] His empirical test did not include the interest rate variable.

products, and uncovered a mutual causality and long-term equilibrium between the two. In a statistical accounting of change in the balance of off-balance-sheet WMPs in Hainan Province, the PBoC Haikou Central Branch Study Group (2013) identified an evident relationship of substitution between the balance of off-balance-sheet WMPs and monthly change in savings deposits. Ding Bo et al. (2012) noted that "among the on-balance-sheet products offered by the four major commercial banks since 2010, those with SHIBOR as pricing benchmark accounted for 71% of funds raised from all products." This fully demonstrates a close relationship between the WMP market and the interbank market. The propensity of WMPs to develop into currency market funds is similar to the interest rate liberalization trend in the US. To break through the Regulation Q's ceiling on deposit interest rates, the US banking sector has developed transferable certificates of deposits (CDs), transferable negotiable orders of withdrawal (NOW) accounts, currency market deposit accounts (MMDA), among other currency market instruments. The only difference in the interest rate liberalization process of both countries is the difference of vehicular instruments.

The above literature shows that China is already in a gradual process of deposit rate liberalization. However, very few studies have been carried out to empirically demonstrate the potential impact of this process (on household savings, bank intermediation interest spread, etc.). This chapter is written to examine the effects of WMP market on household savings. Given the fast-changing economic variables in China's transitional stage, we try to include as many control variables as possible in investigating the effect of interest rate liberalization.

4.2 Selection of Indicators and Empirical Model Specification

This chapter aims to uncover interest rate liberalization's effects on household savings. As far as determinants of household savings are concerned, the traditional deposit savings theory takes into account two variables of income and interest rates. Specifically, we have identified the population-weighted mean of urban household disposable income and rural household net income as the proxy variables for household income; and the actual yield of bank WMPs as the proxy variable for interest rate. Since we consider the aggregate savings in a region, we should also consider demographic burden, whose proxy variable is the gross dependency ratio (GDR). Household consumption is also an important variable of household savings, but is not included in our modelling given that the high correlation between general consumption level and household income may incur a collinearity problem. According to Wang Guogang (2013), China's falling consumption rate (rising savings rate) stems from the absence of consumption upgrade, i.e., housing, travel and education account for a scant share of total household consumption. Hence, we use household consumption on housing travel and education as a share of total housing spending as the proxy variable to investigate the effect of consumption structure on household savings.

We specify the following empirical model:

$$s_{j,t} = \beta_1 Income_{j,t} + \beta_2 r_{j,t} + \beta_3 Depr_{j,t} + \beta_4 ConsStr_{j,t} + u_j + \varepsilon_{j,t} \quad (4.1)$$

In Eq. (4.1), $S_{j,t}$ is the per capita household saving of province *j* in year *t*; $Income_{j,t}$ is the per capita household income of province *j* in year *t*; $r_{j,t}$ is the average yield of home currency credit WMPs of province *j* in year *t*; $Depr_{j,t}$ is the gross dependency ratio (GDR) of province *j* in year *t*; $ConsStr_{j,t}$ is household consumption on housing, travel and education as a share of total household spending of province *j* in year *t*; β_i is coefficient of each variable; u_j is the individual effect of province *j*; $\varepsilon_{j,t}$ is error term.

The specification of Eq. (4.1) indicates that empirical study has selected a panel model, which is based on two considerations: first, compared with the time sequence model, the use of a panel model allows more information to be contained to better reflect the relationship between various indicators, which is desirable considering that our time sequence has a short span from 2006 to 2012, reflecting only seven years of information on the temporal dimension, while the cross section contains information about 31 provinces. Second, household savings are subject to a multitude of factors such as the coverage of social security system and inflation, which can be incorporated into the individual effect in the panel model while omitted variables may appear in a time sequence model, thus affecting the effect of estimation.

Concerning the regression coefficient, we have made the following assumptions:

Assumption 1: β_i is positive, i.e., the higher household income per capita, the higher household savings rate per capita.

Assumption 2: β_2 is negative, i.e., the higher the average yield of home currency credit WMPs, the lower household savings rate per capita. That is to say, WMPs have a substitutive effect on household savings deposits.

Assumption 3: β_3 is negative, i.e., the higher dependency ratio, the lower household savings rate per capita. That is to say, the higher demographic burden, the more consumption of savings.

Assumption 4: β_4 is negative, i.e., the higher the consumption on housing, travel and education as a share of total household spending, the lower household savings rate per capita.

Notably, this equation does not take into account nominal interest rates mainly because nominal deposit interest rates are the same across provinces. After the PBoC raised the ceiling on deposit rates to 1.1 times the benchmark rate on June 7, 2012, small and medium-sized banks followed by raising their interest rates almost to the ceiling, and the four state-owned commercial banks also raised rates on deposits with maturities shorter than one year to close to 1.1 times. Our sample cut-off date is the end of 2012, so this minor difference is neglected.

4.3 Data Source and Data Treatment Explanation

The most complex data treatment in the empirical research section of this chapter is the yield of bank WMPs. First, the data treatment of this indicator will be explained. Basic WMP data employed in this paper is from Wind information. Bank WMPs are invested in a broad range of objects, and the risk-return profiles vary across different products. As far as alternatives to savings deposits are concerned, such products should include low-risk products such as interest rate products, negotiable instruments, bonds and credit products. In practice, we have selected Renminbi-denominated credit products.[2] Since our empirical equation includes cross-sectional information, the issuing regions of bank WMPs should correspond to different provinces. Specific operations may fall into two categories: first, for those products marked with specific issuing provinces, we will indicate the names of those issuing provinces. Second, for most products are marked with "nationwide", "bank-wide" or no indication of their issuing scope, we consider that such WMPs could be purchased at the outlets of the bank's branches and then indicate the issuing provinces of those products.[3] Third, we should divide the contract period into different types of maturities (including maturities shorter than one month, three months, six months, one year, three years, and all products) for the convenience to uncover the effects of products with different maturities on household savings. We refer to the above process as a "screening, separation and labelling" process. Lastly, we should take a simple average of such information at the provincial level to arrive at the mean yield of Renminbi-denominated credit WMPs with different maturities in various provinces in a given year.

Here, we should make additional three explanations: first, we have excluded WMPs for corporate clients while making no distinction between ordinary and VIP clients. Second, Wind information has provided actual yield and upper limit and lower limit on expected yield of WMPs. If the actual yield of the product is available, we will adopt the actual yield; otherwise, we will take the average value of the upper and lower limits of expected yield if both limits exist; in case only the upper or lower limit exists, we will adopt the sole available data.[4] Third, we have excluded

---

[2] Since 2009, a multitude of asset pool WMPs have appeared in China's banks WMPs market involving various types of investment assets. As long as the primary investment assets are not stocks, commodities or exchange rate products and include other credit products, we will categorize them as credit WMPs.

[3] The following circumstances also exist in our statistics, i.e., some banks have operated across provinces during certain statistical periods. Despite the bank-wide issuance of those products at different time points, the geographical scope of issuance was different. In practice, we try to determine the business scope of banks at different time points. For those banks whose business history is not available, we have followed the coverage of provinces in their business operations at the most recent time point.

[4] According to our statistics, the actual yields of over 90% of products reached or exceeded the lower limit of expected yield, and the upper and lower limits on the expected yields of most products were equal. For products with only the upper or lower limit on expected yield and without actual yields, we have collected their data to retain as much information as possible.

negative yields and excessive yields (e.g., above 30%) from the results obtained from Step 2.

Data treatment of other indicators is explained as follows: *Per capita household savings:* first, we obtained the annual household savings deposit balance data of each province and divided such data by the province's population to obtain the per capita balance of household deposit savings; then, we took the differential of the per capita balance of household savings deposits to obtain per capita household savings (flow concept); finally, we took its logarithm. In our calculation, the difference turned out to be negative, so the logarithm could not be taken. Hence, we decided to rearrange our calculation by taking logarithms before difference.

Per capita household income: Since the explained variable corresponds to the per capita level of a province while per capita household income includes two indicators, i.e., urban household disposable income and rural household net income, we took a weighted average of these two variables by the population ratio.

Gross dependency ratio (GDR): data can be directly obtained for each province in all years except 2010. We made up for the missing data of 2010 by performing an interpolation with the simple average between 2009 and 2011.

Spending on housing, travel and education as a share of total household spending: for urban households, consumption on housing, travel and education includes consumption on housing, transportation and communication, education, culture and entertainment, healthcare, miscellaneous expenses and service consumption. The sum of these five items of consumption is divided by urban household per capita consumption to obtain the spending of urban households on housing, travel and education as a share of total household consumption. For rural households, the same items of consumption are employed to calculate rural household spending on housing, travel and education as a share of total rural household consumption following the same approach. Then, we took the weighted average of the two results according to the ratio between urban and rural populations to arrive at the final ratio of household consumption on housing, travel and education. The above data is from Wind information based on NBS data. Table 4.1 provides descriptive statistical results of the variables.

4.4 Empirical Test Results

Before testing the empirical model, we need to determine whether the fixed effect or stochastic effect model should be adopted. The Chi-squared statistic of Hausman's test is 25.12 with a significance level of 0.00, which rejects the null hypothesis. Hausman's test suggests using the fixed-effect model.

Table 4.2 reports the results of fixed-effect panel regression of per capita household savings with different variables. In Model 1, the explanatory variable only includes per capita household income and credit WMP yield. Per capita household income has a positive impact on per capita household savings, i.e., income growth incurs savings growth; credit WMP yield has a negative impact on per capita household savings,

Table 4.1 Descriptive statistical results of the variables

Indicator	Observation value	Mean	Standard deviation	Min	Max
Per capita household savings (logarithmic form)	186	0.0650	0.0253	−0.0207	0.1165
Per capita household income (logarithmic form)	186	4.0435	0.1886	3.6815	4.5774
Yield of credit WMPs (%)	186	3.8616	0.8475	2.3583	5.0087
Gross dependency ratio (%)	186	35.6004	6.6519	19.2700	55.0900
Spending on housing, travel and education as a share of total household consumption (%)	186	45.8200	4.2772	29.3900	52.2400

i.e., a significant relationship of substitution exists between WMPs and household savings. The coefficient of per capita household income is greater than that of credit WMP yield, i.e., the former has a greater impact on savings deposits than the latter.

In Model 2, we have introduced the variable of gross dependency ratio (GDR). The introduction of GDR has improved the equation's goodness of fit while no significant change has occurred in z statistic of the other two variables, which indicates greater robustness of the equation. The estimated coefficient of newly introduced GDR is significant at the 10% level; the sign of its estimated coefficient is inconsistent with

Table 4.2 Effect of credit WMP yield on per capita household savings (fixed effect)

Indicator	Model 1	Model 2	Model 3
Per capita household income (logarithmic form)	0.0422***	0.0647***	0.0859***
	(4.44)	(3.58)	(3.76)
Yield of credit WMPs (%)	−0.0073***	−0.0078***	−0.0097***
	(−5.77)	(−5.65)	(−6.98)
Gross dependency ratio (GDR) (%)		0.0018*	0.0022*
		(1.82)	(1.92)
Spending on housing, travel and education as a share of total household consumption (%)			−0.0057***
			(−4.52)
R^2	0.2380	0.2490	0.3108
Observation value	186	186	186

Note * and *** denote significance at 10%, 5% and 1% significance levels, respectively. Numeric values in parentheses are the values of *z* statistic the model's assumption. Some scholars (Liu Shenglong et al., 2012) explained how GDR affected household savings from a life expectancy perspective. An increase in life expectancy means that people will spend more time in retirement and have to save more in their working age to maintain a certain level of consumption in an extended retirement. This view may explain the positive correlation between gross dependency ratio and household savings.

In Model 3, we further introduce the variable of housing, travel and educational consumption on the basis of Model 2. The introduction of this consumption structure variable has further improved the equation's goodness of fit while no significant change has occurred in z statistic of the other three variables, which indicates a further increase in robustness of the equation. As far as the newly introduced consumption structure variable is concerned, its estimated coefficient is significant only at the 1% level; the sign of its estimated coefficient is negative, which is consistent with the model's assumption expectation. This result coincides with the reality: after over three decades of reform and opening up, China has seen a serious oversupply of industrial products, especially light industrial goods, which means that no stimulus policy, however strong, targeted at such consumption may reduce the savings rate. In contrast, access to healthcare, schooling and housing presents broad challenges across China. With imperfect social security, unequal access to education, healthcare and other public services, as well as the poor availability of financial services, households have to save more in case of future needs.

Overall, the equation's goodness of fit and robustness have steadily increased with the gradual inclusion of new variables. The absolute value of Model 3's estimated coefficient is greater than those of Model 2 and Model 1. That is to say, without controlling of the two variables of the gross dependency ratio and consumption on housing, travel and education, the household savings impact of per capita household income and credit WMP yield will be underestimated. Examined by the absolute value of estimated coefficients, the factors can be ranked by the following descending order in terms of the magnitude of their impact on household savings: household income, financial products that may substitute deposits, consumption structure, and aggregate demographic burden.

We substitute the overall WMP yield with the yields of WMPs with different maturities to find out WMPs of which maturity have the most significant influence on household savings. Table 4.3 reports the results of regression: Model 1 through Model 3 include WMPs with maturities below five years, three years and one year, respectively. Judging by the regression results, there is no obvious change in the estimated coefficients of various equations, test statistics and goodness of fit. The reason is that WMPs with long maturities are too few. We have calculated the percentages of WMPs with maturities between one and three years and between three and five years from 2006 to 2012 in total WMPs to be 1.82% and 0.09%, respectively. Even if the percentages of those WMPs varied across provinces at different time points, their impact remains small.

In Model 4 through 6, the maturities of credit WMPs are increasingly shortened, and the robustness revealed by the equation's goodness of fit and statistic test reached the maximum with WMP yield (one month) as proxy variable. Judging by

Table 4.3 Per capita household savings effect of credit WMP yield with different maturities (fixed effect)

Indicator	Model 1	Model 2	Model 3	Model 4	Model 5	Model 6
Per capita household income (logarithmic form)	0.0859***	0.0860***	0.0870***	0.1046***	0.1163***	0.1275***
	(3–76)	(3–76)	(3–78)	(4–15)	(4–26)	(5–14)
Yield of credit WMPs (%) (all maturities)	−0.0097_ ***					
	(−6.98)					
Yield of credit WMPs (%) (below three years)		−0.0097***				
		(−7.02)				
Yield of credit WMPs (%) (below one year)			−0.0096***			
			(−6.97)			
Yield of credit WMPs (%) (below six months)				−0.0085***		
				(−5.75)		
Yield of credit WMPs (%) (below three months)					−0.0082***	
					(−5.25)	
Yield of credit WMPs (%) (below one month)						−00142***
						(−8.81)
Gross dependency ratio (%)	0.0022*	0.0022*	0.0022*	0.0020*	0.0020*	0.0019*
	(1.92)	(1.92)	(1.92)	(1.76)	(1.71)	(1.83)
Spending on housing, travel and education as a share of total household consumption (%)	−0.0057***	−0.0057***	−0.0057***	−0.0056***	−0.0055″*	−0.0061***
	(−4.52)	(−4.53)	(−4.51)	(−4.25)	(−4.17)	(−4.87)
R^2	0.3108	0.3116	0.3106	0.2771	0.2647	0.3360
Observations	186	186	186	186	186	186

Note *, ** and *** respectively denote significance at the 10%, 5% and 1% levels. Numeric values in parentheses are the values of z statistic the estimated coefficient, compared with the yields on products of other maturities, the yield on WMPs (one month) had the greatest substitutive effect on household savings deposits. In reality, most products with more vibrant SHIBOR interest rate variations have maturities shorter than 14 days (accounting for 95% of all products), and most WMPs follow SHIBOR as pricing basis. Combining these two facts with the above results, we may roughly arrive at the following conclusions: credits WMP products are becoming a bridge linking households with the currency market and have a significant substitutive effect on household savings. In other words, the currency market is a vehicle for China's ongoing interest rate liberalization. After substituting credit WMPs with those with the shortest maturities, the following change occurred in other variables: the household savings effect of per capita household income increased, the household savings effect of gross dependency ratio (GDR) decreased, and the household savings effect of consumption structure (share of consumption on housing, travel and education) increased.

4.5 Concluding Remarks

This paper examines the impact of the WMP market's development on household savings. After controlling other important variables, we found a negative correlation between credit WMP yield and household savings, i.e., the development of bank WMPs has a substitutive effect on household savings. After examining the correlation between WMPs with different maturities and household savings, we found that credit WMPs with maturities shorter than one month had the greatest substitutive effect on household savings. Considering the fact that WMPs follow the currency market as pricing reference, we may draw the following conclusions: the currency market has served as a vehicle for China's interest rate liberalization process. Concerning interest rate liberalization, we have further identified two directions for further research on the basis of this paper. First, the extent to which such substitutive effect adversely impacts upon bank operations can be best revealed by a study on the narrowing of interest rate spread. Second, the issue of "financial disintermediation" requires further discussions. Notwithstanding a reduction in household savings deposits as a result of WMPs, the question is whether the decreased funds have completely left the banking system? In other words, are banks completely free from risks after disintermediation? At least, the principal-protected WMP funds stay in the banking system. For such products, banks have a guarantee responsibility. In 2009, the PBoC set up the "structural deposits" account for principal-protected WMPs. By June 2014, China's structural deposits amounted to 2.3 trillion yuan. Are those products moved out from the balance sheet as trust assets isolated from bankruptcy risks? The US sub-prime mortgage crisis is probably a negative example.

The estimated results of other variables in equation also have important policy implications. First, the primary determinant of household savings is household income. Over the past three decades of reform and opening up, China has maintained spectacular GDP growth. However, the shrinking share of labor compensation in total national income has stoked social discord. In the new normal of China's economy, reasonable national income distribution should be a more important item on the policy agenda if the previous high savings and high investment growth inertia is to be maintained. Second, the gross dependency ratio (GDR) has a positive impact on household savings, which is contrary to theoretical expectations. Some scholars attributed this phenomenon to a longer life expectancy. If this explanation holds, we should beware of the potential inverted U-shaped impact of the elderly dependency ratio on savings given the increasingly limited potentials for life expectancy to rise beyond a high level. Third, if the macroscopic question is observed from the perspective of rebalancing, it can be found that the key to reducing household savings is to improve consumption structure rather than raise consumption level. The government should make greater efforts to improve social security, public services and housing to encourage household consumption of housing, travel and education.

(Cai Zhen, Li Chongyang)

References

Aziz. J., and C. Li: "Explaining China's Low Consumption: The Neglected Role of Household Income", *IMF Working Paper*, 2006.

Ding Bo, Ba Shusong, Ma Xiaoke, Jin Lingling: "Banks' On-Balance-Sheet WMPs Support China's Interest Rate Integration", *Rural Finance Research*, Vol.9, 2012.

Li Yan: "Discussions on the Relationship Between Interest Rates and Household Savings in China", *Economic Research Journal*, Vol.11, 1999.

Liu Shenglong, Hu Angang, Lang Xiaojuan: "Life Expectancy and Household Savings in China", *Economic Research Journal*, Vol.8, 2012.

Nabar, M: "Targets, Interest Rates, and Household Saving in Urban China", *IMF Working Paper*, 2011.

Qi Tianxiang: "Study on Household Savings in China During Economic Transition", *Economic Research Journal*, Vol.9, 2000.

Research Group of Haikou Central Branch, the People's Bank of China: "Evaluation of the Impact of WMPs on Interest Rate Liberalization in China", *Hainan Finance*, Vol.9, 2013.

Sheng Fangfu: "Constraints of Deposit Interest Rate Liberalization China and Way-out", *Enterprise Economy*, Vol.5, 2013.

Wang Dewen, Cai Fang, Zhang Xuehui: "Savings and the Growth Effects of Demographic Transition", *Population Research*, Vol.5, 2004.

Wang Guogang: "Urbanization: Fulcrum of China's Economic Transition", *Economic Research Journal*, Vol.12, 2010.

Wang Jinbin, Yu Chunhai: "Possible Pathways for China's Interest Rate Liberalization Reforms", *Journal of Financial Research*, Vol.12, 2007.

Wang Xiaoya, Bo Yongxiang, Xu Yan: "Empirical Analysis of the Impact of Seven Rate Cuts on Savings, Loans and Money Supply in China", *Economic Research Journal*, Vol.6, 2000.

Wu Jian: "Savings Deposit Bifurcation and Change in Money Structure", *Economic Research Journal*, Vol.4, 2000.

Xu Dongjiang: "Rational Reactions of Chinese Households, Banks and Firms to Interest Rate Liberalization", *The Journal of World Economy*, Vol.5, 2002.

Yuan Zengting, Wang Boying, Cai Zhen: "Innovation Motivations of Bank WMPs and Determinants", *South China Finance*, Vol.11, 2010.
Zhang Ming: "Updates of Research on Savings Rate since the 1990s", *The Journal of World Economy*, Vol.4, 2007
Zhu Hongmei: "Empirical Study on the Pricing of Bank WMPs", *Review of Investment Studies*, Vol.9, 2012.

Chapter 5
Theoretical Analysis of China's Interest Rate Liberalization Reforms

Concluded on November 12, 2013, the Third Plenary Session of the 18th CPC Central Committee—an important event under worldwide attention—adopted the *Decision of the Central Committee of the Communist Party of China on Some Major Issues Concerning Comprehensively Deepening the Reform* (hereinafter "*Decisions*").[1] Judging by the content of the *Decisions*, the key message from the Third Plenary Session of the 18th CPC Central Committee is to balance the relationship between government and market and ensure that the market plays a decisive role in allocating resources. As the most eye-catching and innovative element of the *Decisions*, this principle forms the theoretical basis for deepening financial reforms in China.

Over the past three decades of reform and opening up, China's financial reforms have never been interrupted, and great progress has been made in financial liberalization. Yet China's financial system remains underdeveloped, and a low level of market-based operations or the influence of non-market factors continues to pose the biggest barrier to financial market development. Such underdevelopment is, for instance, manifested in price control and quantitative control in the credit market, barriers to market entry and exit, stock market control, ownership discrimination in the financial sector, and the strict control over two-way cross-border capital flow.[2] Evolved from a planned economy, China's financial system is still subject to administrative control by the government with respect to capital supply, which has severed links between the household and corporate sectors and deprived their financial powers. Absolute dominance and excessive intervention of the government over financial markets prevent the formation of effective market-based price mechanism and resource allocation, making financial markets more vulnerable to systemic and regional risks. The decisive role of the market in allocating resources means that the market should play a decisive role in interest rate formation. As noted by Zhou Xiaochuan, former Governor of the PBoC, noted in his interpretive report *Comprehensively Deepening*

[1] See http://wenku.baidu.com/link?url.

[2] Abiad and Mody (2003).

G. Wang, *A Study on Interest Rate Liberalization in China*, Research Series on the Chinese Dream and China's Development Path,
https://doi.org/10.1007/978-981-97-3644-7_5

Financial Sector Reform and Opening up and Improving Financial Market Systems (*Report*) for the Third Plenary Session of the 18th CPC Central Committee,[3] the most important task in deepening China's financial reforms is to liberalize interest and exchange rate formation mechanisms. Interest rate liberalization reforms are intended to straighten out the price relationship in China's financial market systems and normalize the currently distorted market price mechanism. Hence, interest rate liberalization is a primary task in deepening China's financial reforms.

5.1 The Interest Rate Price Mechanism and China's Financial Markets Are Rife with Tensions

Judging by the Central Bank's interest rate reform arrangements,[4] the first step is to create a Loan Prime Rate (LPR) mechanism, encourage the issuance and transactions of interbank certificates of deposits (CDs), and expand the scope of market-based pricing for liability products offered by financial institutions. The second step is to establish a central bank policy interest rate system and advance the transition of the monetary policy regulation framework from quantitative regulation to price-oriented regulation. The last step is to deregulate deposit interest rate control when appropriate to complete interest rate liberalization, or allow market mechanisms to play a decisive role in interest rate formation.

It is fair to say that such framework and approach have followed the principles of China's interest rate liberalization reforms a few years ago, relying on administrative mechanisms, which include: first, a gradualist approach to the reforms, i.e., a reform should not be carried out until conditions are ready to avoid any misstep; second, the reforms should contribute to stability, i.e., any interest rate reforms should be carried out with minimal impacts on the market; third, the reforms should be incremental, i.e., interest rate liberalization reforms will only increase market interests without altering existing interests or rectifying unreasonable market interests; fourth, the traces of administrative dominance in such reforms are still faintly visible. Given the path dependence of interest rate liberalization reforms and the irreplicability and irreversibility of social and economic life, very few scholars have raised doubts over the reform approach and path of China's interest rate liberalization reforms over the past decade or so, and seldom did they reflect upon the actual effects of those reforms. Hence, we should first conduct an in-depth study and theoretical reflection on previous interest rate liberalization reforms before reassessing initial conditions and pathway for China's interest rate liberalization reforms.

Since 1993,[5] China's interest rate liberalization reforms have never been interrupted. In the views of many, China has made major progress in its interest rate

[3] See Zhou Xiaochuan's article published by *Securities Times* on November 19, 2013.

[4] See Zhou Xiaochuan's article published by *Securities Times* on November 19, 2013.

[5] *The Decisions of the CPC Central Committee on Matters concerning the Establishment of the Socialist Market Economic System* adopted at the third plenum of the 14th CPC Central committee

liberalization reforms over the past two decades. The reason is that very few interest rates are still controlled by the government, and except for the upper limit on bank deposit rates, all other rates have been deregulated. For instance, currency market and bond market rates, including interbank lending, repurchase, Treasury bond, financial bond and corporate bond rates, have been fully deregulated. Foreign-currency deposit and loan rates have also been liberalized. As for bank credit market, the Central Bank only regulates the upper limit of deposit rates after deregulating the lower limit on loan rates in July 2013. While these gradualist interest rate liberalization reforms appeared to have enhanced the role of the market in interest rate formation, the actual effects of reforms are not as good as expected due to the administrative approach, and distortions in market price mechanisms and inefficient resource allocation are still common.

Over the past two decades, interest rate liberalization reforms have failed to straighten out distorted interest rate prices in China and allow an effective interest rate price mechanism to take hold in financial markets. Still less did those reforms transform the resource allocation mode where all financial market resources are concentrated under the deposit and loan mechanism. As a result, no evident improvement was made in the operational efficiency of China's financial system. On the contrary, the rural economy, private economy and SMEs meant to benefit from interest rate liberalization reforms suffered from a more severe credit squeeze.[6] Instead of offering more financial services to the real economy, all sorts of financial innovations that sprang up in this reform process (including market, institutional, product and instrumental innovations) turned out to be instruments for financial institutions to evade regulation and for capital to circulate within the financial system to seek profits. Numerous financial innovations in China have further extended the chain of money supply for excessive credit expansion, taking a toll on the efficiency of financial services in supporting the real economy and exposing the entire financial system to more risks. Distorted financial market price mechanisms and long-overdue interest rate liberalization reforms have led to a swathe of problems in China's financial markets, e.g., runaway bank credit expansion, unchecked "financial disintermediation" and shadow banking, frequent money shortages, rampant local government financing vehicles, distorted financing structure, abrupt rise of Internet finance, serious real estate bubbles, and a "double-track" interest rate system. Before deepening the interest rate liberalization reforms for China's financial markets, therefore, we have to fully take stock of and reflect upon the philosophies, modes, pathways and effects of China's interest rate liberalization reforms in the previous two decades, review the problems, draw upon experiences, and establish a new reform approach for interest rate liberalization.

---

and the *Decisions of the State Council on Financial Reforms* laid out the basic vision for interest rate liberalization reform.

[6] According to Ying Qianwei's study, China's microscopic capital allocation efficiency decreased after the loan interest rate liberalization reform of 2004, and the decrease was more significant in regions with lower levels of financial market development. See Ying Qianwei (2012, p. 8).

Judging by the global experiences of interest rate liberalization, there is no one-size-fits-all solution or general experience for interest rate liberalization reforms given the differences of each country's initial conditions, economic environment, and central bankers' mindsets. It cannot be safely said that a gradualist approach is superior to a radical one or the other way around. The choices were made by individual countries according to their actual conditions. Yet most countries had initiated interest rate liberalization when their financial market price mechanisms were seriously distorted and financial resources allocated inefficiently. In most cases, such reforms led to a gradual formation of price mechanisms in financial markets, adjustments in financial market structure, all-round improvements in the capacity of financial services to serve the real economy, a complete transformation of financial risk management modes, and evident improvement in the financial system's efficiency.[7] Yet some studies suggest that interest rate liberalization may also increase the banking system's fragility and trigger a banking crisis in the reforming country.[8] That is to say, interest rate liberalization reforms are a sure path towards the effective allocation of national market resources despite the absence of general conclusions and risk assessment of interest rate liberalization reforms.

China's first two decades of interest rate liberalization reforms had followed a gradualist approach, liberalizing currency market and bond market interest rates before credit market interest rates. In liberalizing credit market interest rates, China has followed the approach of "taking the first step of reform for foreign currencies before the home currency, loan interest rate before deposit interest rate, long maturities before short maturities and large sum transactions before small-sum ones", targeting at ease tasks before more difficult ones to ensure stability.[9] While allowing interest rate liberalization reforms to be carried out smoothly, China's policymakers expected to minimize the reforms' shocks to financial markets and the real economy. However, such a mode and pathway of interest rate liberalization reforms cannot form effective market price mechanisms in China's financial systems. On the contrary, they have led to serious distortions in China's financial market behaviors, price mechanisms, incentives and restraints. The "double-track" interest rate system continues to exist, and systemic and regional risks keep accumulating in financial markets, causing China's financial markets to be disoriented in an immature stage, i.e., finance has led to excessive credit expansion in various forms, causing capital to circulate within the financial market system, profiteering without serving the real economy. Instead of facilitating China's industrial restructuring, interest rate liberalization reforms have created a crowding-out effect on vulnerable industries, economic sectors and the private sector of economy that are vital to China's national interest and people's livelihoods, plaguing financial markets with inefficiencies. All these undesired effects have to do with financial market price distortions and unsuccessful interest rate liberalization reforms.

---

[7] Zhang Jianhua et al. (2012, pp. 175–196).

[8] Zhang Li (2003, p. 89).

[9] See the PBoC's (2005).

Some recent phenomena in China's financial markets appeared different in nature but stemmed from the same origin, reflecting various price distortions in China's financial markets. They range, for instance, from a dash of bank loan issuance at the beginning of the year[10] to a money shortage in the currency market,[11] from the non-repayment risk facing China Credit Trust Co., Ltd. ("CCTIC") to a surge in bank WMPs,[12] and from the sudden rise of Internet finance to the popularity of bitcoins in China. It is fair to say that a swathe of intractable problems facing China's economy can be attributed to serious financial market price distortions. For instance, China's banking system is embroiled in quantitative rather than price competition and challenged by financial disintermediation, shadow banking, serious maturity mismatch in the currency market, runaway forces of Internet finance, unreasonable financing structure, and real estate bubbles.

For instance, why did Chinese commercial banks rush to issue loans at the beginning of the year without effectively pricing their market risks? In China's banking market, it seems that the government imposes very little price control and fully deregulates loan rates except that the upper limit on deposit rates is not deregulated. In addition, various currency market interest rates are fully market-based rates. However, deposit rates offered by Chinese banks are very different from those offered by banks in mature markets, which are not only interest rate cost constraint for the banks, but also the benchmark rates for financial markets as a whole. That is to say, deposit rates offered by banks not only determine banks' loan interest rates, but also influence price tendencies in the entire financial markets as well (e.g., Treasury bond interest rates and interbank lending rates in the currency market, etc.). If banks' deposit interest rates are regulated, banks tend to engage in a competition of credit scale rather than price. That is to say, at the homogenous price level, credit size determines each bank's competitiveness. Hence, credit expansion has become the biggest impulse of commercial banks in maximizing business performance. The dash to issue loans at the beginning of the year has become an important sign of banks vying to be more competitive.

To curb banks' excessive credit expansion, the government has imposed both price control over the banking market and capped banks' credit size. In response, banks have moved their deposit business out of their balance sheets to shun those price and quantitative controls. Through financial product innovation, banks created numerous wealth management products (WMPs),[13] funneling funds into the real estate market and local government financing vehicles (LGFVs) through various

---

[10] In January of this year, Chinese commercial banks rushed to issue loans worth 1.37 trillion yuan, or 13% of the annual total by the aggregate increase in bank credit in 2013. See http://finance.sina.com.cn/china/jrxw/20140130/130518125983.shtml.

[11] Since the end of June 2013, any tightening in the money market would cause a sharp rise in market interest rates. This market phenomenon is often referred to as a "money shortage."

[12] In 2004, there were only 133 WMPs offered by Chinese banks, which raised less than 50 billion yuan. In 2012, 29,100 WMPs were offered in China, raising 19.01 trillion yuan. In eight years, these figures increased by 218 and 379 times, indicating a maniac surge in those financial instruments. See Yin Jianfeng and Wang Zengwu (2013, p. 4).

[13] Yin Jianfeng, Wang Zengwu: "Shadow Banks and the Shadow of Banks".

investment instruments such as entrusted loans and trust loans,[14] giving rise to a huge shadow banking market in China. In case of a real estate price hike, risks in this gigantic shadow banking system would be concealed. Yet once those entrusted products or trust products run into problems, the risks become swiftly transmitted to the banking system.

Since 2013, the currency market has been struck by incessant money shortages with frequent interbank lending rate hikes, which largely stemmed from a serious fund maturity mismatch of domestic financial institutions operating with high leverage ratios, especially small and medium-sized banks. While some financial institutions borrowed short-term funds to finance for long-term loan issuance (which was the only way for some banks to expand their credit size at the fastest pace), many financial institutions took advantage of the currency market for speculation and profiteering instead of addressing short-term positions. Given these distortions in China's currency market operations, problems and "money shortage" events would surface as soon as the Central Bank intervened. In other words, the currency market will be plagued by endless money shortages as long as the interest rate mechanisms in China's credit market remain distorted. The reason is that not only are currency market speculators able to manipulate interest rate volatility to force the Central Bank to inject liquidity into the currency market, but the financial institutions with a serious fund maturity mismatch are unwilling to change their behavior.

Recent years have seen an upsurge in China's Internet finance development. For instance, Yu'ebao, a popular online WMP, saw its assets under management (AUM) skyrocket to over 400 billion yuan in just half a year. More Internet finance investment instruments have mushroomed. The rapid rise of Internet finance in China can be ascribed to Internet technology innovations and smart phone-enabled market agglomeration strengths, which helped overcome deficiencies in traditional financial business modes. More importantly, however, deposit rate regulation has played a bigger part in the rise of Internet finance. Current interest rate on Renminbi-denominated demand deposits is set to be 0.35% by domestic banks. The annualized interest rate of the best WMPs offered by banks is around only 4%. By January 20, 2014, however, the seven-day annualized yield on Yu'ebao reached 6.46%, and the seven-day annualized yield on Licaitong, Tencent's wealth management platform, stood at 7.338%.[15] Online investment instruments delivered over mobile networks are not only more convenient and accessible to average users, but also offer higher returns. What makes it possible, one might wonder, for Internet finance to yield sharply higher returns for its users? As can be learned from relevant information, those online investment instruments were delivered in partnership with fund management firms under short-term wealth management funds and primarily invested in fixed-return assets or the currency market without much difference from traditional investment channels. That is to say, the lack of progress in interest rate liberalization reforms served as a

[14] Since 2008, trust business in China has also experienced rampant growth. In 2008, China's trust business amounted to 1.2 trillion yuan, which increased by 525% to 7.5 trillion yuan by 2012. See Yin Jianfeng, Wang Zengwu: *Shadow Banks and the Shadow of Banks*, p. 102.

[15] See https://financeprod.alipay.com/fund/index.htm

key driver behind the emergence of Internet finance in China. Unless policymakers follow a new approach to and speed up interest rate liberalization reforms, the development of Internet finance will deal a heavy blow to China's traditional financial market.

A swathe of problems plaguing China's financial system—such as high potential risks and unreasonable financial structure—can be attributed to the lack of progress in interest rate liberalization reforms and distortions in financial market price mechanisms. In China's domestic financial market, which evolved from the planned economy and heavily relies on implicit government guarantee, excessive credit expansion did not occur until in recent few years. Given the limited credit expansion, the risk of a financial crisis was unsurprisingly small. Yet excessive credit expansion in recent years have fueled potential risks (including liquidity risk, shadow banking risk, local government financing vehicle risk, and interest rate risk).[16] Interest rate liberalization reforms and the establishment of a deposit insurance system and a market-based exit system for the banking sector represent a fundamental change in the way Chinese banks compete, putting an end to the competition of scale. Under the cost constraint, commercial banks will have to fundamentally enhance their risk pricing capabilities to survive fierce competition. However, risks in the domestic banking market should still be evaluated cautiously. In this regard, two questions linger: are current regulatory standards sufficient for risk evaluation? What is the magnitude of and how to evaluate financial risks during an economic countercyclical period? That is to say, banking sector risks associated with the real estate sector will not be exposed without cyclical adjustment. In case cyclical adjustment occurs in China's real estate sector, however, problems and risks facing China's banking sector will also be laid bare. Recently, the China Banking Regulatory Commission (CBRC) has issued regulations on straightening out shadow banks and local government financing vehicles (LGFVs) with a view to preventing risks in China's banking sector. To keep such risks at bay, however, we must address the root cause, change our way of thinking and speed up interest rate liberalization reforms, letting market-based price mechanism play a decisive role in allocating financial resources.

As the above explanations suggest, interest rate liberalization reforms are intended to correct the distorted price mechanism in China's financial market, establish an effective price mechanism to determine the flow of financial resources, raise the efficiency of China's financial system operations and enhance the financial market's capacity to serve the real economy, rectify the non-market-based financial system, transform bank-dominated financial resource allocation, allow enterprises and households more choices of financial behaviors, and let the market play a decisive role in allocating financial resources and thus support domestic industrial restructuring and economic development. Judging by the effects of China's interest rate liberalization reforms over the past two decades, the previous approach, methodology

[16] In the 64 years since the founding of the People's Republic of China in 1949, China's credit supply increased by 30 trillion yuan in the first 60 years and close to 40 trillion yuan in the more recent four years. Such rampant credit expansion has led to systemic risks accumulating in the financial market. Data is from *China Statistical Yearbook*.

and pathway of interest rate liberalization reforms no longer apply to the changing landscape of economic development. We should reflect upon past reforms and draw lessons, redefine the initial conditions, methodology and pathway of the ongoing interest rate liberalization reforms, and steer those reforms based on current conditions. In expediting China's interest rate liberalization reforms, there is no general theory and experience to follow. What we can do is to blaze a trail suitable for China's financial market development. Without adequate progress in interest rate liberalization reforms, problems in China's financial market will become more numerous and pose greater risks over time.

5.2 Theoretical Basis of China's Interest Rate Liberalization Reforms

The degree of market-based interest rates as the price of capital directly determines the efficiency of resource allocation in financial markets. Normally, interest rate liberalization refers to the process in which the government takes steps to relax or phase out direct control over interest rates to allow the market to play a decisive role in interest rate formation and variation or allow capital suppliers and borrowers to independently evaluate the credit risks of interest rates. Interest rate liberalization includes the liberalization of interest rate determination, transmission, structure and administration. The goal of interest rate liberalization reforms, therefore, is to establish market-based interest rates, foster interest rate transmission underpinned by the Central Bank's benchmark interest rates and intermediated by currency market interest rates, develop a financing structure determined by market supply and demand, and diversify market interest rate formation mechanisms. As a result of these reforms, market-based resource allocation will become significantly more efficient, financial markets will be put at the service of the real economy, and greater progress will be made in China's economic growth transition and industrial restructuring.

The question that warrants reflections is what makes interest rate liberalization reforms necessary? Why? What are the motivations of the reforms? What kind of indicators should be designed to measure the effects of interest rate liberalization? What is the basis for establishing those indicators? And their scientific justifications? The list of questions may go on and on. Discussions and reflections based on those questions are essential for establishing the theoretical basis of interest rate liberalization.

Normally, interest rate liberalization is contrary to interest rate control and requires the deregulation of interest rate control by the government. The government imposes control over interest rates for two reasons: first, advanced market economies mobilized low-cost financial resources to meet their investment needs during specific periods.[17] For instance, Europe and the US embraced interest rate control to support

[17] Zhang Jianhua et al. (2012, p. 177).

economic reconstruction after the World War II. While newly independent countries established market-based economies, many countries with a planned economy have also shifted towards market-based ones after the 1980s. With nascent market economies and immature financial markets, financial repression became a basic trait of financial markets in these countries, which primarily stemmed from interest rate control.[18] Any type of interest rate control will distort financial market prices and lead to inefficiencies in financial resource allocation, giving rise to potential risks in the financial system. In the 1960s–1970s, financial reform or liberalization became an international trend. A core aspect of financial reforms is interest rate liberalization reforms.

Financial reforms are interest rate liberalization reforms in a more general sense. Investigating the motivations of financial reforms, efficiency measurement indicators and efficiency effects helps deepen our understanding of the theoretical basis of interest rate liberalization reforms. Notably, financial reforms topped policy agenda in many countries in the last three decades of the twentieth century. Although financial reforms in these countries vary greatly in terms of speed, scale, effects and results, Abiad et al. conducted a quantitative study on the different financial policies of 35 countries from 1973 to 1996 and summarized the general theory behind motivations of this round of financial reforms.[19] Abiad et al. identified three drivers of this wave of financial reforms. First, countries prompted by internal and external events to respond by altering its financial policy, thus triggering financial reforms. Second, policymakers learned and renewed knowledge to re-assess how financial markets operated in their respective countries, recognizing the problem of costly and inefficient financial operations. This reality and the underlying vested interests cannot be changed without financial reforms. The third factor is ideological impact.

As can be learned from the literature, scholars have extensively discussed the shocks of specific events that had influenced and motivated financial reforms. In his case studies on developing countries, Krueger[20] noted that most financial reforms occurred in two circumstances: either a new government took office or an economic crisis erupted. He also believed that such shocks also include abrupt change in international economic situations and international financial institutions demanding aid recipient countries to reform.[21] Financial reforms triggered by such shocks can be endogenous or exogenous. For instance, it was widely considered that financial reforms would most likely occur in the early stage after a new government took office ("New Government Hypothesis").[22] The reason is that when a new government takes office, it tends to introduce broad economic reforms to honor its election promises. However, the breadth and scope of such reforms are subject to reform costs and benefits reckoned by the new government. If the cost of reform occurs in a short term while it takes a longer period to materialize the benefits of reform, the

[18] McKinnon (1973).

[19] Abiad and Mody (2003).

[20] Krueger (1993).

[21] Krueger (1997, pp. 1–22).

[22] Haggard and Webb (1993, pp. 143–68).

new government will become less motivated to reform after taking office. According to Haggard and Webb's case studies,[23] democratic parties in Argentina, Bolivia and Brazil tended to adopt more extensive economic reform policies but their actual reform policies were often delayed in the late stage of their tenure. It was also argued that by taking office, a new government would tip the balance of political powers, and incoming political elites would prefer to maintain the status quo in the interest of political stability when the economy was doing well. As soon as their political power became more stable or a crisis occurred, the case for financial reforms became stronger.[24] It is widely proven that countries face different sorts of crises and resort to various approaches to financial reforms. The severity of the crisis, however, determines the difficulty of each financial reform.[25] In fact, both the Dodd-Frank Act adopted by the US in 2010 and the Financial Services Act adopted by the UK in 2012 meant that a swathe of major financial reforms would be introduced.[26] The release of those acts was prompted by the shocks of the US global financial crisis in 2008. Hence, financial reforms are prompted by the shocks of major events, and the only difference is the nature, magnitude, scope and initial conditions of those events, which determines the intensity of driving forces behind financial reforms.

Learning or "learning by doing" is also a driver of financial reforms, on which extensive literature can be found. If relevant parties are not well-informed about the content of a financial reform and its results, even if this reform is beneficial for the society as a whole, relevant stakeholders will lack incentives to reform and even oppose the reform. According to Fernandez and Rodrick (1991),[27] if individuals or vested interests have little idea about who will benefit from a reform, they will oppose the reform and ask for the status quo to be maintained even if this reform is beneficial for the society as a whole and can increase welfare for most people. For instance, it is assumed that two sectors exist in a city, where sector L creates 60% of jobs and sector W creates 40% of jobs. When a reform policy is to be introduced, a possible outcome would be as follows: first, sector L will lose 2 units of interest; second, sector W may add 2 units of return; third, one third of labor force could migrate to sector W. From a social welfare perspective, this reform policy will raise overall social benefits and more than 60% of people stand to gain. However, since no one in sector L knows who will benefit from the reform, those in sector L expect a negative return and decide to oppose this reform. As people in sector L come to realize the possible outcomes of reform, their attitude may reverse. Hence, learning and access to information are the most important drivers of financial reforms. That is to say, no country may expect to accomplish financial reforms at one go. Instead, financial reforms are a process of learning and acquiring information. Similarly, such financial reforms are also a process of interest adjustment and contestation. Krueger considered that any financial reform would entail an adjustment of interests

[23] Haggard and Webb (1993, pp. 143–68).

[24] Tornell (1998).

[25] Drazen and Easterly (2001, pp. 129–157).

[26] Li Wenhong and Wu Zuhong (2013).

[27] Fernandez and Rodril (1991, pp. 1146–55).

and could encounter resistance from vested interests. If the financial reforms put a greater premium on the increment of interests rather than a zero-sum game, resistance from vested interests would be much smaller and in some cases, new interest groups may turn out to support financial reforms.

In addition, financial reforms may also be driven by a variety of other factors such as different ideologies, major political reforms, new technologies, and the level of a country's reform and opening up. For instance, the French Revolution at the mid-nineteenth century not only triggered a wave of sweeping social and political reforms, but also aroused financial reforms in Europe.[28] The French Revolution weakened landlord aristocrats and transferred political power to wealthy farmers and emerging industrialists and commercialists, opening up new markets and technologies. New investment opportunities prompted industrialists and commercialists to explore financing markets as alternatives to traditional sources of capital. In this context, a succession of major financial reforms were carried out, enabling the establishment of limited liability companies, stock exchanges, emerging financial institutions, and new financing instruments. Robust market demand after political reforms served as strong forces behind those financial reforms. Raghuram Rajan et al. also believed[29] that in an economy with a high degree of international trade and investment openness, investment opportunities from openness will reduce domestic opposition to financial reforms, which is conducive to the implementation of financial reforms. Benefiting from an early-mover advantage, foreign financial institutions will push forward financial reforms in those countries. With a higher degree of trade openness, a country will experience faster international capital flow that facilitates financial reforms. Spain in the 1980s to 1990s is a case in point.

In the views of Abiad et al., the efficiency of financial reforms is subject to the depth of such indicators as credit control, interest rate control, market entry barriers, stock market regulation, financial sector privatization, and financial sector openness.[30] They use these indicators to conduct an extensive statistical analysis of the determinants of financial reforms in 35 countries over the span of 24 years. Their general conclusion is that the occurrence of a major event will exert significant shocks to the status quo, and those shocks may induce either financial reforms or a reversal of reforms; learning has played a significant role in the reform process. Learning is not only the initial driver of financial reforms, but also makes further financial reforms possible. In today's world, ideology's impact on financial reforms is not particularly striking. A conducive international market environment helps enhance financial reforms, but a banking crisis leads to the opposite effect.

For China's interest rate liberalization reforms, the shocks of existing conditions and a series of events may also be construed as a learning process. For instance, the

[28] It may induce either financial reforms or a reversal of reforms; learning has played an important role in the reform process. Raghuram Rajan and Luigi Zingales (2004, pp. 139–144).

[29] Raghuram Rajan and Luigi Zingales (2004, pp. 147–151).

[30] They classified indicators into various grades such as Grade 0, Grade 1, Grade 2 and Grade 3, which represent complete repression, partial repression, partial liberalization, and complete liberalization. Different grades denote different levels of market-based operations. Based on these indicators, they estimated the level of market-based operations in a country's financial system.

shocks of a new term of the Chinese government taking office and domestic and international financial market events would force China to accelerate interest rate liberalization, without which China's financial markets would not defuse and withstand crises. China's interest rate liberalization reforms are also a learning process. The reason is that China has no ready experience to follow in setting the initial conditions, pathways and modes of its interest rate liberalization reforms, which cannot be carried out in disregard of the nature of interest rates. In this respect, China's reformers are in a learning process. In the next section, we will interpret the nature of interest rate liberalization reforms based on the laws of interest rate pricing.

5.3 Laws of Financial Product Pricing and the Heterogeneity Of Physical Commodity Pricing

As an important price of the factor market, interest rates are the core mechanism for financial markets to effectively allocate resources. Hence, interest rate liberalization should allow the market to play a decisive role in interest rate formation and variation. What are interest rates? How are interest rates formed? Which factors will influence interest rate variation? Various funds or assets are mutually substitutive or complementary. Interest rates may vary across different modes of financing due to heterogeneous risks, liquidity, maturity date, taxation, transaction cost, among other factors. To explain interest rate formation and the relationship among interest rates, scholars have developed theories on interest rate determination and maturity structure. Instead of providing a summary of literature on those interest rate theories, this paper focuses on the analysis of the mechanism behind interest rate credit risk pricing and its differences with physical commodity pricing for the purpose of reflecting the nature of interest rates as credit risk pricing, which provides theoretical basis for interest rate liberalization reforms.

What are interest rates? According to British philosopher John Locke, interest rate is the price of money[31]; J. M. Keynes considered interest rate as the compensation for giving up liquidity during a specific period[32]; Robert J. Shiller, a laureate of the Nobel prize for economics in 2013, defined interest rate as yield-to-maturity on bonds with payment date T at time t. The payment amount of such bonds may also be vector-discounted into the price of bonds[33]; Der-tzon Hsieh believed that interest rate is the price of credit or loanable funds or the price that must be afforded in using capital. Interest rates as a price are an important variable for distributing financial and physical resources and linking finance with the real-economy sectors.[34] As shown above, researchers may offer different definitions on interest rate from various perspectives. The above-mentioned definitions on interest rate, however, all

[31] Der-tzon Hsieh (1993, p. 634).

[32] Keynes (1997, pp. 142–143).

[33] Shiller and McCulloch (1990, pp. 627–722).

[34] Der-tzon Hsieh (1993, p. 629).

recognize interest rate as the price of the factor market. The only difference lies in the connotations of interest rate, such as the use of funds, forsaken liquidity, bonds and loanable funds.

We believe that interest rates are the price of credit risks, which can be explained under the following mechanism: A primary function of finance is to perform cross-temporal and cross-spatial allocation of resources through specific intermediaries under uncertain conditions, i.e., those with surplus funds transfer funds through a certain intermediary to those with a shortage of funds and willing to pay a price for obtaining such funds. An important aspect of financial research is to examine why and when such cross-temporal and cross-spatial financial transactions would occur, what barriers and problems would confront those financial transactions, how financial transactions evolve, and so on and so forth. In answering these questions, we should be aware that financial transactions are vastly different from the market transactions of ordinary (or physical) goods. For instance, normal market transactions are instantaneous, i.e., payment and goods delivery occur at the same time. Yet financial transactions allocate resources on different temporal and spatial dimensions, involving payments that often reflect future value. The instantaneity of normal transactions allows the seller and buyer to perform a cost–benefit analysis. For financial transactions, however, a transaction's cost and benefit cannot be known in advance and are uncertain. Such futurity and uncertainty determine that financial transactions must be executed and guaranteed with a certain medium such as contracts. All financial transactions rely on contracts to link the parties of transaction and need to be executed with contracts, which represent an organization or individual's commitment or credibility. Creditworthiness varies from person to person with heterogeneous living environment, education, intellectual level, psychological quality and demand preferences. In financial transactions, risks vary across different sorts of credit. Hence, financial transactions can be defined as the risk consideration of credit. As the price of credit risks, interest rates not only share commonalities with market price, but also are very different from the pricing of physical goods (i.e., great difference exists in pricing between investment and consumer goods).[35]

Price is the core issue of modern economics. Professor Zhang Wuchang even ascribed modern economics to the price theory.[36] Although market price is determined by a multitude of factors[37] such as time, space, subjectivity, objectivity, uncertainties, risks, cost of transaction, personal preferences, pricing mode and public

[35] Karl Brunner *et al.* also identified four markets in a modern economy: Product market, physical assets market, money market, and securities market. Three prices exist in the four markets: Product price, physical assets price, and securities prices. Despite correlations, prices in those markets also have their unique pricing basis and modes of operation. See *Monetary Economics: Problems of Monetary Analysis* by Karl Brunner and Allan Meltzer, China Finance Publishing House, 2010, p. 69. By the attribute of transactional goods, however, this paper divides modern economy into two markets, including the physical goods market and the financial product market. Two prices exist in the two markets, i.e., the price of consumer goods and the price of investment goods. Physical assets tend to possess both attributes, i.e., they are both investment and consumer goods.

[36] Zhang Wuchang (1984).

[37] Wang Dingding (2008, pp. 250–264).

psychology, the three basic functions of market price are the same (for instance, to transmit market information, incentivize and restrain scattered decision-makers, and promote the effective allocation of scarce resources). Yet there are differences in how consumer and investment goods are priced in product and financial markets. Those differences serve as an important entry point for making sense of price mechanisms in financial markets.

The transactions of consumer or physical goods are intended to achieve utility or value of use, and those goods are purchased for the purpose of use. Product utility, however, is limited both in objective and subjective terms, and based on the affordability of buyers. Given the heterogeneous utility and affordability of buyers and the existence of information asymmetry and imperfect competition, the market price of products is always the result of buyer–seller consideration, and price discrimination occurs from time to time (i.e., the same product may have different prices in the same market). Through effective competition, however, the equilibrium price can be reached, as is the case for strategic pricing as a common pricing practice in the market.

Take the pricing of residential property for instance, without sufficient information about market demand, land supply and public infrastructure planning, real estate developers may adopt strategic pricing to maximize profitability. Printers, for example, work with powdered ink. Yet demand for printing varies from user to user. The question facing printer makers is which combination guarantees a higher profit? Is it selling printers dearly and powdered ink cheaply or the other way around? If a company wishes to make a profit from organizing a book exhibition, will it earn more profits by raising entrance ticket fees and offering a discount on books or lowering ticket fees while offering a smaller discount on books? The list of questions may go on and on. These are some case studies of strategic pricing, which help us understand how the prices of consumer goods are determined. Professor Oi from the University of Rochester published a classical study on strategic pricing. In 1971, he published an enticing article *A Disneyland Dilemma: Two-Part Tariffs for a Mickey Mouse Monopoly*,[38] which tactfully analyzed how corporate profit could be maximized by strategically pricing Disneyland's admission tickets and rides.

Professor Oi first made the following two assumptions: first, consumer utility derives from the use of product rather than being admitted to a venue, which is comparable to a printer being useless without powdered ink; second, admitting a consumer does not incur additional cost to the producer, but the product has a marginal cost: admitting a consumer to the park incurs little additional cost, but taking rides and watching shows involve costs. Under such assumptions, the question is what type of strategic pricing will maximize profits for the printer maker? Let us assume that two types of customers buy printers: first, those who use printers frequently; second, those who use printers only occasionally. If firms are able to identify those types of buyers, the best way to maximize profits would be selling powdered ink at cost price to encourage customers to print more while selling printers to the two

[38] Oi (1971, pp. 77–96). Also see Zeng Guoping's "Professor Oi's Disney pricing dilemma", *Hong Kong Economic Journal*, January 9, 2014.

types of customers at different prices. At this moment, a firm may sell printers to customers with the highest demand at the highest price and to customers with the lowest demand at the lowest price. Setting differentiated printer prices according to customer traits helps maximize firm profit. If the firm is unable to identify customer demand and preference, or if a high-demand customer pretends to be a low-demand customer, the best way for the company to maximize profit is to price the powdered ink above cost to reduce demand for more customers—even drive some low-demand customers away from the market—and then sell printers at a relatively low price. On the contrary, if customer demand for printers is more or less the same, the company has to sell printers at a high price to extract consumer surplus before selling powdered ink at cost price.

As can be learned from the above case studies, the pricing of consumer goods has the following implications: first, any market price is the result of buyer–seller consideration. Market price is not unique but falls within a range depending on transaction parties' heterogenous bid strategies, preferences, demand and obtained information, as well as product substitutability and complementarity (i.e., price discrimination argued by Professor Zhang Wuchang: the same product can be sold at different prices in the same market). Second, consumer goods can be priced based on the seller's marginal cost and the buyer's demand and affordability, which is the bottom line for product pricing. Normally, a deal cannot occur beyond the upper and lower price bounds. Third, transaction parties are sensitive to price change, which serves as the incentive and constraint for their behaviors. Fourth, equilibrium price, i.e., the market price of consumer goods, is achieved in the process of supply and demand adjustment.

Investment goods or financial products, however, are subject to very different pricing basis and mechanisms. Normally, all investment goods are transacted to obtain expected yield and are purchased with the expectation to sell at a higher price. Contrary to investment goods, consumer goods are likely to depreciate when being resold. Thus, the purchase of consumer goods rarely exceeds demand. The case is not true for investment goods: investors purchase investment goods as much as possible as long as such goods are expected to appreciate in value. That is to say, investment goods are priced based on investors' market expectations, which are determined by investor psychology and risk preference and financial market conditions.[39] In nature, all investment goods are standardized credit contracts reflecting the risk pricing of credit relationships by banks.[40] Under such conditions, investors are not sensitive to asset price.[41] Instead, investors are more concerned with the future price of investment

[39] Financial conditions include the level of financing cost, access to finance, and leverage ratio.

[40] Modern asset and capital pricing theories or pricing models assume that under certain conditions, asset price is determined based on the probability of a future risk event under the law of large numbers. Hence, modern asset pricing theories often fail to take into account how the psychology of investors influences a future risk event. See *Monetary Banking* by Der-tzon Hsieh, San Min Book, 1993, pp. 282–300.

[41] Here, investors being insensitive to asset price means that investors pay more attention to the future change of asset price rather than current asset price when buying assets at the time. For instance, a stock is worth ten yuan upon IPO and increases in value to 100 yuan after three years.

goods. If the price is expected to rise, investors will continue to buy in – even at a higher leverage ratio. If the price is expected to fall, investors will exit the market. Hence, demand for investment goods can range from zero to infinity. As can be learned from the above discussion, investment goods are priced in different ways from consumer goods. With such differentiation, it becomes easier to understand interest rate determination theories and implications of interest rates as the price of credit risk.

As the price of financial market factors, interest rates have been a key topic of numerous studies since the birth of modern economics. Yet the academia tends to classify interest rate theories before the 1970s into three schools, i.e., the classical interest rate theory, the liquidity preference analysis, and the loanable funds analysis.[42] The classical interest rate theory started from William Petty and culminated with Alfred Marshall. By examining the determinants of interest rates and the effects on capital supply and demand in various aspects of economic life such as investment and savings, the classical theory considers savings as an increasing function and investment a decreasing function of interest rate.[43] When interest rate is unequal to expected return, capital will flow between investors and depositors, thus inducing change in interest rates; if interest rate is equal to expected return, the interest rate is the "natural rate" defined by Knut Wicksell.[44] Here, money is neutral and will not cause any impact on interest rate change. The classical interest rate theory overlooks the impact of money on interest rate change because it is predicated upon the law of one price under the gold standard system.[45] Under the law of one price, the prices of all transactional goods—whether investment or consumer goods—are linked to gold. As the price of capital, interest rate is also subject to the supply and demand relationship as are physical goods. Hence, these theories have naturally overlooked monetary and credit factors that determine interest rate.

J. M. Keynes's liquidity-preference theory discusses interest rate issues from the perspective of money supply and demand.[46] He believed that interest rate was the compensation for people to forgo liquidity or the price of money supply. When interest rate is below the equilibrium price, people's cash possession will exceed cash supply, and vice versa. While regulating money supply, monetary policy will change people's policy expectations and thus influence interest rate. On such basis, Keynes also developed the "liquidity trap theory" (i.e., when interest rate drops to a certain level, monetary policy will not achieve expected effects). Here, Keynes

---

At this moment, investors will not stay away from this stock because it rose in value but will make a purchase decision based on their expectations of the stock's future price movement. Investors will decide to buy if the stock is expected to rise in value, and vice versa. By the same token, for a stock worth ten yuan upon IPO but decreasing in value to 2 yuan after three years, although its value has shrunk to 1/5 of its issuing price, investors will still look at its growth expectations as the key factor in deciding whether to buy this stock.

[42] See Lutz (2007).

[43] Marshall (1923).

[44] Wicksell (1907, pp. 213–220).

[45] Brunner and Meltzer (2010, p. 5).

[46] Keynes (1997, pp. 142, 143).

discussed interest rate in isolation from physical factors because his theory is based on the credit money system. Change in interest rate as the price of financial products is subject to the investment rather than physical attribute of transactional goods. This theory surely offers a deeper-level discussion on interest rate compared with the classical theory, but Keynes's liquidity preference theory failed to bridge the transmission between the price of financial goods and the price of products in the physical economy.

Given the shortcomings of the classical interest rate theory and Keynes's liquidity preference theory, Robinson[47] and Ohlin[48] put forth the loanable funds theory. According to this theory, interest rates are jointly determined by the real economy and the financial system and influence the real economy and national income. Interest rate is the price of loan funds, which is subject to the supply and demand of funds in the financial market. The monetary authority may designate short-term loan rate and rediscount rate as official interest rates to guide overall financial market prices. Official interest rates not only determine the interest rate of bank loans, but also influence financial market behaviors and regulate the supply and demand of loanable funds and the short-term and long-term interest rates of market funds via indirect regulation (such as open market operations, national debt amount, and maturity adjustment). Thus, the loanable fund theory has improved the interest rate theory by combining monetary factors with physical factors, but also puts forth a very important concept, i.e., official interest rates serve as a benchmark for the overall market. That is how benchmark interest rates came into being.

Over the past century, the global monetary system has been profoundly transformed. In early twentieth century, monetary unit was determined by precious metals under the gold standard system under the law of one price, which became replaced by the credit money. After the collapse of the Bretton woods system in the 1970s and especially with the development of electronic currency and electronic payment system in the 1990s, the last connection between money and physical goods was jettisoned. Today, we live in a world of money purely as a unit of account, and the value of each unit-of-account currency is dependent on central bank policies.[49] Many new developments in interest rate theories over the past decade have been related to the central bank's benchmark rates. They include, for instance, the theories of interest rate rules, interest rate corridor, and interest rate fine-tuning. However, instead of investigating change in aggregate money supply and determining the appropriate level of short-term nominal interest rates, these theories are concerned with how the central bank's benchmark interest rates influence firms' and households' decisions on future behaviors and thus prices in other financial markets. Hence, China's interest rate liberalization reforms should not only adjust the central bank's monetary policy instruments and change the value orientation, but also transform the government-regulated benchmark interest rate in real earnest. Establishing a new benchmark interest rate system tops the agenda of China's interest rate liberalization reforms.

---

[47] Robinson (1951, pp. 92–111).

[48] Olilin (1937, pp. 423–27).

[49] Woodford (2010, p. 1).

5.4 Interest Rate Pricing and Transformation of the Benchmark Rate System

Since the 1980s, central banks in developed countries have started to shift their monetary policy objectives from money supply to interest rate guidance. What are interest rates? How are interest rates formed? Why are central banks' monetary policy regulation objectives focused on interest rates rather than money supply? The list of questions may go on and on. These questions were raised not because interest rates were easy to control and would significantly influence consumption, investment and exchange rate as some researchers had argued.[50] Rather, those questions stem from an evolving financial market environment and interest rate research innovations and progress. For instance, the theories of interest rate rules, interest rate corridor, and interest rate fine-tuning prevailed in this period because of theoretical innovations, which originate from Knut Wicksell's thoughts. Wicksell noted very early[51] that even in his era of the gold standard system, the observed change in the price level was not chiefly guided by global gold supply but subject to the interest rates controlled by central banks and the natural rate of interest determined by physical factors. Goodhart also said that[52] when two great economists (i.e., J. M. Keynes and Milton Friedman) discussed the policy issues of short-term interest rate levels, they believed interest rates were regulated by the monetary authority rather than decided by the free market. Central-bank-controlled interest rates refer to the benchmark rates in modern monetary policy theories.

In this period, Michael Woodford's theory of interest rate rules was the most representative. He made very clear statements on central bank benchmark rates.[53] He argued that instead of focusing on short-term nominal interest rate, central banks should target at the overnight interest rate as the monetary policy's operational objective, consider the monetary policy as rules for regulating such objective, and establish the basis for a clear analysis under the framework of the inter-temporal general equilibrium theory. He considered that the effect of change in central bank overnight interest rate objectives on spending decisions was completely subject to the impact of such change on other financial market prices. A central bank's ability to influence spending and pricing decisions is subject to its ability to influence market expectations—and not just current level—of the overnight interest rate. As such, market participants well-informed about a central bank's behaviors and intentions will enhance the effectiveness of the central bank's policy decisions, the expectations that influence those decisions, and the stability of monetary policy. Moreover, so long as the importance of future policy change is well understood by the private sector, the market will act largely according to the central bank's intent. In this case,

[50] Bernanke and Mishkin (1992, pp. 183–228).

[51] Wicksell (1907, pp. 213–220).

[52] Goodhart (1989, pp. 293–346).

[53] Woodford (2010, pp. 1–2, 10–11).

a change in future interest rate expectations will entail a much smaller change in overnight interest rate to effectively incentivize financial markets.

In the era of credit money, especially in the era of electronic money and payment systems, a central bank should, aside from guaranteeing credit money, subject its monetary policy to a set of explicit monetary rules to ensure stable price level in the economy. The benchmark rates controlled by a central bank serve as the instruments for achieving this goal. Second, benchmark rates are normally short-term interest rates for the currency market.[54] While such interest rates reflect the most recent supply and demand of money, they also reflect recent risk-free market return (for instance, the US federal benchmark funds rate is close to 10-year Treasury bond yield). Third, the effects of benchmark rates per se are negligible.[55] The real impact of benchmark rates derives from their effects on long-term interest rates, stock market prices, exchange rates, and various other prices in financial markets via the transmission mechanism. Lastly, rules on benchmark rate put a premium on forward-looking guidance of the central bank's expectations management. That is to say, firms and households may adjust their behaviors and decisions according to information from the central bank. While strengthening the role of central bank monetary policy, such active response reduces risks and uncertainties in firm and household behaviors and decisions. In this sense, the theory of interest rate rules is essentially different from the risk pricing of interest rates in the traditional theory of interest rate determination.

Aside from creating a fair, just, transparent and competitive transaction market to enhance financial institutions' independent pricing power and develop a base interest rate system for financial markets, we should create a central bank policy interest rate system, and re-establish benchmark rates to guide and regulate market rates in China's interest rate liberalization reforms. In the absence of a new benchmark rate system, financial assets will lack pricing basis, and the signal of capital supply and demand cannot be reflected in the prices of financial products, making interest rate liberalization an illusory goal. A key step in China's interest rate liberalization reforms should be to create a new benchmark rate system.

The question is why benchmark rates lie at the heart of China's interest rate liberalization reforms? Normally, benchmark rates are investment return free from risk or with minimum risk and serve as pricing basis and reference for financial products. They are commonly accepted interest rates with an important reference value. For such reason, benchmark rates are often seen as the primary instruments and means for capital seekers to measure the cost of financing and for investors to estimate investment return and government macroregulation. Unlike other interest rates, benchmark rates are market-based, fundamental and transmissive. Yet such

[54] Control of benchmark rates as short-term interest rates varies across central banks of different countries. Such control may focus on the money-market overnight lending rate or repurchase rate, among others. Benchmark rates can be divided into statutory benchmark rates and market benchmark rates. While the former are the macroeconomic regulatory objectives controlled by central banks, the latter are the market rates formed under the market quotation mechanism.

[55] For instance, if the benchmark interest rate is overnight lending rate and rose from 5% to 10% in one day and fell back to 5% in the following day, such an increase has a limited impact on the market as it was offset by an equal decrease in the following day.

qualities only indicate importance of benchmark rates in financial markets. Neither can such qualities explain the role of benchmark rates as the linchpin of interest rate liberalization reforms nor can they prove the indispensability of benchmark rates in financial markets. Why, one might wonder, is the basic price level not required for a general market of physical commodities?

It is fair to say that the importance of the benchmark rate system at the heart of China's interest rate liberalization reforms to China's interest rate liberalization reforms is manifested in the following three aspects: first, as far as financial markets are concerned, interest rates as the price of capital are entirely different from the prices of physical goods in terms of their pricing basis, price formation and operation, and the nature of market products, as discussed before. For instance, the price of a physical commodity depends entirely on the demand and supply relationship of such commodity. It varies with the commodity's supply and demand and its transaction is based on the materiality of such commodity. Yet the prices of financial products are the risk pricing of credit, and their transactions are based on the virtuality of credit. The prices of financial products depend on the conditions of financial markets and investors' expectations and assessment about the future. A financial market rife with information asymmetry and uncertainties will leave individuals and firms without a clue about future assessment and even mislead them into irrational conclusions, not to mention making sense of the complex financial products. By influencing the prices of different assets in financial markets, benchmark rates will help average investors and firms reduce risks and uncertainties in their decisions.

Second, since modern governments provide implicit guarantee for financial markets, they have a responsibility to ensure access to open and transparent information, fair transactions and market stability, and to protect vulnerable investors. In this case, government-mandated benchmark rates (i.e., statutory benchmark rates) may serve as basis for financial market to tame price volatility and achieve long-term and steady development and an instrument for governments to guide effective resource allocation under the market price mechanism, which is also an obligation and responsibility for modern governments.

Lastly, despite the great progress in China's interest rate liberalization, especially the liberalization of bank loan rates since July 2013 as a key milestone, the current benchmark rates in China's financial market are one-year deposit and loan rates for the banks. That is to say, the Central Bank exercises direct risk pricing and price control of bank deposits. Under such government control over benchmark rates, not only does the government conduct risk pricing directly for the banks, but the basis and mechanism for benchmark rates are nebulous. In Europe and North America, benchmark rates are either overnight lending rate or repurchase rate, which must be based on the risk-free Treasury bond yield curve while reflecting the recent supply and demand relationship in the financial market.[56] Hence, the most important task of

[56] For instance, modern asset pricing model assumes that at a constant return on risk-free assets, a future event's risk is assessed according to the law of large numbers to determine the price level of an asset. Such risk-free asset yield tends to be the basis of overall risky asset pricing. Treasury bond yield is a risk-free asset yield because the investors' decision-making range is predictable.

China's interest rate liberalization reforms is to create a new benchmark rate system, which should include both the statutory and the market benchmark rates and must be correlated with the risk-free Treasury bond yield curve. Yet we have also noted a question about China's Treasury bond market that has troubled researchers for a long time: why have China's Treasury bond rates stayed above bank deposit rates over the years? Some ascribed such difference to China's underdeveloped Treasury bond market that deviated from market-based operations.[57] We believe that the key reason lies in the fact that one-year bank deposit rate serves as benchmark rate while Treasury bond rates derive from deposit rates rather than the other way around. Whether China's Treasury bond rate is a risk-free yield rate will be questionable in the absence of benchmark rate transition, i.e., from a deposit rate based on the Central Bank's direct risk pricing for commercial banks to an indirect interest rate with indirect effects on financial market asset prices and from a statutory benchmark rate to a market-based one.

Thus, China's current interest rate liberalization reforms are faced with three key issues: First, the establishment of a new benchmark rate system (e.g., by adopting SHIBOR or repurchase rate in the domestic currency market or another new benchmark rate) is a key premise for China's interest rate liberalization reforms. Second, the transition from the old benchmark rates to the new benchmark rates. Third, the establishment of a sound risk-free Treasury bond yield curve for China's domestic financial markets. Under the current conditions, transition from the old benchmark rates to SHIBOR and repurchase rate should not be difficult given that the latter have been in operation for a long time. The challenges are to create a risk-free yield curve for domestic financial markets and establish the benchmark status of those rates, as highlighted in both the *Decisions* and the *Report*. Once established in a scientific way, the risk-free yield curve will provide the new benchmark rates with an effective market pricing basis. That is to say, as long as the Central Bank has established new benchmark rates, it will become easier for bank deposit rate to be deregulated, which is a key message conveyed in this section. Judging by current conditions, this goal is by no means easy to accomplish. It takes more historical data and institutional development to establish the domestic new benchmark rates or the risk-free Treasury bond yield curve. Transition of the benchmark rate system entails the adjustment of vested interests, whose resistance could pose the biggest barrier to establishing a new benchmark rate system.

5.5 Recent Progress and Problems of China's Interest Rate Liberalization Reforms

2013 witnessed rapid progress in China's interest rate liberalization reforms spearheaded by the deregulation of lower limit of loan rates, the launch of the loan prime rate (LPR), the creation of the interbank negotiable certificates of deposit (CDs)

[57] Peng Xingyun (2013, p. 321).

market, among others. Despite this big step forward in interest rate liberalization, an effective market price mechanism has yet to take shape, the financial market price mechanism remains severely distorted, and reforms still need to pick up speed.

First, the PBoC decided on July 19, 2013 to fully deregulate loan rate control for financial institutions as of July 20, 2013. This marks a deepening of China's financial system interest rate liberalization with a considerable impact on China's financial markets. The reason is that credit risk pricing lies at the heart of modern commercial banks. Before the loan rate deregulation, China's domestic banks had very limited powers for credit risk pricing, and banks vied to expand the credit amount rather than engage in price competition. In this context, domestic banks became highly homogeneous and lacked the restraint and motivation to enhance their risk pricing capacity. The deregulation of loan rates requires banks to provide risk pricing for borrowers according to their credit ratings. China's commercial banks should enhance their risk pricing by creating an effective credit rating system. In this manner, competition in the banking industry will transition from credit expansion to risk pricing. Financial market credit may also come into existence in this process and cease to fully rely on implicit government guarantee.

Deregulation of loan rates helps reduce firms' financing cost and thus boost the real economy. Yet such positive effect is envisaged from theoretical analysis and based on experience from sophisticated financial markets. In mature financial markets in Europe and North America with tight restraints on financial institutions' behaviors and a sound credit system, banks' risk pricing is entirely subject to capital supply and demand as long as market liquidity is sufficient, and effective competition holds down firms' financing cost. China's financial markets are still evolving and far from sophisticated. The problem of financial monopoly has yet to be addressed. Firms and individuals have limited access to finance and crave for bank capital, and so does local governments. In this context, deregulating bank loan rates will not reduce financing cost for firms.

Government guarantee of credit in China's financial markets—whether issued to firms, local governments or individuals—has led to excessive credit expansion. Irrespective of market liquidity conditions, those who borrow and lend on credit stand to profit. This expectation has driven all enterprises, individuals and local governments to obtain funds from various sources, resulting in excessive credit expansion. In such circumstances, the flow of capital is often linked with power and connections, leaving small and medium-sized enterprises (SMEs) underfinanced. After loan rate deregulation, China's financial market concepts and vested interests remain unchanged, and credit expansion coexists with a shortage of loanable funds. Instead of competitively lowering interest rates to raise credit scale after loan rate deregulation, the best way for banks to earn more profits would be to raise loan rates, which does little to tame interest rates or the cost of financing. Judging by what happened a few months after loan rate deregulation, the loan-weighted average interest rate increased rather than decreased.[58] The problem is that loan rate is return for banks and deposits are the cost. If interest rate liberalization only deregulates bank profits, when banks have

[58] The People's Bank of China (PBoC) (2013).

full pricing power for loan rates, their excessive credit expansion becomes inevitable. The more bank credit expands, the more profits banks might earn (as their interest rate spread widens under the shortage of loanable funds). While driving up the cost of financing, this may also channel high-cost capital into high-risk assets, thus fueling asset prices.

Second, the loan prime rate (LPR) may serve as a buffer. After liberalizing loan rates, the Central Bank officially launched the loan prime rate (LPR) on October 25, 2013. As a self-regulatory mechanism for banks' risk pricing, the LPR is neither designated by the Central Bank nor formed freely in the market. Instead, it is formed based on quotes from dominant domestic banks recognized by the Central Bank. Under the LPR, domestic commercial banks are required to consider whether their credit behaviors would raise firms' financing cost to the detriment of real-economy development, avoiding raising interest rates to use public financial resources only for the purpose of maximizing their own profits.

Under the current conditions, the loan prime rate (LPR) as a self-regulatory price mechanism for the pricing of bank risks has uncertain price guidance effects on financial markets. As analyzed in the above section, when banks and other financial institutions have excess capital that exceeds demand for loans, the LPR may serve as a last defense for loan rates to prevent vicious competitions among banks and fix the banking sector's interest risk bottom line at the LPR level. In case of a severe credit shortage, the LPR only serves as a symbolic interest rate. Banks may issue some loans at the LPR but only as a symbolic gesture while lending most loanable funds to seek maximal return. That is to say, the LPR's effectiveness would be very limited unless the Central Bank ramps up its regulatory capacity, put an end to the sellers' monopoly in the credit market, and improve constraints for financial institutions.

Should SHIBOR become a benchmark rate for financial markets, the LPR's effectiveness would also be very limited since the most important constraint for commercial bank loan rates is deposit rates that are the cost of banks. Apparently intended to create a self-regulatory loan price mechanism for commercial banks, the Central Bank's LPR is actually expected to delay deposit rate liberalization as much as possible. With such a constraint for loan rates, banks can be guided to determine interest rates more rationally and avoid single-mindedly seeking maximal return.

While discouraging banks from profiteering from loan rates, the LPR also helps reduce the cost of financing without adjusting or liberalizing deposit rates. Suppression of deposit rates to an extremely low level benefits the banks the most, followed by various lenders and the government, at the expense of individual depositors. In the name of interest rate liberalization, the LPR plays a very limited role in facilitating interest rate liberalization and may pose a barrier to China's interest rate liberalization in the future due to institutional dependence since intricate interests are involved.

Hence, China's deposit rate liberalization still has a long way to go. On December 8, 2013, the Central Bank released *Interim Measures for the Management of Interbank Certificates of Deposit* (*Measures*). Interbank certificates of deposit are "negotiable certificates of deposit", i.e., certificates of deposit that can be freely transferred to a third party before deposits mature. Compared with ordinary deposits, certificates of deposit (CDs) are issued by banking depository institutions recognized by the

Central Bank. Although no withdrawal is permitted prior to maturity, CDs may be transferred to others banks in exchange of liquidity. Aside from an additional financial instrument in China's currency market, CDs also serve as a financing conduit that reflects the supply and demand of capital.

Judging by the *Measures*, CDs are an electronically traded standardized, highly liquid and transparent product with SHIBOR as the pricing benchmark. It is fair to say that the issuance of CDs offers an additional financial product and instrument for China's currency market and an alternative interbank financing conduit, which helps banks' liability management and enhances SHIBOR's benchmark status. CDs may also regulate the grey areas of interbank financing business, reduce potential financial risks that may arise from "quasi-credit business", and thus reduce the risk of a credit crisis in China. In this sense, the launch of CDs marks a key step in China's interest rate liberalization reforms, particularly the Central Bank's deposit rate deregulation.

However, over-expectations are unwarranted. The *Measures* has yet to clarify many issues, not least the uncertainties in the issuance mechanism of interbank CDs, risk weighting, and differences from existing interbank deposits. These uncertainties will weaken the effects of CDs. The following aspects are more important: first, China's interest rate liberalization is repeating the path of many developed countries in Europe and North America, i.e., loan rate is liberalized before introducing interbank negotiable certificates of deposit (CDs) and issuing time certificates of deposit to phase out deposit rate control. Whether this path suits China or not is rather uncertain. Moreover, a country's path of financial reforms and economic development is unique and irreversible. Once a path is followed, a cost–benefit analysis would be meaningless afterwards. Second, the pricing of interbank CDs is subject to SHIBOR benchmark, which is conducive to enhancing SHIBOR's benchmark status. But we should recognize that SHIBOR's benchmark status is a completely different concept from those of interest rates like London Interbank Offered Rate (LIBOR). The reason is that China's benchmark interest rate is one-year bank loan rate rather than SHIBOR. SHIBOR may influence interest rate change of short-term capital in the currency market, but one-year deposit and lending interest rates remain the benchmark for domestic currency market interest rates. If one-year deposit and loan rate is regulated by the Central Bank, SHIBOR should also be regulated under the transmissive effect. If SHIBOR's benchmark status is questionable, it would be problematic to use SHIBOR as pricing basis for interbank certificates of deposit (CDs). The more twisted path interest rate liberalization follows, the higher the cost for interest rate liberalization reforms would be. As such, the current interest rate liberalization reforms should proceed from one-year deposit rate.

Obviously, a multitude of interest rate liberalization reforms introduced by the central bank over the year made little real progress but triggered thought-provoking problems.

5.6 Reorienting the Approach of China's Interest Rate Liberalization Reforms

The Third Plenary Session of the 18th CPC Central Committee has established the decisive role of the market in resource allocation. A market-based price mechanism is essential for the market to play a decisive role in resource allocation. In order for interest rates as the factor price of financial markets to effectively allocate resources, the market should play a decisive role in the interest rate price formation. Hence, interest rate liberalization tops the agenda of China's financial reforms. That is to say, China should take opportunities of the new government taking office and the Third Plenary Session of the 18th CPC Central Committee to accelerate financial market interest rate liberalization reforms.

In 2014, the US exited the quantitative easing (QE) policy that had been in place for five years, putting an end to a five-year feast of cheap capital in global markets and heralding fundamental transformations in global market risk appetites, capital flows, and market interests. The shocks of those changes spell myriad uncertainties in global markets, including China. To mitigate the shocks of such uncertainties, China must build a more resilient financial system—a key step of which is interest rate liberalization reforms.

Meanwhile, it should be noted that China's financial markets are fraught with intractable problems. Among them are excessive bank credit expansion, financial disintermediation, rampant shadow banking, money shortages, unchecked local government financing vehicles (LGFVs), distorted financing structure, an abrupt rise of Internet finance, real estate bubbles, barriers to the transition of economic growth, a reasonable economic structure, and excess capacity. All these problems more or less have to do with serious distortions in financial market price mechanisms and long-overdue interest rate liberalization reforms. Unless China speeds up interest rate liberalization reforms with the opportunities of the Third Plenary Session of the 18th CPC Central Committee, the above-mentioned problems will greatly impede China's economic development and modernization.

The following five aspects of work must be carried out properly to deepen interest rate liberalization reforms:

First, policymakers must fully reflect upon the concepts, modes, pathways and effects of China's interest rate liberalization reforms over the past two decades, draw upon the lessons, summarize experience and develop a new approach to China's interest rate liberalization reforms, which have achieved some successes in stabilizing market development over the past two decades but at the expense of letting shadow banks and real estate bubbles go unchecked. China's financial market development would pay an even greater price if those problems fail to be defused, thus triggering a financial crisis.

Second, the top priority of current interest rate liberalization reforms is to deregulate the upper limit of deposit rates, which present the biggest barrier to China's interest rate liberalization reforms. Deregulating deposit rates involves the following priorities: first, introduce legislation on the deposit insurance system as early as possible; second, deregulate risk pricing for commercial bank deposits or increase the flexibility of deposit rate volatility; third, create conditions for the transition of the statutory deposit and loan benchmark rates with which the Central Bank conducts risk pricing directly for commercial banks into one with which the Central Bank indirectly influences financial market asset prices; fourth, fully deregulate deposit rates, without which a market-based interest rate price mechanism cannot take shape. Both the rapid development of shadow banks and the explosive growth of Internet finance force the Central Bank to quicken its pace of deposit rate deregulation. To be sure, deposit rate reform may generate broader effects and thus requires relevant conditions to be ready. For instance, the Central Bank should enhance its capabilities to regulate money and finance by leveraging assets, turn commercial banks into risk-bearing entities, and provide households and enterprises with more diverse financing options. When the conditions are not ready, deposit rate liberalization should follow a more prudent approach.

Third, re-establish China's benchmark interest rate system focusing on the following priorities: (i) the statutory deposit and loan benchmark interest rate with which the Central Bank prices risks directly for commercial banks should be transformed into one with which the Central Bank indirectly influences financial market asset prices; (ii) enhance SHIBOR's reference status for financial product pricing and transactionality; (iii) re-design the benchmark interest rate to make it reflect current economic conditions more precisely and truthfully and reduce and eliminate factors that may cause price distortions and conflict of interest; (iv) create a sound and systematic benchmark rate system that suits the domestic market.

Fourth, transform the Central Bank's monetary policy approach in an all-round way. Judging by the current situation, China's central bank monetary policy is trapped under the traditional approach. It is more concerned with the aggregate monetary supply or liquidity, how liquidity influences financial market prices, and the policy goal of money supply. Yet money supply and liquidity are *ex-post* information and cannot guide monetary policy and market expectations, and there is a certain time lag. Information about financial market capital supply and demand cannot be reflected in asset prices and cannot be used to develop an effective financial market price mechanism. As such, policymakers should reconsider China's current central bank monetary policy approach.

Fifth, create conditions for a diverse and multi-tiered financing system, giving priority to corporate bond market development and financial product innovation, and shift from a credit-led financial system to a diversified one that provides more financial products to firms and households and facilitates interest rate liberalization reforms.

In a word, interest rate liberalization reforms are a major transition of China's financial markets. This important transition requires theoretical research and preparations and resolute actions to tackle key challenges to reforms. For instance, we should develop a contingency plan to deal with the potential impacts and shocks, overcome barriers and ensure the deepening and successful implementation of China's interest rate liberalization reforms, which are essential for the sound development of China's financial system.

(Yi Xianrong)

References

Abdul Abiad and Ashoka Mody: "Financial Reform: What Shakes It? What Shapes It?" *IMF Working Paper* 70, 2003.

Bernanke, B. S. and F. Mishkin, Central Bank Behavior and the Strategy of Monetary Policy: Observations from Six Industrialized Countries, in O. J. Fischer (eds), *NBER Macroeconomics Annual 1992*, Cambridge: MIT Press, 1992, pp. 183–228.

Der-tzon Hsieh: *Monetary Banking*. San Min Book, 1993.

Drazen, A. and William Easterly, "Do Crises Induce Reform? Simple Empirical Tests of Conventional Wisdom", *Economics and Politics*, 13(2), 2001, pp. 129–157.

Fernandez, R. and Dani Rodrik, "Resistance to Reform: Status Quo Bias in the Presence of Individual-Specific Uncertainty", *American Economic Review*, 81, December 1991, pp. 1146–55.

Goodhart, C. A. E., "The Conduct of Monetary Policy", *Economic Journal*, 1989, pp. 293–346.

Haggard, S., and Steven Webb: "What Do We Know About the Political Economy of Policy Reform?" *World Bank Research Observer*, 8(2), 1993, pp. 143–68.

Karl Brunner and Allan H. Meltzer: *Money and the Economy Issues in Monetary Analysis*, China Financial Publishing House, 2010.

Keynes, J. M.: *The General Theory of Employment, Interest, and Money*, The Commercial Press, 1997.

Krueger, Anne O.: *Political Economy of Policy Reform in Developing Countries*, Cambridge, Massachusetts: MIT Press, 1993.

Krueger, Anne O.: "Trade Policy and Economic Development: How We Learn," *The American Economic Review*, 87, 1997, pp. 1–22.

Li Wenhong, Wu Zuhong: "Updates and Inspirations of Financial Regulatory Reforms in the UK", *Comparative Studies*, Vol. 66, CITIC Press, 2013.

Lutz, Friedrich A.: *The Theory of Interest, A Division of Transaction Publisher*, New Brunswick and London, 2007.

Marshall, A.: *Money, Credit and Commerce*, London, 1923.

McKinnon, R., *Money and Capital in Economic Development*, Brooking Institution, Washington, 1973.

Michael Woodford: *Interest and Prices: Foundations of a Theory of Monetary Policy*, China Renmin University Press, 2010.

Oi, Walter Y.: "A Disneyland Dilemma: Two-Part-Tariffs for a Mickey Mouse Monopoly," *Quarterly Journal of Economics*, 85(1), 1971, pp. 77–96.

Ohlin, B.: "Alternative Theories of the Rate of Interest," *Economic Journal*, XL(VII), 1937, pp. 423–27.

Peng Xingyun: *Principles of Finance*, Shanghai People's Publishing House, 2013, p. 321.

Raghuram Rajan, and Luigi Zingales: *Saving Capitalism from the Capitalists*, CITIC Press, 2004.

Robinson, J., "The Rate of Interest", *Econometrics*, XIX, 1951, pp. 92–111.

Shiller, R. J. and J. H. McCulloch: "The Term Structure of Interest Rates", Collected in *Handbook of Monetary Economics*, Vol.1. Chapter 12, North-holland, 1990, pp. 627–722.

The Decisions of the CPC Central Committee on Matters concerning the Establishment of the Socialist Market Economic System adopted at the Third Plenary Session of the 14th CPC Central Committee and the *Decisions of the State Council on Financial Reforms*, http://wenku.baidu.com/link?url.

The People's Bank of China (PBoC): *China Monetary Policy Report*, Q4 2013, the PBoC's Website.

The People's Bank of China (PBoC): *Report on Steadily Advancing Interest Rate Liberalization*, PBoC's Website, January 2005.
Tornell, A.: "Reform from Within", *NBER Working Paper* 6497, Cambridge, Massachusetts: National Bureau of Economic Research, 1998.
Wang Dingding: *Lecture Notes on the History of Economics Philosophy*, Century Publishing Group, Shanghai People's Publishing House, 2008.
Wicksell, K.: "The Influence of the Rate of Interest on Prices," *Economic Journal*, 17, 1907, pp. 213–220.
Yin Jianfeng, Wang Zengwu: *Shadow Banking and Bank's Shadow*, Social Sciences Academic Press (China), 2013.
Ying Qianwei: *China's Loan Interest Rate Reform and Capital Allocation*, Economy & Management Publishing House, 2012.
Zhang Jianhua et al.: *Global Experience of Interest Rate Liberalization*, China Machine Press, 2012.
Zhang Li: *Analysis of Financial Liberalization Effects*, China Financial Publishing House, 2003.
Zhang Wuchang: *Words of an Orange Peddler*, HKEJ Publishing Ltd., 1984.
Zhou Xiaochuan: "Comprehensively Deepening Financial Reforms and Opening up and Improving the Financial Market System", *Securities Times*, November 19, 2013.

Chapter 6
Deposit Rate Liberalization and Exchange Rate Reforms

In an open economy, exchange rate and interest rates influence and restrain each other and affect the internal and external equilibria of the economy. Interest rates influence exchange rate in direct and indirect ways. Under the direct effect, the flow of international arbitrage capital induces exchange rate variations. With other conditions being constant, when interest rate in a home country is above the international level, short-term capital will flow into the home country, whose currency appreciates as demand for its currency increases in the foreign exchange market. Otherwise, there will be a capital outflow, causing its currency to depreciate. Under the indirect effect, interest rates influence the exchange rate level by altering domestic aggregate demand. When investment return is constant, higher interest rates will drive up investment cost and reduce money supply and price level in a country, which is conducive to exports. Meanwhile, a reduction in investment demand and foreign exchange expenditure under the current account will cause the home currency to appreciate against foreign currencies as long as foreign exchange supply is constant.

Exchange rate influences interest rates through price level and short-term capital flow. Home-currency depreciation will cause the prices of imported products to increase, driving up price inflation, suppressing real interest rates, and giving rise to upward pressures on nominal interest rates. In addition, home-currency depreciation will also trigger a short-term capital flight, causing domestic capital supply to decrease and interest rate to hike.

In China's exchange rate liberalization reforms, therefore, we should investigate the correlation between exchange rate and interest rates so as to unravel the effects of interest rate liberalization on the exchange rate policy and the effects of exchange rate reforms on the interest rate policy, shedding light on how exchange rate and interest rates can be made best use of to regulate the economy and achieve internal and external equilibria of the economy.

G. Wang, *A Study on Interest Rate Liberalization in China*, Research Series on the Chinese Dream and China's Development Path,
https://doi.org/10.1007/978-981-97-3644-7_6

6.1 Brief Review of Literature

In *A Tract on Monetary Reform*, J. M. Keynes (1923) noted that: "The difference between forward exchange rate and spot exchange rate, if expressed in percentage rate, tends to be the interest rate spread between two financial centers. The difference between forward interest rate and spot interest rate will fluctuate around the interest rate parity according to supply and demand. J. M. Keynes was the first to put forth the interest rate parity theory.

After Keynes, British economist Paul Einzig (1930) investigated the relationship between exchange rate and interest rates from a dynamic perspective, elaborated the intrinsic correlation between interest rate and exchange rate, and found exchange rate to be subject to the relative yield of both countries' currencies. Einzig identified interest rate spread as a key driver of exchange rate variations, thus providing a powerful tool for forecasting forward exchange rate and improving the classical interest rate parity theory.

Ronald I. McKinnon and Kenichi Ohno (1999) created their own theoretical model from the perspective of how exchange rate would influence interest rates. They pointed out that inflation lasted for a longer period in the floating exchange rate era, causing long-term interest rates to fluctuate in a broader band compared to short-term interest rates in the floating exchange rate era.

In addition, numerous international scholars have also conducted extensive empirical research on the correlation between interest rates and exchange rates in various countries. Macroeconomic effects of interest rate and exchange rate vary with the degree of interest rate liberalization.

Many Chinese academics have also examined the relationship between interest rate and exchange rate over the years. From the perspective of capital account convertibility, Jiang Boke (1994) discussed the importance of interest rate control to exchange rate, recognizing the importance for China to develop a sophisticated short-term currency market. He identified a positive correlation between interest rates and exchange rate.

By testing and analyzing the correlation between China-US interest rate difference and Renminbi-US dollar exchange rate variations, Du Jinmian and Zheng Lingyun (2001) concluded that the interest rate parity theory could hardly apply to the current determination of Renminbi exchange rate. Based on such a conclusion, they further delved into the reasons why Renminbi exchange rate had deviated from the interest-rate parity in light of the interest-rate parity theory's limitations and China's reality and discussed the interest rate parity theory's applicability to the determination of China's exchange rate.

Xue Hongli (2002) reviewed the interest-rate parity model's evolution in China. Under fully effective financial market conditions, the interactions among interest rates, exchange rate and international capital flow form a self-balancing mechanism, and the interest-rate parity model is an abstract manifestation of such mechanism. For China in economic and financial transitions, such a self-balancing mechanism has yet to take shape, and the relationship among the three is unbalanced. As China's financial reforms deepen, however, the self-balancing mechanism will gradually become established in China. Based on his analysis of the interest-rate parity model's applicability to China, Xue Hongli introduced the institutional friction coefficient into his model to derive an interest-rate parity model that suits China's national conditions and explained the gradual establishment of the self-balancing mechanism through the equation's evolving process. After analyzing China's institutional environment, he examined the unbalanced relationship among interest rates, exchange rate and international capital flow, and forecasted pressures on Renminbi exchange rate to appreciate/depreciate. The PBoC Research Group (2001) performed an empirical test on the correlation between exchange rates and interest rates in Southeast Asian and Latin American countries, and offered valuable conclusions on China's interest rate and exchange rate reforms.

Based on empirical analyses on the exchange rates and interest rates of East Asian countries, Xu Shaoqiang and Li Lina (2001) noted that the interest rates-exchange rate relationship of East Asian countries is not as strong as described in theories. After reviewing domestic and international research on the relationship between interest rate and exchange rate, Wang Aijian (2003) summarized the mechanism of the correlation between interest rate and exchange rate and performed the Granger causality test to examine the correlation between Renminbi interest rates and exchange rate. After analyzing the reasons behind the low correlation between Renminbi's interest rates and exchange rate, he offered reflections on China's interest rate and exchange rate reforms.

6.2 Brief Descriptions of Relevant Theories

In international economics and financial theories, the interest rate parity theory offered the first description of the relationship between interest rate and exchange rate. Interest rate parity generally includes the uncovered interest-rate parity (UIP) and the covered interest-rate parity (CIP). CIP postulates that arbitrageurs may profit from the interest rate differential between two countries through simultaneous reverse operations in the spot and forward foreign exchange markets if both countries possess well-developed financial markets and complete financial instruments and are free from transaction cost regulation and capital control with complete substitutability between domestic and foreign securities. Since these conditions are absent in China, this section only discusses UIP.

6.2.1 Uncovered Interest-Rate Parity (UIP)

Uncovered interest-rate parity (UIP) means that when investors make an uncovered foreign exchange investment, their profit equals return free from exchange rate risk, i.e., expected return. Assuming that i_t, i_t^* are the interest rates when investing the home currency and a foreign currency from period t to period $t + 1$, respectively, E_1 is the spot exchange rate in the foreign exchange markets, and E_{t+1}^e is expected spot exchange rate of t in $t + 1$ period. Then,

$$(1 + i_t)/\left(1 + i_t^*\right) = E_{t+1}^e/E_t \tag{6.1}$$

It can be learned from logarithmic rules that for the smaller x, Ln $(1 + x) \approx x$. We make $x =$ (y-2)/2, which gives us:

$$\ln\left[1 + (y - 2)/2\right] \approx (y - 2)/2 \tag{6.2}$$

Taking logarithm on both sides of Eq. (6.1) gives us:

$$\ln(1 + i_t) - \ln\left(1 + i_t^*\right) = \ln\left(E_{t+1}^e/E_t\right)$$

The logarithmic approximation can be obtained using Eq. (6.2):

$$i_t - i_t^* = \left(E_{t+1}^e - E_t\right)/E_t \tag{6.3}$$

where, $\left(E_{t+1}^e - E_t\right)/E_t$ is referred to as the expected exchange rate variation. Based on exchange rate evaluation, only when all the expected returns are equal, i.e., the interest rate parity is satisfied, will there be no coexistence between the oversupply of deposits in one currency and the excessive demand for deposits in another currency. At this moment, the foreign exchange market can be considered as in the equilibrium state. Based on the interest rate parity theory and currency market equilibrium, we may develop an analytical framework for the relationship between interest rate and exchange rate, which consists of the following theoretical equations:

$$i_t = i_t^* + \left(E_{t+1}^e - E_t\right)/E_t \text{ (Interest - rate parity condition)} \tag{6.4}$$

$$\frac{M_s}{P} = L(i, Y) \text{ (Monetary market equilibrium condition)} \tag{6.5}$$

where, i is home-country interest rate, Y is home-country real output, M_s is money supply, and P is general price level.

The interest-rate parity theory considers the relationship between interest rate and exchange rate from the perspective of capital flow and analyzes the impact of interest rates on exchange rate by creating an interest-rate parity equation. However, the interest rate parity theory also has flaws when applied to analyze the effects of interest rates on exchange rate. For instance, the assumption of interest-rate parity is too idealistic to be satisfied in reality. Interest-rate parity analysis only reflects part of the multifaceted effects of interest rates on exchange rate, among other problems.

6.2.2 Interest Rate and Exchange Rate in Purchasing Power Parity (PPP)

The purchasing power parity (PPP) theory originated from the Spanish School of Salamanca in the sixteenth century. It was not until the 1920s that a relatively complete PPP theory was developed by Swedish economist Karl Gustav Cassel. His theory holds that the demand for a currency is underpinned by its purchasing power. When a country provides its currency for other countries, it provides residents in those countries with the power to purchase its goods and services. Hence, the price of a currency is subject to its power to purchase goods and services, and the exchange rate between currencies is decided by their respective purchasing powers. The purchasing power ratio is the purchasing power parity (PPP). The PPP theory includes two hypotheses of absolute purchasing power parity and relative purchasing power parity. The following are their theoretical expressions:

$$E_t = P_t / P_t^* \text{ (absolute purchasing power parity)} \tag{6.6}$$

$$E_t = \left(P_t / P_t^*\right) \times k \text{ (relative purchasing power parity)} \tag{6.7}$$

where, P_{t} is the price of a benchmark basket in the home country in period t; P_{t}^* is the price of a benchmark basket in a foreign country in period t; k is constant, $k = E_0 P_1 / P_0$, P_0 is the home country's general price level in the base period; E_0 is the two-way exchange rate in the base period; E_{t} is the exchange rate in the calculation period. Relative PPP correctly reflects the relationship between exchange rate variation as a percentage and the difference of inflation. Such reflection is correct even if the two countries select different composition and scope of commodities for calculating their respective price levels.

Based on the PPP and the money supply and demand function, a theoretical methodology for analyzing the long-term exchange rate effects of interest rates, money supply and output can be put forth. Since this theory only considers the determinants of money supply and demand, it is referred to as the exchange rate monetary analysis methodology, which holds that the exchange rate between two currencies, i.e., relative price, depends entirely on their relative supply and actual demand. Changes in interest rates and domestic output will induce change in exchange rate only by influencing monetary demand. As a long-term analysis, monetary analysis is free from the assumption of price rigidity and has the following basic expression:

$$E = \frac{P}{P*} = \frac{M_s / L(i, y)}{M_s^* / L(i*, Y*)} \tag{6.8}$$

According to Eq. (6.8), when interest rates on Renminbi assets increase, China's real monetary demand will fall, long-term price will rise, Renminbi/US dollar exchange rates will rise, and Renminbi will depreciate against the US dollar by the same proportion. According to the interest rate parity theory, when a home country's interest rate increases, Renminbi/US dollar exchange rates will fall, and Renminbi will appreciate. The results of the two theories appear opposite, and this tension stems from different assumptions of price adjustment speed. Based on the interest rate parity analysis, under the sticky price assumption, when money supply falls, price level cannot decrease immediately in response to diminishing money supply. Interest rate will inevitably rise if currency market equilibrium is to be maintained. Rising interest rate is associated with lower inflationary pressures and long-term currency appreciation and results in an immediate rise in monetary value. Based on PPP analysis, however, rising interest rate is associated with higher inflationary pressures and long-term currency depreciation and results in an immediate decrease in monetary value.

6.2.3 Summary

According to the above two basic models and research results from other perspectives, we have summarized the correlation between interest rate and exchange rate as follows:

First, the effects of interest rate variations on exchange rate. Interest rate variations influence exchange rate in direct and indirect ways. Under the direct effect, the flow of international arbitrage capital causes exchange rate to increase or decrease. With other conditions being constant, when the home country's interest rate is higher than a foreign country's interest rate, the home country will attract an inflow of short-term capital that seeks higher return, causing demand for the home currency in the home country's foreign exchange market to exceed supply. In this case, the home currency's spot exchange rate will rise, and foreign exchange rate will fall. On the contrary, when the home country's interest rate is low, there will be an outflow of capital, causing the home currency's exchange rate to change in the reverse direction. Under the indirect effect, interest rates influence the exchange rate level by altering domestic aggregate supply and aggregate demand. For instance, when a country's interest rate is high and investment return is constant, a high interest rate policy by the government will raise investment cost, drive down investment demand, reduce the home country's money supply, subdue inflation, and increase the price competitiveness of export commodities. Meanwhile, investment demand and aggregate demand will fall accordingly, thus reducing current-account foreign exchange spending.

When foreign exchange supply is constant, an oversupply of foreign exchange will cause foreign exchange rate to fall and home-currency exchange rate to rise.

The role of expectations in interest-rate-to-exchange-rate transmission - whether via direct or indirect conduits - cannot be overlooked. Adjustment to a country's interest rates will trigger an expectation in the household sector about change in the home country's currency, thus influencing the exchange rate. The role of expectations comes into play normally in conjunction with other factors and sometimes generates a multiplier effect. In a word, rising monetary interest rates will cause the country's spot exchange rate to appreciate and forward exchange rate to depreciate through the flow of short-term arbitrage capital, and vice versa.

Second, the effects of exchange rate variations on interest rates. Exchange rate variations influence interest rates primarily through two conduits of price and short-term capital flows, especially through the price effect for exports and imports. From an import perspective, a home currency's depreciation will cause imported goods to be more expensive in the home currency. Meanwhile, goods processed with imported raw materials will also become more expensive. If the country has a very small elasticity of demand for or no substitute to such imports, the prices of those imports increase without any reduction in demand, and such imports account for a significant share of the country's GDP, there will be an increase in the prices of final products due to the rising cost of production, which fuels a domestic consumer goods price hike. From an export perspective, the home currency's depreciation boosts the price competitiveness of the home country's exports, thus expanding the home country's exports. With the supply elasticity of exports being relatively limited, demand for domestic commodities exceeds supply, causing an excess of money to go after a limited amount of goods and services and thus triggering a continuous increase in the general price level, i.e., demand-driven inflation.

The exchange of depreciation of home currency will lead to a domestic price hike and drive down real interest rates, which is favorable to debtors and unfavorable to creditors and will trigger a supply and demand imbalance of loan capital, giving rise to upward pressures on nominal interest rates.

In addition, expectations also influence the transmissive effects of exchange rate variations on interest rates. The home currency's depreciation begets expectations for the exchange rate to further decrease, prompting a short-term capital flight. Diminishing domestic capital supply will cause interest rates to hike. However, falling exchange rate will also create an expectation for a rebound in the exchange rate, thus attracting a short-term capital inflow to increase domestic capital supply and induce an interest rate decline.

Variations in the exchange rate expectations are subject to the gap between forward and spot exchange rate levels and changing relative economic strengths of the two countries. In China's reality, the key determinant of Renminbi appreciation or depreciation is the relative foreign exchange supply and demand and the Central Bank's exchange rate policy. Since Renminbi's exchange rate stability is the key objective of the Central Bank's exchange rate policy, Renminbi exchange rate variations are expected to be very small. Under such expectations, Renminbi exchange rate has a limited effect on the increase or decrease of capital flow, weakening its transmissive effects on interest rates.

6.3 Interest Rate and Exchange Rate Relationship in China's Case

The above section offers two fundamental theoretical models as the basis for a brief discussion of the relationship between interest rate and exchange rate. Yet it should be noted that all these models are predicated upon open economy and perfect market, i.e., the capital market is fully liquid, prices fully elastic, and economic entities have sufficient expectations, etc. China does not meet those conditions and the liberalization of its interest rate and exchange rate remains relatively limited. In this context, the relationship between interest rate and exchange rate is different from what is revealed in the basic model.

6.3.1 The Correlation Between Interest Rate and Exchange Rate Under Different Degrees of Market-Based Operations

The correlation between interest rate and exchange rate varies across different degrees of interest rate liberalization and various types of exchange rate regimes. Next, we will briefly discuss the correlation between interest rate and exchange rate under the two scenarios of interest rate control and complete interest rate liberalization and the two exchange rate regimes of fixed and floating exchange rates.

6.3.1.1 The Correlation Between Interest Rate and Exchange Rate Under the Interest Rate Control and Floating Exchange Rate Regime

Interest rate control means that a country's interest rates are determined by its central bank or monetary authority rather than determined by the market. Interest rate control is a type of price control with the purposes of restricting vicious competition between banks and ensuring financial system security. There are two forms of interest rate control: first, unitary control, i.e., either deposit rate or loan rate is regulated; second, multi-rate control, i.e., in addition to deposit and loan rate controls, the discount rate, processing fees and other service prices are also regulated. Since interest rate control is normally tied with credit, it can be considered that interest rate liberalization in the broad sense should include the cancellation of direct credit, i.e., interest rate liberalization in the broad sense is a process of removing price control and quantitative restraint. By controlling interest rates, the government may alter financial resources allocation and ensure financial market stability.

Under the floating exchange rate conditions, monetary assets are freely convertible, and capital may flow sufficiently between the home-currency asset market and the foreign exchange market. With other conditions being constant, if the central bank ramps up money supply, the initial nominal interest rate will remain constant due to interest rate control. However, an increase in money supply will cause price level and inflationary expectations to rise, thus holding down real interest rates. With the falling real interest rates on assets denominated in the home currency, real return on assets denominated in the home currency will decrease, prompting capital to seek new investment opportunities in the foreign exchange market and convert to foreign currency assets. This will result in a greater demand for foreign currencies and cause the home currency to depreciate and the relative prices of imported products to increase, giving rise to an imported inflation. The joint effect of such imported inflation and the inflationary expectations stemming from an increase in money supply may create pressures on the central bank's monetary policy, forcing the central bank to adjust interest rates to hold down inflation.

6.3.1.2 The Correlation Between Interest Rate and Exchange Rate Under Interest Rate Liberalization and the Fixed (Managed) Exchange Rate System

Since the exchange rate is determined by the government, its floating band is tightly regulated. When the international pricing power of a country's currency changes while its exchange rate is fixed, the home currency will be overvalued or undervalued. If the home currency is under pressures to appreciate, the monetary authority will be forced to purchase huge amounts of foreign currencies in the foreign exchange market. The resultant decrease in foreign exchange reserves and base money will push up domestic interest rates. The transmissive mechanism of interest rate effects on the exchange rate will create an excess demand for the home currency and an excess supply of foreign currencies, attracting international short-term speculative capital inflows for arbitrage and fueling pressures for the home currency to appreciate (Figs. 6.1 and 6.2).

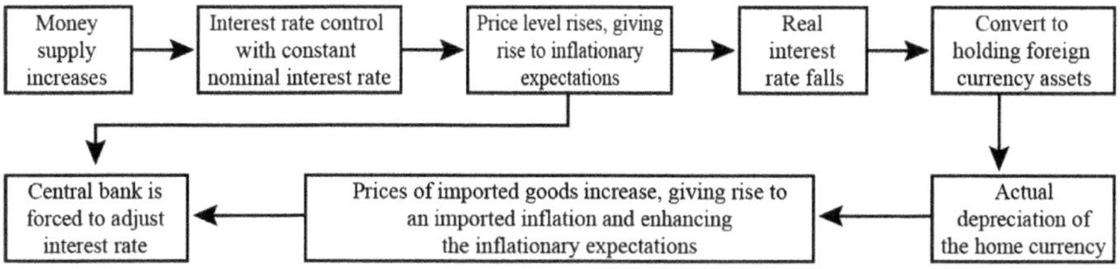

Fig. 6.1 Interest rate regulation and the floating exchange rate system

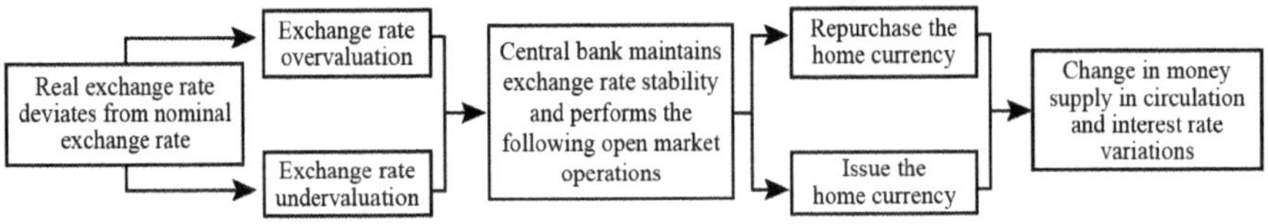

Fig. 6.2 Interest rate liberalization and fixed exchange rate

6.3.2 China's Practice: Dilemma Between Interest Rate Objective and Exchange Rate Objective

Over the past decade, the change in the correlation between China's interest rate and exchange rate largely stemmed from a combination of the above two situations, i.e., the Central Bank not only regulated interest rates, but also controlled exchange rate policies to a large extent. In the context of increasing opening up and capital flows, however, these objectives contradict with each other (i.e., the so-called "impossible triangle"), causing the monetary policy to be in a dilemma. With the existence of the domestic and foreign interest rate spread and strong expectations for Renminbi appreciation, the PBoC had to purchase US dollars under the foreign exchange settlement and sales system, which would cause foreign exchange reserves to increase, thus forming the base money input (and funds outstanding for foreign exchange). If the Central Bank took no hedging actions, there would be more liquidity in the banking system, and interest rates would be lowered to narrow the domestic and international interest rate spread. This would obviously lead to an overexpansion in money supply, creating inflationary pressures or asset bubbles. With increasing funds outstanding for foreign exchange, the PBoC stepped up hedging operations, ranging from the central bank notes in 2003 to the statutory reserve ratio, to withdraw market liquidity. By maintaining interest rates at the previous levels, such hedging operations have, to some extent, prevented external disequilibrium from affecting the domestic macroeconomic policy, but at the expense of spurring an inflow of arbitrage funds. The above logic of actions has underpinned China's monetary policy operations over the past decade (Table 6.1 and Fig. 6.3).

Table 6.1 Progress of China's exchange rate reforms

Time	Exchange rate adjustment measures
July 2005	Implemented a floating exchange rate system with a floating band of 0.3%
May 2007	The floating band was increased from 0.3% to 0.5%
December 2008	Pegging Renminbi to the US dollar
June 2010	Unpegging Renminbi to the US dollar
April 2012	The floating band was increased from 0.5% to 1%
March 2014	The floating band was increased from 1 to 2%

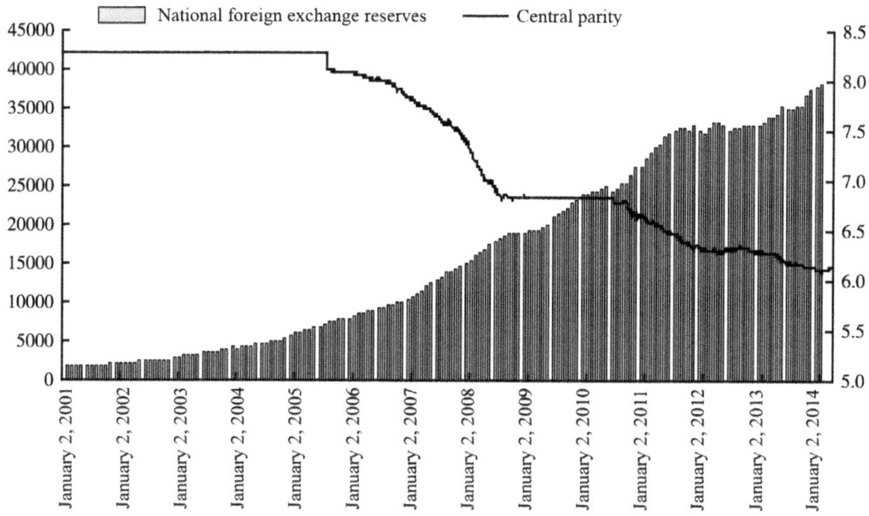

Fig. 6.3 China's foreign exchange reserves and Renminbi exchange rate (*Note* Foreign exchange reserves (100 million USD); Renminbi exchange rate (USD against RMB))

In the context of current account and capital account surpluses and an inflow of foreign exchange fund, hedging has become the most important policy operation for the Central Bank to address the tension between interest rate stability and exchange rate stability: specifically, the Central Bank had to use various policy instruments to withdraw base money issuance arising from funds outstanding for foreign exchange. Judging by the Central Bank's balance sheet, the Central Bank employed roughly three methods to offset the impact of increasing foreign currency assets on money supply. The first approach is to maintain constant liabilities and reduce the balance of "claims on government", "claims on other depository corporations", "claims on other financial corporations", "claims on non-financial corporations" and "other assets", so that their reduction equals the increase in "foreign assets". The second approach is to increase total liabilities, i.e., after the change in "foreign assets", no adjustment would be made to assets other than adjustment to liability items such as "reserve currencies", "bond issuance" and "government deposits", so that the change in liabilities equals the increase in "reserve assets". The third approach is to adjust asset and liability items simultaneously, i.e., maintain quantitative and structural equilibria of the balance sheet on the basis of the first and second adjustment approaches. Judging by the correspondence between the above three approaches and the monetary policy instruments, the first approach involves open market operations, rediscount, relending, the Central Bank's overdraft to public finance, among other monetary policy instruments; the second approach entails such monetary policy instruments as the deposit reserve policy, central bank bill issuance, and fiscal deposits; the third approach requires price and structural offsetting instruments such as exchange rate policy, interest rate policy and capital flow in addition to the quantitative offsetting instruments mentioned in the first and second adjustment approaches.

Judging by China's monetary offsetting practice, the PBoC's monetary offsetting was dominated by the first approach before 1998, i.e., mainly by adjusting asset structure; after 1998, the second approach held sway, i.e., adjustment of debt amount and structure. Since 2003, in particular, the Central Bank has relied the most on central bank bills and statutory reserve ratio (Table 6.2).

First, central bank bill offsetting: the Central Bank has launched massive open market operations since 2002. At the beginning, open market operations focused on spot buyouts of primarily Treasury bonds and repo operations. Given the limited bond stock on the Central Bank's balance sheet, the Central Bank found itself in an embarrassing situation of having no bonds to sell after a brief period of one-way operations. In this context, the Central Bank converted unmatured sell repos in its open market operations into central bank bills on September 24, 2002 as an alternative before using them in repo operations. Central bank bills thus officially entered China's bond market. Since April 2003, central bank bills started to be issued on a large scale and was allowed to circulate in the interbank market as an important bond. Since then, the central bank bill issuance has swelled with an increasing variety of bills. In 2008, the outstanding balance of central bank bills peaked at 4.8 trillion yuan, and due to cost increases, the Central Bank shifted the focus of its hedging operations to raising the statutory reserve ratio, resulting in a sharp decline in the balance of central bank bills after 2009. By the end of 2013, the outstanding balance of central bank bills fell to 776.2 billion yuan (Fig. 6.4).

It is fair to say that central bank bills have played a key role in China's financial reforms and macroregulation and served as a realistic option for the Central Bank to effectively implement its monetary policy in the context of the ongoing reforms in relevant fields particularly when coordination between fiscal and monetary policies

Table 6.2 PBoC's balance sheet

Assets	Liabilities
Foreign assets	Reserve currency
Foreign exchange	Monetary issuance
Monetary gold	Deposits from financial corporations
Other foreign assets	Deposits from non-financial corporations
Claims on government	Bond issuance
Claims on other depository corporations	Foreign liabilities
Claims on other financial corporations	Government deposits
Claims on non-financial corporations	Self-owned funds
Other assets	Other Liabilities
Total assets	Total liabilities

Source PBoC's website

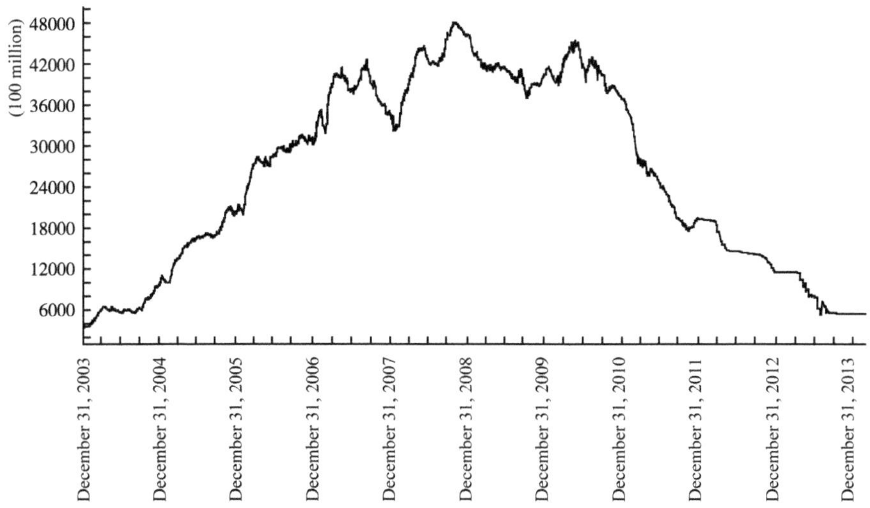

Fig. 6.4 Outstanding balance of Central Bank bills

was yet to be improved. In this sense, it represents a financial innovation with Chinese characteristics.

Second, the statutory reserve ratio: compared with the central bank bills, adjusting the statutory reserve ratio serves as a means of administrative regulation with more direct offsetting effects at lower costs. However, the potential distortions to the financial market cannot be overlooked. Relevant issues will be discussed in the subsequent section and will not be elaborated here. From September 21, 2003 to February 24, 2011, the Central Bank has adjusted the statutory reserve ratio 32 times (four reductions in 2008, one reduction in 2011, and two reductions in 2012). Currently, the statutory reserve ratio for large financial institutions is 20%, and that for small and medium-sized financial institutions is about 16%, and the frozen commercial bank funds amount to some 20 trillion yuan.

Third, monetary sterilization and central bank balance sheet: the purchase of foreign exchange assets and the subsequent sterilization operations have led the central bank balance sheet to swell with significant structural changes in liabilities and assets. From 2003 to the end of 2013, China's central bank balance sheet expanded by five times from 6200.4 billion yuan to 31,727.8 billion yuan with an annual growth rate of about 45% (see Table 6.3). Meanwhile, major changes also occurred in the Central Bank's balance sheet structure. On the asset side, the amount of foreign assets—mainly foreign exchange assets—spiked from 3114.1 billion yuan in 2003 (including foreign exchange assets worth 2984.1 billion yuan) to 27,223.3 billion yuan by the end of 2013 (including foreign exchange assets worth 26,427 billion yuan), up close to nine times by the end of 2013, and the share of foreign assets in the Central Bank's total assets rose from 50% in 2003 (including foreign exchange assets that accounted for 48%) to 86% in 2013 (including foreign exchange assets accounting for 83%). Meanwhile, major changes also occurred in the Central Bank's liability structure. In early 2003, the Central Bank's biggest liability was monetary issuance, which accounted for 44% of the Central Bank's total liabilities, followed by deposits from financial institutions and government, which accounted for 30% and 7%, respectively. At the end of 2013, deposits from other depository financial institutions became the Central Bank's largest liability with a balance reaching 20,604.2 billion yuan, accounting for 65% of the Central Bank's total liabilities. The share of monetary issuance shrank to 20.5% as the second largest central bank liability. After 2009, central bank bills as a share of total central bank liabilities nosedived from 15.6% to 2.4% in 2013.

6.3.3 Problems in the Current System

Judging by the quantitative results, the Central Bank's sterilization policy worked well and had isolated China from external economic shocks. It should be noted that the fundamental problems behind internal and external disequilibria remain unresolved. As sterilization continued and expanded, the adverse effects kept building up.

First, the Central Bank's regulatory capacity reduced. Modern monetary policy is implemented by the central bank primarily by regulating the cost and amount of financing for the government and financial institutions including commercial banks. When a central bank has a favorable position of claims on both the government and financial institutions, it may effectively regulate the amount of money and credit through interest rates. However, when a central bank is indebted to both the government and financial institutions, its policy space becomes highly limited. As can be seen from the abovementioned central bank balance sheet, the Central Bank was a net debtor to the government and financial institutions, and its liabilities to financial institutions (including reserve funds and central bank bills) made up 68% or so of the Central Bank's total liabilities.

The implication is that under the current reserve management system, automatic increases in home-currency funds resulting from foreign capital inflow would provide sufficient funds for financial institutions' development. Judging by their financial ties, the daily operations of China's financial institutions are increasingly separated from the Central Bank. The Central Bank's "twin deficits" to the government and financial institutions—especially to financial institutions—have gradually undermined the potency of its monetary policy, making it unable to influence the behaviors of financial institutions and regulate monetary and credit supply through market-based operations. As a result, the Central Bank had to resort to administrative interventions for direct control.

Second, distortions in financial market operation mechanisms. Currently, the Central Bank freezes banks' liquidity mainly by raising the statutory reserve ratio. While reducing the financial cost pressures for commercial banks, this operation has its drawbacks, resulting in a large amount of idle funds and capital price distortions. By freezing huge sums of capital on its own account, the Central Bank inevitably

Table 6.3 Composition of the PBoC's balance sheet, 2003–2013 (Unit: 100 million yuan)

Year	2003	2004	2005	2006	2007	2008	2009	2010	2011	2012	2013
Net foreign assets	31,141	46,397	62,697	84,846	123,877	161,810	184,571	215,419	237,898	241,416	272,233
Including: Foreign exchange	29,841	45,940	62,140	84,360	115,168	149,624	175,154	206,766	232,388	236,669	269,215
Claims on government	2901	2969	2892	2856	16,317	16,196	15,662	15,421	15,399	155,313	15,312
Claims on depository institutions	10,619	10,424	8167	6516	7862	8432	7161	9485	10,247	16,701	13,147
Claims on other financial institutions	7255	8865	17,750	21,949	12,972	11,852	11,530	11,325	10,643	10,038	8907
Claims on non-financial institutions	206	136	66	66	63	44	44	24	24	24	24
Other assets	8516	9300	11,459	11,412	7098	8027	7799	7597	6763	11,041	7652
Total assets	62,004	78,093	103,034	127,648	168,192	206,363	226,768	259,274	280,977	294,537	317,278
Reserve currencies	52,841	58,856	64,343	77,757	101,545	129,222	143,985	185,311	224,641	252,345	271,023
Monetary issuance	21,240	23,104	25,854	29,138	32,971	37,115	41,555	48,646	55,850	60,645	64,980
Deposits from financial institutions[a]	22,558	35,672	38,391	48,459	68,415	91,515	102,429	136,665	168,791	191,699	206,042
Deposits from non-financial institutions	9042	79	97	159	158	591	624	657	908	1348	1330
Bond issuance	3031	11,079	20,296	29,740	34,469	45,779	42,064	40,497	23,336	13,880	7762
Government deposits	4954	5832	7527	10,210	17,121	16,963	21,226	24,277	22,733	20,753	28,610
Self-owned funds	219	219	219	219	219	219	219	219	219	219	219
Other liabilities	474	2106	10,648	9719	14,837	13,586	18,648	7592	6334	4525	6244
Total liabilities	62,004	78,093	103,034	127,648	168,192	206,363	226,768	259,274	280,977	294,537	317,278

Note[a] the PBoC's liabilities to other financial institutions are relatively limited and can be equated to the reserve funds of depository financial institutions.
Source: the People's Bank of China

distorts capital supply and demand and triggers deviations in capital pricing, which results in a host of tensions. For instance, while capital supply is sufficient for the banking system (steady M2 growth), the private sector suffers a capital shortage. To make up for the opportunity cost from the freezing of capital, banks would widen the deposit and loan rate spread to increase asset yield, which not only raises the cost of capital for firms but also might increase risks for the financial system. These results are obviously unfavorable for the stable operation and resource efficiency of the financial system and goes against the direction of interest rate liberalization reforms followed by China over the years.

Third, cost and sustainability issues.

In addition to creating market distortions, the Central Bank's hedging operations also face cost and sustainability problems. From a financial perspective, the sheer cost of the Central bank's hedging operations is staggering without considering the return from foreign exchange asset operations and foreign exchange losses.

Central bank bills: between 2003 and 2013, the Central Bank had conducted 833 issues of central bank bills, including 350 issues of three-month bills, 57 issues of six-month bills, 319 issues of one-year bills, and 107 issues of three-year bills. The amount of central bank bill issuance increased steadily over the years, peaking in 2008. As a result, the central bank's payment of interest on central bank bills grew from 7.98 billion yuan in 2003 to a peak of 225.2 billion yuan in 2008. Put together, the Central Bank's total payment of interest on central bank bills should amount to roughly 713.6 billion (Table 6.4).

Compared with central bank bill issuance, the cost of raising the statutory reserve ratio is much smaller. According to the Central Bank's current regulations, the interest rate on the statutory reserve funds is 1.62%, which is far smaller than that on central bank bills. As such, the statutory reserve ratio plays an increasingly important role in the Central Bank's hedging operations. Despite the low interest rate, interest payment remains staggering due to the increasing amount of reserve funds. Between 2003 and 2010, the Central Bank paid a cumulative amount of around 800.5 billion yuan in interest on the reserve funds of commercial banks (including interest on excess reserves).

In combination of the two costs, the Central Bank's direct financial cost for offsetting liquidity amounted to some 1.5 trillion yuan between 2003 and 2010. Such a massive cost is undoubtedly a heavy burden for the Central Bank. As China's foreign exchange reserves continue to increase, hedging policy sustainability is questionable. More importantly, with the continuous increase in the stock of central bank bills and the record-high levels of the statutory reserve ratio, the space and marginal efficiency of both policy operations are shrinking (Table 6.5).

Source the People's Bank of China (PBoC)

Table 6.4 Estimation of Central Bank bills cost, 2003–2010

Year	Maturity	Number of issues	Issuance amount (100 million yuan)	Interest rate range	Payment of interest (100 million yuan)
2003	Three-month	33	4150	2.80–2.15	25.1
	Six-month	23	2588	2.99–2.19	33.2
	One-year	7	900	2.43–2.32	21.5
	Sub-total	63	7638	2.99–2.15	79.8
2004	Three-month	43	5649	2.88–1.87	35.4
	Six-month	11	1840	3.40–2.23	23.4
	One-year	42	7172	3.57–2.59	227.3
	Three-year	3	300	4.15–4.11	37.2
	Sub-total	99	14,961	4.15–1.87	323.4
2005	Three-month	44	9430	2.58–1.05	31.2
	Six-month	13	2372	2.88–1.23	21.6
	One-year	52	12,310	3.40–1.33	247.4
	Three-year	16	3550	4.15–3.00	365
	Sub-total	125	27,662	4.15–1.05	665.2
2006	Three-month	43	10,150	2.54–1.73	51.8
	Six-month	2	950	2.70–1.82	9.1
	One-year	52	25,423	2.89–1.83	600.5
	Sub-total	97	36,523	2.89–1.73	661.4
2007	Three-month	47	10,220	3.41–2.50	69.7
	Six-month	49	16,356	4.06–2.80	490.8
	Three-year	46	13,995	4.52–2.97	1456.6
	Sub-total	142	40,571	4.52–2.50	2017
2008	Three-month	46	12,230	3.41–1.01	99.1
	Six-month	8	735	3.70–3.70	13.6
	One-year	43	20,315	4.06–2.25	815.6
	Three-year	25	9680	4.56–4.52	1324.2
	Sub-total	122	42,960	4.56–1.01	2252.5
2009	Three-month	47	29,500	1.33–0.97	84.16
	One-year	24	8740	1.76–1.50	151.94
	Sub-total	71	38,240	1.76–0.97	236.1
2010	Three-month	47	16,630	2.01–1.36	280.2
	One-year	50	15,380	2.51–1.76	328.3
	Three-year	17	10,340	3.00–2.65	292.1

(continued)

Table 6.4 (continued)

Year	Maturity	Number of issues	Issuance amount (100 million yuan)	Interest rate range	Payment of interest (100 million yuan)
	Sub-total	114	42,350	3.00–1.36	900.6
Total payment of interest on central bank bills		7136			

Note the calculation of interest on central bank bills does not consider cross-year interest payment, i.e., all interest payments are current-year payments made in the same year of central bank bill issuance, and such an assumption does not affect the calculation of aggregate interest payment
Source the People's Bank of China

Table 6.5 Estimation of the reserve requirement policy's cost between 2003 and 2010 (Currency unit: 100 million yuan, %)

Year	Balance of deposits	Statutory reserve ratio	Interest on statutory reserve funds	Excess reserve ratio	Interest on excess reserves	Total
2003	189,486	6.5	233	5.9	182	415
2004	224,290	7.3	307	5.3	193	501
2005	263,847	7.5	374	4.7	139	513
2006	311,302	8.3	485	4.5	138	623
2007	362,403	11.8	805	4.1	149	953
2008	427,787	16.7	1334	4.3	178	1512
2009	531,972	15.2	1310	4.1	158	1468
2010	665,557	17.3	1865	3.2	155	2020
Total	—	—	6713	—	1292	8005

6.4 Policy Recommendations

Open economic and financial systems are vulnerable to external shocks amid interactions with global financial markets, giving rise to internal and external economic imbalances and financial crisis with ripple effects on the real economy. Over the past two decades, the "twin surpluses" of China's trade balance and capital account have coexisted with an overheating domestic economy, resulting in tension between interest rate and exchange rate objectives and a host of associated problems. As China's market-based reforms progress, a key question facing China's financial reforms in the new era is how to reform interest rate and exchange rate formation mechanisms to remove the existing distortions and regulate economic imbalances.

A sure choice in China's monetary policy implementation is to seek the best interest rate and exchange rate policy combination to give play to the interplay between Renminbi interest rate and exchange rate and the synergy between interest rate policy and exchange rate policy. As conditions for Renminbi interest rate and exchange rate liberalization become increasingly mature, China should implement the following policy initiatives to promote exchange rate and interest rate coordination.

First, determine a reasonable prioritization of financial reforms. Market-oriented reforms should not be too fast as to disrupt the reasonable sequence of financial reforms and should promote the synergic effects of financial reforms. Inappropriate prioritization of financial liberalization reforms will not raise the efficiency of financial liberalization and may induce financial fragilities and even a financial crisis. In China's financial reforms, the first step is to liberalize interest rates before deregulating the capital account and thus completing exchange rate liberalization, so as to minimize external shocks on the financial system. Interest rate liberalization is the foundation for monetary stability. The free flow of international capital can be allowed only when domestic lending can be performed at a balanced exchange level and domestic inflation is effectively curbed to make exchange rate depreciation unnecessary. Based on such indicators as the benchmark interest rate, market interest rate, the international balance of payments and foreign exchange reserves, the Central Bank should regulate the currency market and thus influence foreign exchange market change and the exchange rate to avoid excessive shocks of simultaneous interest rate liberalization and capital account deregulation to investment and output.

Second, create a monetary policy combination. A flexible and effective financial macro-regulation mechanism is predicated upon market-based interest rates that give play to their "built-in stabilizer" effect in close coordination with a resilient exchange rate regime. Through various interest rate and exchange rate operations, the Central Bank should perform swift, timely and accurate policy transmission and safeguard financial market stability and economic security through well-functioning currency market and foreign exchange market. Although the interest rate mechanism cannot fully defuse pressures for Renminbi to appreciate, a market-oriented interest rate formation mechanism may serve as an "built-in stabilizer" to ease currency value pressures amid growing international currency reserves. When real interest rates rise, the monetary authority must expand the floating band of exchange rate accordingly to enhance the regulatory efficacy of monetary policy. Meanwhile, necessary restrictions on international capital flows should be maintained to beef up monetary policy regulation capacity.

Third, expedite the interest rate liberalization process as appropriate. China should create a flexible mechanism of transmission between interest rate policy and exchange rate policy to give play to their synergic effect. Interest rate liberalization is a basic precondition for the exchange rate and interest rate policy combination. Without interest rate liberalization, the rising money supply and inflationary pressures due to an inflow of foreign speculative capital cannot be eased by interest rate variations. Similarly, a capital flight cannot be stopped by raising interest rates.

Fourth, propel the market-based interest rate and exchange rate linkage to prevent financial turbulence. Given that forming a reasonable exchange rate system is the priority and difficulty of China's current exchange rate reforms, it is necessary to deepen Renminbi exchange rate reforms and continue expanding the flexibility and floating band of Renminbi exchange rate. In creating a balanced exchange rate mechanism and deregulating the capital account, it becomes more complex to coordinate interest rate and exchange rate policies. Hence, the choice of an exchange rate regime and the establishment of a benchmark exchange rate are critical to interest rate and exchange rate coordination. Flexible and effective interest rate and exchange rate coordination is essential to enhancing monetary policy flexibility and curbing inflows of short-term speculative capital. In case of an unexpected shock to the real economy such as a plunge in exports or a mass capital flight, the combination of an open capital account and a floating exchange rate regime is obviously superior to one with a fixed exchange rate regime. Meanwhile, the possibility of a consequent financial turbulence must be considered in such processes.

Fifth, create a broad and deep foreign exchange market and develop a resilient Renminbi exchange rate regime. Many developing countries and transitional countries lack financial infrastructure to support a deeper and more extensive foreign exchange market. Without official exchange rates as guidance and relevant policy support, they cannot provide stable assurances for economic operation. The same is true for China's reality. China's financial infrastructure has yet to offer an extensive, deep and resilient market vehicle for a reasonable and balanced exchange rate regime. The foreign exchange market is, therefore, a key component of China's Renminbi exchange rate reform. China's foreign exchange market breadth and depth are far from compatible with the micro-structure of market-based and resilient spot exchange rate formation. To advance the formation of a flexible forward exchange rate, China needs to further improve the market maker system of its commercial banks, develop a reasonable forward foreign exchange pricing mechanism, and further propel the formation of a resilient Renminbi exchange rate regime.

Sixth, accelerate the reform of the foreign exchange reserve system to prevent the impact of an external disequilibrium on the internal economy. As mentioned before, problems in China's existing systems stem from not only the internal and external disequilibria at the economic level, but also the current mode of foreign exchange administration that makes it likely for external disequilibrium to affect the internal economy. Hence, we should advance interest rate and exchange rate liberalization reforms and enhance policy coordination, in which the most fundamental task is to reform the exchange rate reserve management system. Specifically, the following three possible options of reform are available.

1. China's foreign exchange reserves can be transferred to the Ministry of Finance to establish a foreign exchange stabilization fund under the Ministry of Finance. The Ministry of Finance may use special Treasury bonds to swap the Central Bank's foreign exchange assets. Nevertheless, Article 29 of the *Law of the People's Republic of China on the People's Bank of China (Amended in 2003)* prescribes that the "PBoC shall not overdraft to government finance and shall not directly subscribe for or underwrite Treasury bonds and other government bonds." Such swap cannot be conducted directly and requires a special institutional arrangement, which may follow the method for establishing the China Investment Corporation (CIC). As foreign exchange reserves keep increasing, the stabilization fund can be used to issue financing bills to raise Renminbi cash for purchasing foreign exchange.

Provided that foreign exchange reserves are under the management of the Ministry of Finance, the Central Bank may still be appointed to perform the daily management of foreign exchange reserves and foreign exchange market interventions. The Ministry of Finance may determine the basic principles for foreign exchange management for the Central Bank to hammer out and implement detailed rules.

This mode is closer to Japan's system and has the following benefits: first, allocating foreign exchange reserves to the stabilization fund may sever the direct linkage between foreign exchange variation and money supply. Second, putting the Ministry of Finance in charge of foreign exchange reserves means that after China's exchange rate liberalization, the Ministry of Finance will be responsible for making the exchange rate policy and relevant international financial policies. For large countries, allocating internal and external equilibrium objectives to different departments helps address tensions between those objectives and enhance the independence and stability of their economic operations. Lastly, revealing the financial cost of the existing exchange rate policy may help propel China's exchange rate market reforms.

2. Split China's foreign exchange reserves into two parts. One part may be separated from the Central Bank to establish a new foreign exchange investment fund, and carved out from the central bank balance sheet. The Ministry of Finance needs to intervene in the carve-out process and swap those assets by issuing special Treasury bonds. The remainder will be held by the Central Bank to maintain stability in exchange rate and foreign exchange market. Further growth in foreign exchange reserves should be purchased by the foreign exchange stabilization fund with home-currency capital raised from issuing financing bills. Under such a system, the foreign exchange rate policy is still administered by the Central Bank, and the key significance of the Ministry of Finance's participation (in the management of foreign exchange increment) is to sever the impact of foreign exchange reserve variations on the home country's policy-making.

This mode of reform has the following benefits: first, it severs the direct link between foreign exchange reserve variations and domestic money supply; second, the Central Bank reserves the ability to intervene in the foreign-exchange market, and the institutional reform has smaller market shocks; lastly, the cost of exchange rate system will be made explicit to some extent.

3. Turn the State Administration of Foreign Exchange (SAFE) into an independent agency (in charge of the foreign exchange stabilization fund) and keep its business administration within the remit of the Central Bank. It is a central bank-led approach. The fund is subject to review and audit by the Ministry of Finance. The foreign exchange stabilization fund has three major functions: to issue financing bonds to raise Renminbi capital to purchase excess foreign exchange; to maintain and increase the value of foreign exchange assets under management; to coordinate with the Central Bank for market interventions according to policy requirements in special times. In this mode, the Central Bank may keep some foreign exchange reserves for stabilizing foreign exchange rate and foreign exchange market.

The key to the above three modes lies in the establishment of an independent agency whose financing and asset purchase behaviors will replace the Central Bank's direct foreign exchange purchase, thus severing the correlation between foreign exchange reserve variations and money supply. In this respect, the above three modes achieve similar short-term effects.

Nevertheless, these three modes involve different administrative authorities and vary in terms of reform difficulties and long-term effects. Without doubt, the first mode is ideal but entails great resistance with relatively big potential short-term shocks to the market; the third mode is easier to implement with fewer shocks. Under the third mode, however, the Central Bank is still responsible for both internal and external equilibrium objectives. Besides, a realistic barrier is a potential objection from the Ministry of Finance to provide state credit guarantee for the financing bonds issued by the foreign exchange stabilization fund over which it has no direct administrative power. Comparatively, the second mode is a more realistic option.

(Zeng Gang)

References

Xu Shaoqiang, Li Lina: "A Tentative Analysis of Renminbi Exchange Rate's Rational Tendencies", *China Forex*, Vol.3, 2001.

Xue Hongli: "A Brief Analysis of the Evolution of the Interest-Rate Parity Model in China", *Journal of Finance and Economics*, Vol.2, 2002.

Chapter 7
Conditions and Supporting Policies for Interest Rate Liberalization

Interest rates are the core benchmark of financial markets. Since China's economic reforms are yet to complete, financial transactions in China during the transition period have been more or less guided by a distorted interest rate system controlled by administrative forces, which seriously impedes the improvement of financial resource allocation efficiency. For this reason, the Third Plenary Session of the 18th CPC Central Committee called for "expediting interest rate liberalization and improving the Treasury bond yield curve to reflect market supply and demand." Obviously, advancing interest rate liberalization to give play to the role of finance in resource allocation will be a key element of China's financial reforms for some time to come. Advancing Renminbi deposit and loan rate liberalization is a complex and systematic project that is predicated upon a host of conditions and relevant policies, which, if unmature or not in place, will not only hinder the process of RMB deposit and lending interest rate liberalization but also may make it difficult to be advanced.

7.1 Background and Relevant Literature

7.1.1 Research Background

Theoretically, the connotations of interest rates are explicit and clear-cut: interest rates can be regarded as the benchmark price of capital. In the real world, however, interest rates are not just an abstract and empty concept but a diverse and complex system. Each interest rate corresponds to a certain financing activity and reflects such attributes as the riskiness of financing activities. Accordingly, interest rate liberalization is not simply government deregulation but a systematic project of great complexity. It includes at least the following highlights: (i) Interest rate liberalization is the change of the capital pricing mechanism with the goal to ensure that the

G. Wang, *A Study on Interest Rate Liberalization in China*, Research Series on the Chinese Dream and China's Development Path,
https://doi.org/10.1007/978-981-97-3644-7_7

interest rate level and maturity structure are determined through free price negotiation and perfect competition between capital seekers and suppliers. (ii) Within a country's interest rate system, various interest rates are correlated with and influence each other, and one or a few interest rates have a decisive impact on change in the interest rate system. As an essential component of interest rate liberalization, those interest rates are the benchmark for the entire market, promote the development of the currency market and the benchmark interest rate system. To give play to these effects, we should break through market segmentation and develop an effective interest rate transmission mechanism. (iii) Taking maintaining macroeconomic stability into consideration, the monetary authority should have sufficient and effective market-based instruments at its disposal to achieve the objectives of regulating the interest rate level and structure. (iv) Interest rate liberalization essentially entails change in the financing price mechanism with a distinctively gradualist feature of starting with certain financing activities before gradual implementation to cover other financing activities. The double track characteristics of the interest rate pricing mechanism are inevitable for a certain period of time.

The change in the interest rate price mechanism profoundly affects the return, costs and risks of capital seekers and suppliers and various financial institutions, which are hard to manage. Initiated over 30 years ago, China's interest rate liberalization has progressed from the informal financial sector to the formal financial sector and from narrower and easier areas to broader and more difficult ones. The steady reform strategy has led to great progress in China's financial markets, offering an increasingly diverse range of financial products. Resistance to further interest rate liberalization has diminished. Many financial institutions have become willing to adopt market-based financial pricing mechanisms that serve their interests.

To date, China's interest rate liberalization reforms have made great progress. By the early twenty-first century, China's financial markets (including the corporate bond market, the Treasury bond market and the financial bond market) had generally achieved interest rate liberalization. The currency market has also liberalized interest rates. Conditions have been ready for liberalizing interest rates in the foreign currency market as well. In this manner, the liberalization of Renminbi deposit and lending interest rates has become the centerpiece of China's interest rate liberalization reforms at the beginning of this century. Specifically, the floating band of bank loan rates should be continuously expanded to achieve market-based loan pricing; meanwhile, steps should be taken to liberalize bank deposit rates to achieve deposit rate liberalization as the ultimate goal.

On July 20, 2013, the PBoC removed the lower limit on loan interest rate for financial institutions except for commercial personal housing loans, relaxed control on discount rate, and ceased to set upper limit on loan rates for rural credit cooperatives (RCCs). This marks the completion of much of China's loan rate liberalization, and the new loan rate formation mechanism tests commercial banks' loan risk pricing power.

After removing the lower limit on loan rates, the Central Bank established the self-regulatory mechanism for market rate pricing by financial institutions on September

24, 2013. In line with national regulations on interest rate management, this mechanism enforces self-regulatory management of currency market, credit market and other financial market interest rates autonomously determined by financial institutions to maintain fair market competition and promote standard and healthy market development. On October 25 of the same year, the loan prime rate (LPR) centralized quote and publish mechanism was officially put into operation after a month of trial operation. The LPR is the loan rate for the highest-quality customers of commercial banks, and other loan rates can be determined through markup or markdown of the LPR. On the basis of LPR quotes from quoting banks, the designated issuer will calculate the weighted average of quotes to form the average LPR rate of quoting banks and announce it to the public. We believe that since the LPR based on quotes from major banks in China is of important reference value for banks' loan and asset businesses, and the official operation of the LPR centralized quote and publish mechanism is conducive to improving the Central Bank's interest rate regulation mechanism and laying the institutional foundation for further interest rate liberalization reforms.

After deregulating the lower limit on loan rates, deposit rate liberalization became the central task in China's interest rate liberalization reforms. In November 2014, the upper limit of deposit rate floating band was raised to 1.2 times the benchmark rate. In October 2015, the upper limit of deposit rate floating band was scrapped for commercial banks and rural cooperative financial institutions, which marks the near completion of interest rate liberalization. Complete deposit rate liberalization poses new challenges to both commercial banks and the Central Bank. Policy coordination and innovation in various aspects are required for deposit and loan rate liberalization reforms to undergird the success of China's overall interest rate reforms. Proceeding from the favorable and unfavorable conditions facing Renminbi deposit and loan rate liberalization reforms, this chapter discusses the institutional environment and policy orientation for steadily advancing those reforms to provide a basic approach and pathway for the ongoing reforms.

7.1.2 Brief Descriptions of Relevant Theories

US economists Ronald I. McKinnon and Edward S. Shaw have made groundbreaking contributions to research on interest rate liberalization in developing economies. According to Ronald I. McKinnon, financial repression extensively exists in developing countries, causing market segmentation and inefficient resource allocation (McKinnon, 1998). Edward S. Shaw noted that financial repression led to less financial accumulation, falling domestic savings rate, and shrinking financial markets (Shaw, 1998). Based on the above assessment, McKinnon and Shaw believe that developing economies should implement financial liberalization reforms underpinned by interest rate liberalization. Some empirical studies have supported their assessment. For instance, Fry (1989) found that real deposit rate edging closer to the market equilibrium level will induce an increase in economic growth rate. For another instance, Gelb (1989) noted that countries with excessively low real interest rates in the 1970s also experienced low economic growth rates.

With the eruption of financial crises in countries after liberalizing interest rates under the financial liberalization theories, however, some scholars have reflected upon the drawbacks of interest rate liberalization. Stiglitz and Weiss (1981) considered that moral hazard and adverse selection in the credit market prevent banks from identifying and screening projects under the self-regulatory effect of interest rates. Hellman et al. pointed out that with insufficient central bank regulatory capabilities, developing economies must artificially suppress interest rates to remove moral hazards and maintain financial stability.

With rapid financial innovation, economists have generally recognized that interest rate control will only distort resource allocation and hamper long-term economic growth. Interest rate liberalization is an irresistible trend. The associated problem of market failure can be addressed by more effective regulation (Hellman et al., 1994). Referencing Knut Wicksell's natural rate of interest theory, Woodford (2003) argued that short-term interest rates should be lowered when the economy was in a downswing, and when interest rate was close to zero and could not be further lowered, the best way to revitalize the economy was to maintain interest rates at a close-to-zero level, so that such low interest rate expectations, coupled with a higher inflation rate, might stimulate investment and spending.

Recent empirical literature offers vigorous support to the conclusion that financial liberalization reforms are conducive to economic growth. With capital market openness and private capital flow as proxy variables of financial liberalization, Ranciere et al. (2006) created an econometric methodology for decomposing growth and crisis effects for an analysis of financial liberalization in 60 countries during 1980–2002, and found that the positive effects of financial liberalization on economic growth had far outweighed the adverse impact of crises. Referencing Ranciere et al. (2006), Lee and Shin (2008) tested the relationship between such financial freedom indicators as interest rate liberalization and economic growth, and found that the positive growth effects of relaxing financial regulation had far outweighed the adverse impact of crises. Using financial liberalization indicators including interest rate liberalization, Abiad et al. conducted a microscopic observation of five Asian countries, and found that financial liberalization could effectively improve capital allocation efficiency. With all-round consideration of financial liberalization including interest rate liberalization, capital account openness and trade opportunities, Kaminsky and Schmukler (2003) uncovered based on a regression analysis of 28 developed and developing countries between 1973 and 1999 that the relaxation of financial regulation was followed by an expanded boom-bust cycle, but in the long run, financial liberalization reinforced financial market stability and was conducive to economic development. Based on an analysis of panel data of 15 EU member states between 1960 and 2001, Romero-Avila (1981) uncovered that capital account openness and interest rate liberalization had both significantly contributed to economic growth.

Implementation of interest rate liberalization reforms has spurred extensive research in China on the topic of interest rate liberalization. Earlier studies have focused on the necessity, feasibility and international experience of interest rate liberalization (e.g., Wang, 2001; Zhou and Yao, 2002, et al.). As China fully liberalized currency market interest rates and only retained interest spread management on deposit and loan rates, Chinese academics have started to investigate the relationship between the effectiveness of interest rate policy and interest rates under different systems. For instance, Porter and Xu (2009) and He Dong and Wang Honglin (2011) et al. examined the relationship between fully liberalized capital market interest rates and the regulated deposit and loan benchmark rates, and found that China's currency market interest rates were the most sensitive to the benchmark deposit rate, the regulation of loan interest rates had restricted the price signal of the currency market. Li Bin (2014) uncovered that China's currency market interest rates could sensitively respond to output gaps and price change, and that an evident chain of transmission existed between various interest rate products, which created favorable conditions for further implementing interest rate liberalization reforms.

7.1.3 Correlation Between Interest Rate Liberalization and Deposit and Loan Rate Liberalization

As noted before, most scholars believed that bank deposit and loan rates were the last bastions to be liberalized, aside from which interest rate liberalization had more or less been achieved in China's bond market, interbank currency market, and domestic foreign exchange market. The reform path identified by the Central Bank in 2002 also followed this approach, i.e.: taking the first step of reform for foreign currencies before the home currency, loan interest rate before deposit interest rate, long maturities before short maturities and large sum transactions before small-sum ones. We believe that judging by the nature of interest rate, current understanding makes some sense but has limitations. Interest rate is the price of money transactions, and the nature of interest rate liberalization is to basically eliminate government administrative interventions in money transactions and allow various entities to engage in money transactions freely, thus forming the prices of funds with different maturities and risk attributes. If the government wishes to influence interest rates, it may only act as a market entity to exert an indirect influence via regular transactions. This situation cannot be achieved simply by realizing the free float of bank deposit and lending interest rates. What also matters is to create other necessary conditions to bring deposit and loan rate reforms to fruition and fashion a truly effective pattern of interest rate liberalization.

Based on the above considerations, China should deepen its interest rate liberalization reforms in a flexible and orderly manner until the interest rate liberalization reforms achieve their goal. In particular, further improvements have yet to be made to the transmission mechanism under which the Central Bank guides interest rates, the interest rate formation mechanism, and the Treasury bond yield curve, among other reforms.

We should also recognize that complete deposit rate liberalization poses new challenges to both commercial banks and the Central Bank. For commercial banks, competitive pressures could goad state-controlled commercial banks and other systemically important financial institutions into opportunistic behaviors, giving rise to financial instability. Hence, deposit rate liberalization will further improve the incentives and restraints of China's commercial banks, highlighting the urgency to reform the broader financial regulatory system. From the Central Bank perspective, deposit and loan rates will cease to serve as important monetary policy instruments. When issuing bonds, many Chinese companies have followed the Central Bank's one-year deposit rate as their pricing basis. That is to say, after deposit rate liberalization, many companies will have to seek other interest rates as pricing basis for issuing bonds. The Central Bank must establish a new monetary regulation mechanism after fully deregulating the upper and lower limits on deposit and loan rates, which at least include: seeking a portfolio of more effective, flexible and independent monetary policy instruments; and establishing more effective benchmark rates for smoother and more effective monetary policy transmission (Peng and Dong, 2014).

In addition to considering commercial banks' risk pricing and risk management capabilities, China should also create a sound interest rate risk transaction market and a set of central bank macro-regulatory mechanism for overall interest rates as basic institutional assurance for deposit and lending interest rate liberalization. As far as interest rate risk transaction markets are concerned, China has already established such derivatives markets as forward interest rate agreement and interest rate swap markets, allowing financial institutions to enhance interest rate risk management by leveraging derivatives markets. From a macro-regulatory perspective, the PBoC as the central bank needs to establish a set of monetary policy operation systems to guide and influence overall interest rates and interest rate structure to express its intentions via monetary policy operations in an environment of fully liberalized interest rates, influence aggregate demand by altering overall interest rates, and influence the structure of credit funds in the broad sense by adjusting the interest rate structure (including maturity structure and risk structure). Among these priorities, the most urgent one is to create the benchmark rate for China's monetary policy.

7.2 Basic Conditions for Advancing Deposit and Lending Interest Rate Liberalization

According to international experience, deposit and lending interest rate liberalization tends to accelerate under the following economic conditions:

First, accelerating financial disintermediation due to a changing macroeconomic environment. In the stagflation in the 1970s, real interest rates in Western developed countries often turned negative since bank interest rates were artificially controlled, prompting depositors to withdraw cash from the banks and causing financial disintermediation. In response, regulated banks and other financial institutions strongly demanded interest rate control to be removed.

Second, in the context of financial globalization, the sharp difference between regulated domestic interest rates and interest rates in the international markets led to massive inflows and outflows of cross-border capital, which seriously disrupted domestic financial stability, as was often the case for the UK and France in the 1960s.

Third, financial institutions subject to interest rate regulation evaded regulation by inventing innovative financial instruments. For instance, some US investment companies such as Merrill Lynch Securities and Fidelity Investments created currency market funds to meet market needs. The basic role of those funds was to invest deposits in products free from interest rate regulation such as commercial bills (CPs), large negotiable certificates of deposits (CDs), short-term Treasury bonds, repurchase agreements and bank acceptance bills, whose yield varies with market interest rates. Compared with banks subject to interest rate regulation, currency market funds successfully evaded restrictions under Regulation Q, allowing funds to yield higher interest rates with better liquidity, payment and transfer functions.

Based on such international experiences, the above three conditions for interest rate liberalization are initially ready for China.

First, financial disintermediation intensifies with the rapid development of Internet finance. The government must strive to develop direct finance to absorb liquidity released from the banking system and allow direct money transactions between capital seekers and suppliers. This makes it possible for China to expand the business scope of banks, allow mixed operations, move capital operations outside banks' balance sheet, and complete deposit interest rate liberalization through the investment of deposits in investment funds.

Second, the recent exit of the US quantitative easing (QE) policy has led to abrupt changes in the direction and scale of international and domestic capital flows; and the consequent interest rate difference will intensify interest-seeking international capital flows, giving rise to "interest spread transactions" seeking financial return and causing significant uncertainties to China's domestic financial markets.

Third, wealth management products (WMPs) and Internet finance have transformed interest rate determination mechanisms outside banks, getting capital seekers and suppliers, financial institutions and companies all involved in the interest rate determination process. The linkages between official lending and private lending and between formal finance and shadow banking will optimize capital allocation on a broader scale. This reminds the government that various arbitrage behaviors in the current financial system stemmed from barriers and inconsistent interest rates between markets. Guided by the guiding principles of the Third Plenary Session of the 18th CPC Central Committee, a consensus has been reached among all circles that deposit and lending interest rate liberalization must be expedited to break through those barriers and provide effective price signals for financial organizations and markets to guide the effective allocation of financial resources and provide the Central Bank with accurate information and effective means for performing macro-regulation.

Without a doubt, many institutional barriers stand in the way in China's deposit and loan rate liberalization.

At the microscopic level, the soft budgetary constraint and administrative interventions have caused SOEs to be insensitive to interest rate change, compromising the capital allocation function of interest rates. Similarly, the availability rather than cost of capital is the top concern for local governments subject to the soft budgetary constraint. With China's current public finance system yet to be fully established, the thirst for cash among local governments is another adverse factor against interest rate liberalization. The absence of bank governance structure means bankers are not held accountable for bank performance, and implicit government guarantee has disincentivized financial institutions' risk control. Insensitive capital demand has also led to excessively high interest rates, increasing financial institutions' profit-seeking motivation. In such a competitive environment, moral hazard prevails since unscrupulous financial institutions are more likely to develop faster. The gradual weakening of prudent project management in the financial system has led to serious capital misallocation.

At the macroscopic level, first, the Central Bank's macro-regulatory mechanism cannot effectively regulate the positions of commercial banks and guide change of market rates. This has to do with China's current deposit reserve system and is also a manifestation of the Central Bank's underdeveloped payment and settlement system; second, the policy system with money supply as the intermediate goal is highly dependent on the stability of bank deposits, and interest rate liberalization will cause deposits to be more volatile. This tension may slow China's interest rate liberalization process. Third, China's deposit rates have over the years served as the benchmark rate, but the assumption of this function in the long run is hampered by the derivative nature and limited maturity structure of deposit rates. We should strive to develop the currency market and debt instrument markets to smoothen the transmission mechanism of benchmark rates and establish a market-based benchmark rate system.

7.3 Analysis of Practical Conditions for Interest Rate Liberalization Reforms in China

In China's case, deposit and lending interest rate liberalization reforms are faced with favorable and unfavorable conditions.

First, conditions for the development of financial products. Financial products are important vehicles for short-term and long-term money transactions. Aside from capital allocation and risk management, both simple investment and financing products and sophisticated derivatives or structured products must reflect the price discovery function to identify the equilibrium transaction price of financial markets.

The rapid development in WMPs and Internet finance has made China's interest rate determination outside the banking system increasingly market-oriented.

According to the annual reports of listed companies, hundreds of listed companies have purchased WMPs with surplus funds, suggesting more diversified investment modes for capital suppliers. It should also be noted that China's bond products are relatively few, and mainstream products such as municipal bonds funds in overseas markets have yet to appear in China's bond market. In addition, the derivatives market developed more slowly, and basic products such as forwards, futures, options and swaps remain small in transaction volumes, not to mention more sophisticated innovative products. Financial products are the objects of transactions and an important assurance for the formation of market rates. Given the absence of risk management instruments and diverse products in the bond market, interest rate liberalization is far from complete. In a currency market without short-term Treasury bonds, the monetary authority finds it hard to conduct normal interest rate operations. China's market-based interest rate system is marred by a severe shortfall of derivative products.

Second, conditions for the development of financial institutions. The development status of China's financial institutions as market transaction entities is insufficient to ensure smooth interest rate liberalization.

On the one hand, any financial market must have numerous traders to gather enough supply and demand information and trends, so that transactions will converge towards the intrinsic prices of currencies or assets, reflecting the role of market mechanisms. The reality is that financial institutions—especially nonbanking financial entities—are lacking in China's interbank lending market, bond market, foreign exchange market, derivatives market and exchange market. Markets that require nonfinancial entities to participate have yet to be deregulated, and foreign entities are subject to more stringent restrictions.

On the other hand, as an important premise for interest rate liberalization, entities including banks should be able to not only autonomously determine deposit and loan prices, but also more freely design and innovate other sorts of products and acquire a greater pricing power. We should further improve the governance structure of commercial banks, pursue financial innovations, encourage financial institutions to develop non-deposit and non-lending businesses to take the initiative to advance liberalization of deposit and loan rates.

Without these two conditions, market-based interest rates cannot be established in real earnest for limited transactions conducted by limited entities.

Third, conditions for financial market development. Highly liquid financial markets with effective price information feedback are essential to improving the Central Bank's interest regulation system and transforming the regulatory mode. Even with sound products and entities, financial markets as money transaction venues must have a sufficient influence, without which financial market interest rates will only be limited market-based rates. In the interbank lending market, for instance, problems in market structure and mechanisms have resulted in wild volatility of interbank lending rates compared with bond repurchase rates, making them vulnerable to the shocks of single large transactions. China's bond market remains under the administration of multiple agencies and fraught with myriad problems such as separate regulatory supervision between interbank and exchange markets, inconsistent rules and standards, and insufficient product innovations. Compared with global foreign exchange markets, China's foreign exchange market features smaller volumes and less freedom of transactions and are subject to explicit and implicit policy restrictions. Hence, it is difficult for China's foreign exchange market to achieve effective foreign exchange flow and effectively support Renminbi price equilibrium. Outside the formal financial system, vibrant transactions of massive private lending capital have taken place, and numerous equity funds are setting their own pricing outside the capital market.

These phenomena require us to broaden the scale and boundary of financial markets when discussing interest rate liberalization. International experience also suggests that financial market development plays a fundamental role in interest rate liberalization: US government bond market, corporate bond market and interbank currency market were relatively sophisticated before the US phased out interest rate limits; at the inception of its interest rate liberalization reforms, Japan also vigorously expedited bond market development (Lian Ping, 2013).

Fourth, conditions for the development of financial policy mechanisms, the most important of which is that the monetary authority must withdraw from direct market interventions. Otherwise, interest rate liberalization will be a mere illusion. At the fundamental level, the monetary authority should appear in the market as a non-profit transaction entity under the optimal conditions for interest rates liberalization and achieve monetary policy goals through free transactions. On the one hand, this requires a weakening of such policy instruments as administrative window guidance, credit rationing and financial product quotas and fewer government interventions in the personnel arrangements of financial institutions; on the other hand, the Central Bank should be more independent and reinforce its non-profit attribute. For instance, it should accelerate the exit of central bank bills and reference the practice of the US Federal Reserve in submit production profits in excess of its operating expenses, among other initiatives.

In addition, interest rate liberalization reforms should also create a conducive macroeconomic environment and monetary policy environment. For instance, such reforms should further relax the upper limit on deposit rates and be carried out when market liquidity is relatively easy and in a relaxed monetary policy environment to avoid excessive pressures for deposit rates to rise. Last but not least, those conditions cannot be used as an excuse for postponing reforms.

7.4 Policy Environment for Deposit and Loan Rate Liberalization Reforms

The success of China's deposit and lending interest rate liberalization reforms hinges upon the policy environment. In this sense, policy coordination has become an important and indispensable task.

7.4.1 Policy Coordination in the International Deposit and Loan Rate Liberalization Process

In international experience, US government strategies in coping with financial disintermediation are especially worth referencing. Against the institutional background of regulated deposit rates, segregation of financial business and underdeveloped direct finance, the development of US currency market funds has allowed capital to move out from banks' balance sheets and enter financial markets for direct transactions. This has given capital seekers and suppliers an opportunity to reveal their true preferences in financial markets and engage in perfect competition, thus advancing interest rate liberalization. At the beginning of financial disintermediation, the US monetary authority had attempted various methods to attract capital from financial markets back to the banking system. Yet instead of containing the trend of disintermediation, these attempts impeded US financial innovation and modernization (Li Yang, 2008). As a result, the US fell behind Japan and Germany in terms of economic competitiveness for a while. In the early 1980s, the US monetary authority reversed its regulatory strategy amid deepening disintermediation. The most important change is that scrapping the tradition of interest rate regulation and separate financial business operations, the US monetary authority decided to follow the trend of financial innovation by deregulating, liberalizing interest rates, linking banks with financial markets, and blurring the boundary between direct and indirect finance to develop direct finance.[1]

The US interest rate liberalization process demonstrates that currency market funds appeared in the market as a financial innovation to evade interest rate regulation. When currency market funds offer much higher rates than banks' deposit rates, depositors will be lured to withdraw cash from the banks and invest the same in currency market funds. Regulators should follow the trend to relax banking sector regulation, encourage financial innovation, and allow capital to be moved out from banks' balance sheets and enter financial markets. This will allow financial institutions to compete with each other sufficiently and set the prices of financial products freely, reflecting the investment and financing preferences of both capital seekers and suppliers. In this manner, the equilibrium price of capital will be naturally determined under market mechanisms, allowing interest rate liberalization process to be completed successfully (Li Yang and Dong Yun, 2014).

More generally speaking, the following basic experience can be drawn from the policy orientation of interest rate liberalization process in various countries.

First, all countries have established the deposit insurance system while liberalizing interest rates, improved the mechanisms for preventing and defusing financial risks,

[1] Alan Greenspan's testimony at the Congress in 1997 elaborated the monetary authority's regulatory approach. He said to the effect that: "Financial modernization must undo those obsolete, meaningless and economically inefficient constraints to realize more efficient competition among banking institutions in their respective markets and fashion a more effective financial system that provides the public with better services (Financial Crisis Inquiry Commission (FCIC), 2012).

and established regulatory mechanisms for mixed operations to ease the shocks of interest rate liberalization.

Second, with changing intermediate and operational goals of monetary policy in many countries in their interest rate liberalization process, central banks shifted from direct interest rate regulation modes to indirect interest rate regulation modes, and open market operations received greater importance.

Third, developing financial markets, improving the financial ecosystem and encouraging financial innovation are essential conditions for achieving interest rate liberalization. In this process, financial regulators must strive to foster numerous and multitiered qualified entities at the microscopic level, establish a financial market system with sufficient competition, and improve the financial regulatory system.

7.4.2 Status and Problems of China's Existing Financial Policies

In this section, we identify the problems and potential improvements of China's existing financial policies adopted by the government and regulators in the ongoing interest rate liberalization process.

Interest rate liberalization has been a main task throughout China's financial development and reforms over the years. The Chinese government has followed a gradualist approach of interest rate liberalization, i.e., while exercising all-round interest rate regulation, policymakers have left gaps to introduce non-state and market-based new elements to the periphery of state economy and financial sector before taking steps to bring results of interest rate liberalization to the formal financial system and force reforms to be further deepened.

Under this policy approach, government administrative control over interest rates has significantly waned. Currently, China's currency market interest rates and loan rates have become fully deregulated. Control over deposit rates has also been gradually relaxed starting with large deposits. The rapid development of bank WMPs and Internet finance exempt from deposit and loan rate regulation have exerted pressures for deposit rate liberalization to be pushed forward. Under the gradualist reform strategy, China's interest rate liberalization has been steadily advanced under the Central Bank's overall regulation, and the reorganization of banking sector governance has prompted financial institutions to call for independent determination of capital price, and thus greatly reducing resistance to interest rate liberalization.

However, if interest rate liberalization is regarded as a process of phasing out government intervention in money transactions and allowing various entities to engage in money transactions freely to allocate resources more efficiently, the effect of China's interest rate liberalization policy is far from achieving this goal. For instance, China's interest rate liberalization in recent years has been accompanied by a rising financial sector leverage ratio, rapid risk accumulation in the financial sector, solidification of the economic structure, a lack of effective support of financial resources for the private economy and small and micro businesses, as well as a massive inflow of capital into real estate and infrastructure sectors through various channels.

Bank deposit and lending interest rates are critical factor prices with a broad and far-reaching influence. Without all-round progress of economic reforms in various areas, liberalizing deposit and loan rates will hardly achieve the goal of optimizing resource allocation, and if implemented when conditions are not ready, interest rate liberalization will bring about numerous adverse effects. Those supporting reforms should be carried out to define a clear boundary between the government and market, establish a deposit insurance system, enhance the interest rate sensitivity of borrowers, promote the development of direct financing, foster reasonable competition and exit mechanisms for financial institutions, and advance market-oriented reforms of factor prices.

7.4.3 Priorities and Approaches for Improving Relevant Policies

Policymakers must bear in mind the intrinsic attribute of interest rates when formulating supporting policies for advancing interest rate liberalization. We believe interest rates are formed through repetitive and massive transactions of financial products in financial markets. Hence, interest rate liberalization should provide a competitive mechanism to allow sufficient competitions between capital seekers and suppliers to form market-based interest rates. If financial resources are dominated by banks offering deposit and loan services, no country would be able to achieve interest rate liberalization. The reason is that banks as financing intermediaries separate capital seekers from capital suppliers, preventing them from showing investment and financing preferences and making it hard to identify the equilibrium price. As such, interest rate liberalization should start with deregulating financial product transactions instead of adjusting bank deposit and loan rates. An essential condition for interest rate liberalization is to allow capital to move out from the banks' balance sheets and enter the capital market for transactions on a mass scale. Mixed operations in the financial sector, off-balance-sheet bank capital operation and shadow banking development under the condition of risk mitigation are the only path towards the introduction of alternatives to deposits and loans and deposit and lending interest rate liberalization.

Intuitively, commercial banks should be the beneficiaries of deposit interest rate cap. Yet with the increase of off-balance-sheet bank capital and disintermediation, coupled with shocks from currency market funds such as Yu'ebao, banks welcome the removal of regulated deposit rates and are ready to participate in a more competitive market.

Hence, regulators should leave shadow banks and Internet finance a moderate space for development and at the same time expand the business scope of banks and allow mixed operations, so that the off-balance-sheet operations of bank capital and the fund investment of deposits will promote market-based interest rates.

In addition, the development of a loan alternatives market offers a useful reference for the government evaluation of loan interest rate liberalization risks, expediting loan rate liberalization reforms. Deposit alternatives may also propel China's deposit rate liberalization reforms. One option is to develop large negotiable certificates of deposit (CDs) and other deposit alternatives on commercial banks' balance sheets as a reference for assessing deposit rate liberalization risks.

After determining the basic reform approach, the next step is to identify the division of responsibilities between various government agencies for advancing interest rate liberalization reforms, which is essential to enhancing policy effectiveness. The central government needs to reduce government administrative interventions in fund allocation, tighten the budgetary constraint for local governments and SOEs, and increase their sensitivity to capital price.

Among various agencies, the Central Bank takes the most onerous reform tasks. First, international experience suggests that during interest rate liberalization reforms and within five years after their completion, small banking institutions become much more likely to go bust, and the deposit insurance system is of great importance to preventing a bank run and crisis contagion. As such, China should lose no time in creating a deposit insurance system under market mechanisms: financial institutions should participate in the deposit insurance scheme under consistent standards and contribute a percentage of their deposits as premiums. Should any participating financial institutions become insolvent, the deposit insurance institution shall be responsible to take over and indemnify against the deposit losses. While effectively protecting depositors' interests, the deposit insurance system will allow financial institutions of all sorts to fairly compete at the same level. Second, China should establish a system of monetary policy operations to guide and influence overall interest rate levels and interest rate structure, seek a more flexible, independent and effective policy instrument portfolio, and create a more effective interest rate benchmark system. Third, China should follow and assess shocks from internal and external environments to deposit and lending interest rate liberalization and try to seize the opportunity when the cost of reform is the least to reduce the adverse effects on economic and social stability.

Banking regulators should systematically, comprehensively and prudently monitor and cope with various risks emerging from interest rate liberalization reforms. In particular, banking regulators should enhance regulation, conduct risk analysis and assessment, improve financial institutions' risk management, and prepare response plans. Specifically, banking regulators should consider introducing innovative capital instruments to help the banking sector comply with the new capital management regulations and improve the loan-to-deposit ratio and intermediate business regulation. Banking regulators may consider replacing the loan-to-deposit ratio with the net stable funding ratio (NSFR) and the comprehensive liquidity analysis and review (CLAR).

Deposit and lending interest rate liberalization affects the banking sector the most, and China's financial system is dominated by the banking sector. Hence, interest rate liberalization is expected to trigger significant systemic shocks to China's financial system. Research indicates that with rising level of economic development, a country's economic development becomes less sensitive to changes in the banking sector and more sensitive to capital markets (Justin Yifu Lin, Xu Lixin, 2012). As such, securities regulatory authorities should further step up the development of multitiered capital markets, moderately lower the threshold of equity financing, strive to develop the bond market to increase the share of direct finance, encourage financial product innovation, and expand the coverage of market-based interest rates to lower interest rate liberalization risks.

For interest rates as the price system that reflects capital scarcity, the ultimate goal of interest rate reforms is to raise the operating efficiency of the real economy. Based on such considerations, government authorities in charge of development and reform should push forward integrated market-based reforms of the production factor price formation mechanism, coordinate reforms of capital price and various other factor prices, and reform the resource allocation mechanism of China's economy. Specifically, government authorities in charge of development and reform may continue to deepen market-based reforms of natural resource sectors such as water supply, electric power, coal, petroleum and natural gas, and prepare for advancing the market-based reforms of land, labor and other factor prices.

On the basis of clarifying their division of responsibilities, government agencies should also step up coordination with the following priorities: first, enhance the rule of law. The legal and judicial systems, as well as basic market disciplines, are of great significance to crisis prevention. On the one hand, banks take advantage of loopholes in the national accounting standards of certain countries to conceal their high NPL ratios; on the other hand, bankruptcy procedures for banks in developing countries are often protracted and impede the timely disposition of problem financial institutions. As such, the improvement of laws and regulations related to the bankruptcy, antimonopoly, accounting and disclosure of financial institutions requires coordination from financial regulators, the development and reform commissions and fiscal and judicial authorities. Second, China shall take the Shanghai Free-Trade Zone as an opportunity to expedite the development of a market-based interest rate system in the experimental area. Priority should be given to monitoring market-based interest rates on market-based home and foreign-currency funds on household and non-household free-trade accounts within the experimental area. Qualified institutions should be included within the scope of priority institutions for issuing large-sum negotiable certificates of deposit (CDs). When conditions are ready, regulators may consider uncapping interest rates for small-sum foreign currency deposits on corporate accounts. During the interest rate liberalization pilot reforms for the free-trade zone, we should follow the basic principle of putting finance at the service of the real economy and avoid intense interest rate volatility with adverse effects on real-economy enterprises.

(Yang Tao, Dong Yun)

References

[US] Edward S. Shaw: *Financial Deepening in Economic Development,* translated by Shao Fujun *et al.*, Shanghai Sanlian Bookstore, 1998.
[US] R. I. McKinnon: *Money and Capital in Economic Development*, translated by Lu Cong, Shanghai Sanlian Bookstore, 1998.
Fry, Maxwell J.: "Financial Development: Theories and Experience", *Oxford Review of Economic Policy,* 1989.
He Dong, Wang Honglin: "Double-Track Interest Rate System and China's Monetary Policy Implementation", *Journal of Financial Research,* Vol.12, 2011.
Hellmann, T., K. Murdock and J. Stiglitz: "Deposit Mobilization through Financial Restraint", *Paper for the Workshop of Financial Development and Economic Growth: Theory and Experiences from Developing Economies,* the University of Groeningen,7–9th, December, 1994.
Justin Yifu Lin, Xu Lixin: "Progress of Latest Research on Correlation between Financial Structure and Economic Development", *Financial Regulation Research,* Vol.3, 2012.
Kaminsky, G. and S. Schmukler: "Short-Run Pain, Long-Run Gain: The Effects of Financial Liberalization", *NBER Working Paper,* No. 9787, 2003.
Lee, I. and J. Shin: "Financial Liberalization, Crises and Economic Growth", *East Asian Bureau of Economic Research Working Paper,* No. 22030, 2008.
Li Bin: "Central Bank's Interest Rate Regulation Mechanism and Interest Rate Liberalization", *Comparative Economic & Social Systems,* Vol.1, 2014.
Li Yang, Dong Yun: "Understanding Internet Finance", *Working Paper of the Economics Department of the Chinese Academy of Social Sciences (CASS),* 2014.
Li Yang: "Disintermediation: New Challenges Facing China's Financial Reforms and Development", *Three Decades of China's Financial Reforms,* Social Sciences Academic Press (China), 2008.
Lian Ping: "Strategic Reflections on China's Interest Rate Liberalization Reforms", *Financial Regulation Research,* Vol.6, 2013.
Peng Xingyun, Dong Yun: "China's Monetary Policy and Financial Situation", appeared in *Analysis of China's Economic Outlook 2014,* Social Sciences Academic Press (China), 2014.
Ranciere, R., A. Tornell and F. Westermann: "Decomposing the Effects of Financial Liberalization: Crises vs. Growth", *Journal of Banking and Finance,* 30(12), 2006.
Romero-Avila, D.: "Liberalization of Capital Controls and Interest Rates Restrictions in the EU—15: Did it Affect Economic Growth? ", *Applied Financial Economics,* 19(20).
Stiglitz, J., and A. Weiss: "Credit Rationing in Markets with Imperfect Information", *American Economic Review,* 71(June), 1981.
US Financial Crisis Inquiry Committee: *US Financial Crisis Inquiry Report,* CITIC Press, 2012.
Wang Guosong: "Interest Rate Regulation and Liberalization in China", *Economic Research Journal,* Vol.6, 2001.
Woodford, M.: *Interest and Prices.* Princeton University Press, 2003.
Zhou Sufang, Yao Zhizhong: "Interest Rate Liberalization Theory and Practice", *Journal of World Economy,* Vol.3, 2002.

Chapter 8
Interest Rate Liberalization and China's Financial System Reforms

As noted at the Third Plenary Session of the 18th CPC Central Committee, the underlying issue of China's economic system reform is how to strike a balance between the role of the government and that of the market, let the market play the decisive role in allocating resources, improve the mechanism whereby prices are mainly determined by the market, and let the government play its functions better. From a financial perspective, we should give play to the decisive role of market mechanism in allocating various financial resources and improve the financial system in which financial product prices are primarily determined by market mechanism. This policy statement lays bare the drawbacks of China's financial system and financial markets and identifies the directions and priorities of financial reforms, development and innovation.

While recognizing China's great achievements in financial development over the past decades, we should also be mindful of the grave drawback that China's financial system is increasingly detached from the real economy. Over the years, most financial reforms discussed by financial regulators and the public were individual reforms, including Renminbi deposit and loan rate liberalization reforms, the deposit insurance system, the business transition of commercial banks, asset securitization, capital market development, capital account openness, Renminbi exchange rate reform, among others. Those discussions made no mention of financial system reform from a national economic perspective. China's financial system that started to develop in the late 1970s is an externally embedded financial system for the real economy. It has deprived the real-economy sector of most financial powers, forming an external self-circulating system absorbing resources from the real-economy sector. The US financial crisis has prompted calls for putting finance at the service of the real economy. Yet China's externally embedded financial system is becoming even more detached from the real economy. China's economy is entering a new era. The establishment of China (Shanghai) Pilot Free-Trade Zone has unveiled a new stage of reform and opening up. At this critical juncture, it has become inevitable for China

G. Wang, *A Study on Interest Rate Liberalization in China*, Research Series on the Chinese Dream and China's Development Path,
https://doi.org/10.1007/978-981-97-3644-7_8

to reform the externally embedded financial system, bring finance at the service of the real economy, and create an endogenous financial system.

8.1 Financial System is Endogenous to the Real Economy

The following statement appears in any *Macroeconomics* textbook: In a two-sector model, the household sector is the capital surplus sector, and the industrial sector is the capital deficit sector. Capital flow from the household sector to the industrial sector is essential to supporting real-economy enterprises to create wealth and maintain economic operation. Hence, financial activities take place between the household sector as capital supplier and the industrial sector as capital seeker in economic operations. Here, three questions need to be specified: the first question is how household sector funds are ploughed into the industrial sector, or in other words, how the industrial sector obtains funds from the household sector? Initially, the household sector invested funds in the industrial sector primarily through equity investment and lending; with the development of financial relations, the household sector started to provide funds for the industrial sector through purchase of bonds, stocks and other securities; then, with the expansion of those financial activities and the establishment of commercial banks and other financial institutions, the household sector started to provide funds for the industrial sector through such pathways as deposits while the above-mentioned conduits continued to function. Obviously, the household sector and the industrial sector originally had financial powers.

The second question is whether the capital supply and demand relationship exists in the industrial sector? The relationship of credit-based commercial exchanges exists among real-economy enterprises. In a business transaction, either a payment is made before the ordered goods are delivered or the other way around due to the separation of time and space. This transaction process is facilitated with the invention of financial products such as promissory notes, post-dated cheques and bills of exchange. Since some large equipment purchased by industrial enterprises are not continuously in use 24/7 while other industrial enterprises may need such equipment for processing components on an ad hoc basis, equipment leasing naturally occurs between industrial enterprises. As this phenomenon becomes more common, financial leasing business among industrial enterprises takes shape. Since some industrial enterprises have idle funds while other downstream or upstream enterprises are in a shortage of funds, those industrial enterprises started to develop lending relations based on commercial credit for mutual benefit. In addition, industrial enterprises also started to carry out capital investment, acquisition through debt, acquisition through equity and project financing amid market development. This suggests that industrial enterprises originally had sufficient powers for financial operation. The third question is whether there is any backflow of funds from the industrial sector to the household sector? While households invest in industrial enterprises in the form of equity, industrial enterprises reward households with investment return; while households purchase bonds of industrial enterprises, which repay bonds in principal and interest to households. These phenomena suggest that both industrial enterprises and households are key elements of the real-economy sector with financial powers and interactions that derive from the real economy and are indispensable to real-economy operations, meanwhile, such financial powers and interactions are extended through continuous financial innovations and become increasingly complex and specific.

Finance is the sum of equity transactions to obtain future proceeds from assets.[1] In economic operation, assets and their proceeds all stem from the real economy. Before industrial enterprises sell financial products such as stocks and bonds to households, they are not in direct possession of the corresponding funds or assets of those financial products. By selling those financial products, industrial enterprises obtain funds and assets for business operation. That is to say, industrial enterprises sell future return on assets. In such transactions, households purchase the rights of future return on those funds (assets) in real-economy enterprises' business operations. Similarly, the transactions of stocks, bonds and other financial products in the secondary market are also intended to claim the future return on assets. Since household and real-economy investments are linked to the future return on assets, uncertainties (risks) are inevitable. Real-economy enterprises' business performance also varies. While some generate return on assets, others break even, and still others operate at a loss. Risk appetites vary considerably in the household sector. Although households seek high return when making a financial investment, many are risk-tolerant and accept losses. On the whole, the complex and multi-tiered structure of household investment risk appetites roughly matches the diversity of risks in the real-economy sector, and such compatibility is conducive to economic operation and development.

With the increasing volume, product categories and modes of financial transactions in the real-economy sector in Western countries, individual enterprises found it hard to maintain those transactions as part of their day-to-day operations, making it natural for those financial businesses to be separated as professional financial institutions. The professionalization of financial services occurred as early as in the first half of the nineteenth century. The following century witnessed rapid development of financial products, markets and institutions, and despite frequent economic and financial crises, the government still acted as a night watchman. The Great Depression of the 1930s has taught the world a costly lesson, prompting countries to introduce financial regulation for the first time in economic history. Since then, a complete financial system has gradually taken shape, consisting of financial rules, financial regulation, financial products, financial markets and financial institutions. Notably, the real-economy sector (non-financial enterprises and households) should not be deprived of their financial powers in the formation of the financial system. The household sector still has sufficient financial product options for investing consumption surplus funds; real-economy enterprises also retain a sufficient power of electing to issue bonds, borrow funds, issue shares, acquire financial leasing and trust funds, and create investment funds. Moreover, the real-economy sector's financial powers

[1] See Wang Guogang's "A Brief Discussion of the Relationship among Money, Finance and Capital", *Chinese Review of Financial Studies*, Vol.2, 2011.

are a fundamental part of a complete financial system to function as an indispensable sector of the economy.

One basic principle has been demonstrated by both theory and practice: finance is endogenous to the real-economy sector, and financial development is underpinned by real-economy development at the fundamental level. The financial powers of the real-economy sector are a fundamental component of the financial system. In this sense, finance is rooted in the real economy. Without the real economy, finance will become "water without a source, or a tree without roots." A lesson from the US financial crisis is that the financial system had detached from the real-economy sector and formed an independent self-serving and self-circulating system. Once finance is detached from the real economy, financial bubbles become inevitable.

8.2 Causes and Characteristics of China's Externally Embedded Financial System

In the three-decade planned economy era, there was no financial activity in China, not to mention financial system. Back then, administrative and fiscal mechanisms dominated almost all activities in the economy. In the planned economy, financial linkages between households and real-economy enterprises were severed by state intervention, such as the fiscal allocation of funds to state-owned enterprises, state planning of supply and distribution, production according to planned quotas, state-prescribed employee compensation, submission of total profits to the state and state coverage of enterprise losses. Under such conditions, banks were established like fiscal cashiers, and financial institutions such as securities, trust, investment fund and financial leasing companies were non-existent, not to mention financial regulators. These institutional arrangements had deprived China of the fundamental conditions for financial activities and the financial system. Under such an economic pattern, on the one hand, industrial enterprises received funds supplied primarily by the government instead of from the household sector, and were prohibited from such financial activities as equity investment and capital lending. Their operating profits were entirely submitted to public finance. No financial interactions existed between households and real-economy enterprises. On the other hand, real-economy enterprises lacked the most fundamental economic rights, not to mention financial rights. Hence, the basic conditions for financial mechanisms to exist and develop were non-existent.

China's financial system started to develop in the late 1970s at the beginning of reform and opening up. Back then, China chose to introduce an externally embedded financial system out of the five considerations: first, in the planned economy where administrative mechanisms held sway in economic operations, real-economy enterprises and households had neither financial powers nor financial awareness. Even the word "finance" was unheard of. A striking example is that in the mid-1980s, running a business on debt was widely publicized and encouraged as a groundbreaking innovation dubbed as "borrow a hen to lay eggs", and running a business on debt fully on debt was wide promoted.

Second, as a legacy of the review and approval system under the planned economy, the establishment of financial institutions, the creation of financial products and the amount of financial transactions (and even customers of financial institutions) were subject to strict administrative review and approval. In the financial sector, all activities continued to be subject to administrative review and approval (such review and approval tended to be more detailed after the late 1990s). The Industrial and Commercial Bank of China (ICBC), the Agricultural Bank of China (ABC), the Bank of China (BOC) and the China Construction Bank (CCB) were established as specialized banks in 1984, but they still undertook government-assigned projects.

Third, while China's reformers created financial institutions following the example of developed countries with the expectation to narrow the gaps with those countries, they did not recognize the financial powers bestowed to the real economy as they were less visible.

Fourth, before the mid-1990s, China's reformers were still discussing the organizational system of SOE reform and the transition from permanent to contract employment system. Companies "responsible for their own profits and losses and seeking self-development" were in their nascent stage, and the enterprise financial system underpinned by the accounting statement was shifting to one with the balance sheet at the heart. Without the concept and system of assets and liabilities, enterprises were not able to issue such financial products as stocks and bonds as the basis for acquiring financial power.

Fifth, before 1998, bank credit still had to follow state planning and was characterized by specific administrative preferences in terms of the amount and recipients of credit supply. Under state planning and rules, stocks and bonds could only be underwritten by financial institutions. Real-economy enterprises and households still lacks the basic financial product options. Over the past three decades of reform and opening up, China has attempted to develop finance from outside the real economy, giving rise to what we call an "externally embedded" financial system, which has the following eight characteristics.

1. The real-economy sector (including non-financial corporations and household) almost had no financial product options. Households barely had any alternative to invest their consumption surplus funds other than depositing them in banks, which meant that those funds could not reach real-economy enterprises without the intermediation of financial institutions, and that real-economy enterprises had few conduits other than loans to acquire funds from the financial market. Various rights to financial activities have become the exclusive rights of financial institutions. Without the permission of financial institutions and regulators, real-economy enterprises would be more or less cut off from the supply of household sector funds.
2. China's institutional framework offers no space for financial activities to be carried out within the real economy. Real-economy enterprises faced various

hurdles in accessing financial services, ranging from the prohibition of borrowing funds at the beginning of reform to barriers to issuing commercial bills for short-term financing and the ban on financial leasing among real-economy enterprises. A real-economy enterprise would breach the law and face penalties if it directly engages in any of the above-mentioned financial activities.

3. Real-economy enterprises are not entitled to independently issue securities, which must be approved by financial regulators and underwritten by financial institutions. Those financial institutions underwriting securities not only determine whether a real-economy enterprise has the right to issue securities, but also wield considerable influence in the pricing of securities.
4. Direct financial instruments have turned into indirect financial instruments. Corporate bonds are a primary direct financial instrument issued by real-economy enterprises to households for the purpose of accessing household funds. In China, however, corporate bonds have turned into an indirect financial instrument: almost all corporate bonds issued by real-economy enterprises are purchased by commercial banks and other financial institutions with the consumption surplus funds from urban and rural households in the form of savings deposits.
5. China's commercial banks and other financial institutions see deposits as their fundamental strength. They vied to attract deposits as a decisive business in maintaining and supercharging their business operations. The financial operations of commercial banks and other financial institutions are mainly subject to the amount of available funds and the sustainability of fund supply. After the mid-1990s, the consumption surplus funds of urban and rural households have become a major source of capital for commercial banks and other financial institutions and a key aspect of their competition strategy.
6. Financial markets—especially the currency market—have largely become markets of financial transactions among financial institutions themselves, with few direct ties with the real-economy sector. The interbank market is China's primary currency market, in which most players are financial institutions. Naturally, transactions in the interbank market are also dominated by financial institutions.
7. Financial institutions and financial regulators have formed an interdependent system, restricting the real-economy sector's claims on financial powers under various excuses such as financial stability, risk control, professionalism and the public nature of financial services. In the process of establishing financial systems, financial regulators usually need to consult financial institutions for their opinions but seldom ask real-economy enterprises for feedbacks. As a result, those financial systems are more reflective of the financial institutions' interests, ignoring requests from real-economy enterprises.
8. Although financial product innovations stem from demand from the real-economy sector, they are largely motivated by financial institutions' business development and profit-seeking considerations.

As can be seen from the above characteristics, China's financial system is a structure between real-economy enterprises and urban and rural households that is embedded into the real economy under administrative mechanisms. While absorbing consumption surplus funds from urban and rural households at very low prices in the form of savings deposits, China's financial system profiteers from expensive loans to real-economy enterprises. Such financial system that severs direct financial ties between households and real-economy enterprises is essentially different from an endogenous financial system.

This externally embedded financial system has played a positive role in China's development in the reform era over the past more than three decades. First, it supplied much-needed capital for China's economic growth and facilitated the development of financial products and markets through the financial intermediation mechanisms of commercial banks, including lending and other financial activities. Despite an extreme shortage of fund at the beginning of the reform era, China's economy has avoided a poverty trap. Without a doubt, China's externally embedded financial system has made positive contributions to the country's economic development over the past more than three decades. Second, it has leveraged administrative mechanisms to stabilize the financial order, avoided financial turbulence amid rapid economic development, effectively withstood the shocks of the Asian Financial Crisis and the global financial crisis that first erupted in the US, and prevented losses that financial turbulence would otherwise incur to capital suppliers (primarily household) and capital seekers (primarily real-economy enterprises). Third, it has bought time and space for establishing a financial system with Chinese characteristics, allowing China to avoid repeating the twists and turns of developed countries in creating their financial systems in over two centuries and reducing the otherwise tremendous costs of establishing a financial system in a chaotic market with disorderly competition. Fourth, it has demonstrated the fundamental role of market mechanism in allocating financial resources through competitions among financial institutions of all sorts, creating conditions for China's further financial reforms and development. Fifth, it has explored a new path for developing countries to escape financial repression, advance financial deepening, and break through the old path of Western countries in establishing their financial systems, offering a new approach for financial development in developing countries and regions.

8.3 Drawbacks of the Externally Embedded Financial System

Just like anything in the world has pros and cons, the externally embedded financial system also has its intrinsic drawbacks in the national economic system. The intrinsic drawbacks of China's externally embedded financial system are particularly evident in the context of China's efforts to deepen reforms, give play to the decisive role of market mechanism in allocating resources, expedite economic restructuring, and enhance economic sustainability and its overall national strength—particularly against the backdrop of China's implementation of an open economic strategy, proactive integration into the global economy and increasing openness of financial system. These drawbacks can be reflected in the following aspects:

First, the otherwise integrated economic activities are divided into unrelated sectoral activities with fragmented resources. Such fragmentation has not only taken a toll on the real-economy sector's efficiency and competitiveness, but also exposed the financial system to additional risks.

Consumer finance is endogenous to shopping activities. By integrating cash flow, logistics flow and customer information flow, commercial institutions bring shopping conveniences to consumers and financial and customer information to merchants. With such information, merchants may become more competitive and adjust their business structure. In China, however, bank cards remain the sole vehicle for consumer finance. While banks manage cash flow and commercial institutions are responsible for logistics flow, customers' information is left in no one's hands. On the one hand, when applying for a loan to expand business, merchants are required to provide adequate collaterals to the banks and accept exorbitant interest rates, and the process is protracted and inconvenient; on the other hand, without access to customer information, merchants are unable to provide customized services and maintain their customer base. Lack of customer information restricts competition among merchants to provide better services. Except for offering price discounts, merchants could do little to improve service quality and homogeneous business strategies have a severe impact on the development of multi-tiered commercial markets.

Supply chain finance is endogenous to correlated real-economy enterprises. Supply chain finance means that real-economy enterprises at the core of (or in the central position) in the supply chain may provide cash and other financial support for downstream and upstream enterprises according to the needs for the industry's development. Such cash or other financial support is underpinned by a host of factors, including goods supply, commercial credibility, information sharing, technical support and market exploration, and represents an important direction in the development of modern finance. In China, however, supply chain finance has become a conduit for commercial banks to issue loans to real-economy enterprises in the supply chain or an option for pivotal supply chain enterprises to entrust their funds to commercial banks that offer loans to borrowers on their behalf. In issuing such loans, commercial banks only care about the security of principal and interest and pay little attention to—and are not able to assess—how their lending decisions contribute to supply chain robustness and efficiency. Unable to supply funds, core supply chain enterprises have lost the cohesive powers to enhance goods supply, business credibility, information sharing, technical support and market exploration and cannot effectively coordinate supply chain relations. In this manner, the chain of financial relations has been turned into "point-to-point" financial services offered by commercial banks.

Second, the dominance of deposit and loan business has led to tensions and inefficiencies in financial resource allocation, creating financial barriers to the development of the real-economy sector.

Efficiency in financial resource allocation is not measured by whether financial institutions generate higher revenues and profits. Instead, financial resource allocation becomes more efficient when real-economy enterprises access finance at a lower cost. Under the externally embedded financial system, access to finance is restricted and expensive for most real-economy enterprises. On the one hand, due to the lack of financial product options, large and medium-sized enterprises face loan rates above corporate bond interest rates in the same period, i.e., access to finance is expensive. As large and medium-sized enterprises take the lion's share of loans, access to finance is both restricted and costly for small and micro businesses. The high cost of capital has raised the bar for many investment and business activities to be carried out in the real-economy sector, hampering the efficiency of resource allocation. On the other hand, commercial banks and other financial institutions have reaped hefty profits. On the other hand, as China took steps to open up its financial sector as part of its WTO commitments, China's commercial banks have seen a surge in their after-tax profits over the past decade, which is in sharp contrast to tepid profit growth of real-economy enterprises. Some media agencies have ascribed "banking sector profiteering" to monopoly. It should be recognized that institutional innovation and bank personnel's hard work after China's banking sector reform have contributed to the rapid growth in profits of the banking sector. Yet another key factor is the lack of financial options for real-economy enterprises that has allowed commercial banks to profit from the deposit and lending interest rate spread. The guaranteed return from deposit and interest rate spread has been a key driver of commercial banks and other financial institutions' scramble to attract deposits. In addition, deposit interest rates remained low for urban and rural households as depositors. With little alternative to depositing their savings in banks, urban and rural households have piled up their savings deposits despite low interest rates and shared little in the huge dividends paid by real-economy enterprises to the financial system.

As long as deposit and loan business remains dominant financial services in China, it is almost impossible to transform China's financial industry pattern where indirect finance holds sway. The development of direct finance requires necessary financial powers to be granted to real-economy enterprises, which is contradictory with the vested powers of financial institutions and regulators. As a result, the policy proposal tabled 15 years ago to vigorously develop direct finance and suppress the share of indirect finance has never been implemented in real earnest, leaving commercial banks free from worries about financial disintermediation. Indirect finance still accounts for a significant share in China's financial system. Funds accessed by real-economy enterprises through direct finance still represent a major share of aggregate financing to the real economy. Meanwhile, the impulse to establish new commercial banks is increasing.

Third, the mismatch of funds between the real-economy sector and the financial sector intensified. In their daily operations and fixed-asset investment, real-economy enterprises require funds of different nature, maturities and liquidity. Essentially, the structural financial assets should be compatible with these requirements. In China's practice, however, the fund and financial product structure of the financial sector differs greatly from these requirements, giving rise to a serious mismatch.

In China, the funding mismatch includes the following five aspects: (i) mismatch of entities: the allocation of financial resources that should otherwise take place between households and real-economy enterprises turns out to occur between households and commercial banks and between commercial banks and real-economy enterprises; (ii) mismatch of fund nature, i.e., mismatch between capital funds and debt funds; (iii) maturity mismatch, i.e., mismatch between short-term and long-term funds; (iv) product mismatch, i.e., mismatch between direct financial instruments such as bonds and indirect financial instruments like deposits and loans; (v) market structure mismatch, i.e., mismatch between capital market and currency market transaction functions. These types of mismatch are explained in detail as follows:

First, mismatch of entities: originally in economic and financial operations, funding allocation took place between urban and rural households and real-economy enterprises. Numerous urban and rural households have demonstrated a complex and diverse structure of risk appetites, which is compatible with the complex and diverse risk profiles arising from the business performance of real-economy enterprises. This is a process of composite selection through the competition mechanism of financial markets. In China's financial system, however, the entities of funding allocation have turned into financial institutions such as commercial banks. While obtaining funds from depositors at the lowest possible interest rates, these financial institutions lend funds to real-economy enterprises at the most exorbitant interest rates possible (irrespective of the length of financial chain) to seek sellers' monopolistic return. The market function of financial resource allocation is thus usurped by commercial banks and other financial institutions, which have become expanding intermediaries embedded between capital suppliers and capital seekers. Their interventions have led to incessant and serious mismatches between entities in funding allocation.

Second, mismatch of funding nature: in economic and financial operations, funds can be roughly divided into capital funds and debt funds. Among them, capital funds are the basic condition for the assumption of debt funds and the timely repayment of debt as the basis for maintaining market credibility and order. In China's economic and financial operations, however, capital funds are extremely difficult to form. The amount of capital funds formed with the profits and depreciation allowance, stock-market financing, equity fund investment and foreign investment each year falls far below the amount of capital funds required for fixed-asset investments each year according to the prescribed ratio of the capital fund system. On the one hand, this has led to a serious shortfall of capital funds to support the business operations of real-economy enterprises, forcing them into the dilemma of seeking short-term debt funds from bank credit. On the other hand, China's economic and financial operations have thus been accompanied by an expansion of debt funds with lengthening and increasingly complex debt chains, giving rise to the accumulation of various operational risks.

In China's economic and financial operations there has been mismatch between capital funds and debt funds for a long time, typically evidenced by a serious shortfall of capital funds. In 2013, the absolute amount of China's fixed asset investments stood at 48 trillion yuan (and continued to grow at a rate above 17%). At the 30% capital ratio of fixed asset investment, these fixed asset investments should be supported by capital funds worth close to 17 trillion yuan. Even assuming that the annual after-tax profits of real-economy enterprises (around 5 trillion yuan) were invested as capital funds into fixed asset investment, together with stock-market financing, investment with depreciation allowance funds, foreign investment and fiscal investment, the annual shortfall of capital funds for fixed asset investment would amount to 7 trillion yuan or so. This shortfall is not particularly alarming if it is limited to a specific year. Yet the severe shortfall of capital funds has persisted for more than two decades with a cumulative amount in excess of tens of trillions of yuan. In addition to their chronically high debt-to-assets ratios, many real-economy enterprises have invested bank credit funds in their registered capital. This shortfall of capital funds is a key reason behind the lack of long-term assets underpinning China's economic operations.

Instead of the shortfall of consumption surplus funds in the household sector, the dearth of capital funds stemmed from the fact that commercial banks absorbed the vast majority of those funds in the form of deposits and issued loans to borrowers. Since the loan conduit only generates debt funds, the household consumption surplus funds thus entered real-economy enterprises in the form of debt capital. A manifestation of capital fund shortfall is the maturity mismatch between deposits and loans. In terms of maturity structure, demand deposits and time deposits each account for about 50% of depository funds absorbed by commercial banks in China, but short-term loans only account for around 40% while mid-and long-term loans make up about 60%. In addition, many short-term loans were used as long-term loans. Loans are commercial banks' risk assets. The longer the loan maturity, the greater the risks. For this reason, commercial banks in major developed countries seldom issue mid-and long-term loans. Since real-economy enterprises in China are deprived of their financial powers and unable to acquire long-term operating funds directly from financial markets, they have little choice but to use bank loans in fixed asset investment. As commercial banks issue mid-and long-term loans in large amounts, the scarcity of short-term capital became more acute, culminating in the "June 20" banking liquidity crisis of 2013.

Third, maturity mismatch: bank credit is essentially short-term debt capital (although "mid-and long-term loans" account also exists in the lending business of China's commercial banks and other financial institutions, such funds are issued according to the progress of investment projects). For risk-averse financial institutions including commercial banks, the longer loan maturity, the greater the risks are. The preference to issue short-term credit capital is contradictory with long-term investment projects. The "money shortage" in China's interbank lending market on June 20, 2013, the fight among banks to attract deposits after November 20, 2013 and the interest rate spike that occurred after January 10, 2014 all stemmed from a fund maturity mismatch. Such a fund maturity mismatch has led to a strange phenomenon of "easy monetary policy, money shortage, and high interest rates."

Fourth, product mismatch: in geometry, the shortest distance between two points is a straight line; in finance, this is reflected in the lowest financial transaction cost of direct finance. The financial system should, therefore, be dominated by direct financial products and supplemented by indirect financial products. Nevertheless, in China's financial system, the amount of direct financial products such as corporate bonds is disproportionate and distorted compared with indirect financial products such as deposits and loans of financial institutions including commercial banks. As shown in Table 8.1, real-economy enterprises only held 15.218 billion yuan out of the total balance of bonds worth 25,910.849 billion yuan, and urban and rural households only held 486.642 billion yuan. The rest 95% were held by financial institutions. In economic and financial operations, financial institutions are not capital suppliers. They use "various deposits" of households and real-economy enterprises to purchase bonds. In this manner, bonds have morphed from direct financial instruments into indirect ones, i.e., transforming from alternatives into supplements to savings and deposits (this explains why the rapid increase in China's bond issuance over the past decade posed little challenge to financial institutions including commercial banks).

Fifth, market mismatch. Financial markets can be divided into currency market and capital market. In international financial markets, capital market transaction volume is far greater than currency market transaction volume. In China, financial markets include the interbank market and the stock exchange market. Transactions in short-term financial products (equivalent to currency market transactions) in the interbank market far exceed stock exchange market transactions. Meanwhile, participants in the interbank market can only be financial institutions. For these reasons, the interbank market has become a market for financial institutions to trade financial products and raise short-term funds among themselves with few direct ties with real-economy enterprises and urban and rural households.

These fund mismatches have intensified financial institutional tensions accumulated over the years. Subject to institutional constraint, a swathe of variant business modes have derived from commercial banks and other financial institutions' on-balance-sheet businesses, including bank-trust cooperation, bank-securities cooperation, bank-insurance cooperation and bank wealth management products (WMPs).

Table 8.1 Structure of China's Bond Holders, 2012–2013 (Currency unit: 100 million yuan)

Item	Balance in 2013	Growth in 2013	Balance in 2012
Special settlement members	17,005.67	−12.61	17,018.27
Commercial banks	166,818.11	9176.33	157,641.78
Including: Nationwide commercial banks	137,781.97	5400.28	132,381.69
Credit cooperatives	5942.12	655.10	5287.02
Non-bank financial institutions	752.08	−50.74	802.82
Securities companies	1586.77	−3.03	1589.80
Insurance companies	23,229.19	1131.94	22,097.25
Investment fund companies	26,758.20	3114.38	23,643.82
Non-financial institutions	152.18	−126.96	279.14
Individual investors	4866.42	1830.29	3036.13
Stock exchanges	8855.82	4253.24	4602.59
Others	3141.93	1571.44	1570.50
Total	259,108.49	21,539.38	237,569.11

Source the official website of China Central Depository & Clearing Co., Ltd. (CCDC)

No matter how the financial chain is lengthened and financial institutions' performance improves, real-economy enterprises have seen their financing costs continue to rise, and the dilemma for China's finance and real economy deepens.

Fourth, the currency market has become a market of financial transactions among financial institutions themselves, with few direct ties with the real-economy sector.

The interbank market is the dominant component of China's currency market. On the one hand, entities permitted to trade in the interbank market include state-controlled commercial banks, other commercial banks, other financial institutions and foreign-funded commercial banks, excluding real-economy enterprises and households. Hence, the interbank market is the venue for transactions of short-term funds and short-term financial products among financial institutions. In transactions, state-controlled commercial banks are major capital providers, and other commercial banks and financial institutions are mainly capital receivers. On the other hand, products in the interbank market primarily include interbank lending, bond spot trading, bond repurchase and bills. In 2012, the transaction volume in the interbank market reached 295.2 trillion yuan, including that of bills worth only 31.6 trillion yuan, or 10% of the total transaction volume. Bills directly related to the short-term funds of real-economy enterprises only accounted for a tiny proportion of currency market transactions.

In 2013, China further expanded the scope of asset securitization pilot program. Judging by the asset securitization of the China Construction Bank (CCB) and the China Development Bank in 2005, however, what happened was that asset securities issued by one bank were purchased by other banks. If this situation continues, asset securitization will be a game between financial institutions including commercial banks, causing the financial system to be further detached from the real economy.

Fifth, progress in various financial reforms has stalled: these reforms either scratched the surface or stayed on paper.

Monetary policy reform has so far made slow progress. Over the past decade, China's administrative regulation of deposit and loan benchmark rates and the amount of new loans to be issued has contributed to financial stability at the expense of keeping the financial system independent from the real economy.

With the tremendous amount of deposits accounting for a significant share of aggregate financial products and representing the most fundamental business for commercial banks in China, the deposit insurance system, once implemented, is likely to cause deposits to be concentrated at large commercial banks, leaving small commercial banks and small deposit and loan financial institutions (such as rural credit cooperatives) cash strapped with serious ripple effects on the financial system as a whole. For this reason, the introduction of the deposit insurance system has been repeatedly delayed.

The formation of deposit and lending interest rates following market mechanisms is a key element of interest rate liberalization. To date, however, China's interest rate reforms have been confined to the administrative interventions to expand the floating band of deposit and lending interest rates, neither failing to induce adjustment in the asset structure, business transition and change of profit model of commercial banks and other financial institutions, nor granting more financial options to urban and rural households and real-economy enterprises.

China's commercial banks vowed to embark upon business transition over a decade ago, but judging by their balance sheets, "various deposits" remain their biggest source of funds and represent a higher share than before. In the asset portfolio, "various loans" still represent the most important use of funds, and despite a slight decrease in the share of loans, there is little change in the real proportion if the amount of bonds mutually held by commercial banks is included. Limited change in debt structure and asset structure reflects that commercial banks' business transition has stayed on the surface and hardly made substantive progress.

Progress has yet to be made in opening the financial account as part of the capital account. Opening the financial account is not just an issue of currency convertibility. There should be sufficient financial products available for international financial operators (including institutions and individuals) to make investments in order to bring a backflow of overseas Renminbi to China and integrate domestic financial markets with international financial markets. The functions of these financial products cannot be fulfilled by Renminbi deposits and loans or undertaken by the financial system underpinned by financial institutions.

China's externally embedded financial system is plagued with many drawbacks, showing that it must be reformed. Yet the reform is by no means easy. Any misstep is likely to cause a serious financial turmoil or even crisis. Therefore, the reform must be carried out with great caution.

8.4 Intrinsic Implications of Finance's Return to the Real Economy

In pushing finance back to the real economy, China does not have to reinvent the wheel, i.e., China's financial system development does not have to repeat the path that has been taken for over two centuries for Western countries to complete since the nineteenth century. Besides, repeating this process is impossible from a historical or realistic perspective. Yet this does not mean that nothing can be done to change the situation and China's financial system has to continue its old path. What "return" means here is to expand the financial options of real-economy enterprises and urban and rural households in the real-economy sector, i.e., to return the financial powers that originally belonged to real-economy enterprises and urban and rural households back to the real economy sector and advance the development of endogenous finance.

There are two pathways for finance to be endogenous to the real-economy sector. The first pathway is through financial institutions, i.e., financial institutions specialized in financial business activities become an independent sector amid the real-economy's development; the second pathway is through financial markets, i.e., real-economy enterprises and households are allowed to directly enter financial markets for issuing and trading various financial products in their own names. Under China's current financial systemic and institutional mechanisms, the extent to which finance is "brought back" to the real economy is determined by how much real-economy enterprises and urban and rural households are permitted to enter financial markets directly for issuing and trading relevant financial products in their respective own names. It is not about how many financial institutions are established by real-economy enterprises. The intrinsic logic is that, on the one hand, under the condition that the issuance and transactions of financial products are basically monopolized by financial institutions, even if real-economy enterprises establish financial institutions, those financial institutions will only continue to follow the business trajectory of existing financial institutions and thus cannot increase the financial options of real-economy enterprises; meanwhile, since not all real-economy enterprises are able to establish financial institutions (in other words, very few real-economy enterprises have the resources to invest in creating financial institutions), those real-economy enterprises unable to set up financial institutions remain deprived of financial options. On the other hand, no matter how real-economy enterprises establish financial institutions, they cannot expand urban and rural households' financial options, i.e., it cannot solve the problem about how capital suppliers invest their consumption surplus funds into real-economy enterprises through financial markets. In this sense, the crux of the problem is how to allow real-economy enterprises and urban and rural households to directly enter financial markets.

In a market of perfect competition, price is determined by neither the seller nor the buyer but through two-way competition between buyers and sellers. A question worth considering is which entities in the financial system are competing with commercial banks and other financial institutions? Are they securities companies, trust companies, insurance companies, asset management companies or other financial institutions? The simple answer is no. These financial institutions need to absorb funds not only from the real-economy sector—such as equity investment funds, trust plan funds and insurance policy funds, but also from other financial institutions such as commercial banks—such as loans, debt-issuing funds and shadow banking funds. In the deposit and loan market and even the financial system as a whole, the real competitors to commercial banks and other financial institutions are real-economy enterprises and urban and rural households of the real-economy sector. On the one hand, provided that the household sector has the powers to use consumption surplus funds in financial operations, each household or resident will, at their own discretion, invest their cash in stocks, bonds, funds or other financial products, or deposit their savings in banks. At low deposit interest rates, commercial banks and other financial institutions will lose a huge amount of depository funds, forcing them to determine deposit interest rates at their competitive price level of financial markets. On the other hand, real-economy enterprises may raise funds by independently issuing bonds, stocks and other financial products, or by applying for a loan from the bank. Yet when commercial banks and other financial institutions lend to real-economy enterprises at interest rates above market price, they will face the risk of running short of borrowers. This forces them to price their loans at competitive price levels of financial markets. When the real-economy sector is in possession of financial powers, therefore, the price system of financial products tends to improve amid competition.

To bring the real-economy sector back to financial markets, we must deepen our understanding about the market risk attributes of primary financial products. In financial operations, primary risk products include bonds, stocks, deposits and loans, from which most other financial products are derived. Bonds and stocks are standardized financial products, whose issuance and transactions occur in the open market. Their price tendencies are restrained by publicly disclosed information and investors voting with their feet, and their risks are shared among investors. Deposits and loans are non-standardized financial products and normally cannot be continuously traded, and such information as the volume, direction and effect of their fund flows is not disclosed with risks primarily borne by financial institutions such as commercial banks. Since investors that hold bonds and stocks include real-economy enterprises, urban and rural households and relevant financial institutions, corresponding risks are scattered among and taken by among commercial banks and other financial institutions, which assume most financial risks of deposits and loans. Also, risk scattering is a key principle of financial operation. From the perspective of assumption of financial risk, a logical institutional arrangement is to develop financial products such as bonds and stocks with great efforts while putting a brake on the expansion of such financial products as deposits and loans. The externally embedded financial system, however, is opposite to the above-mentioned portfolio of diverse financial products. Its institutional arrangement is based on the logic that the possession of bonds, stocks and other financial products by numerous real-economy enterprises and urban and rural households would make it harder for the government to exercise administrative control; on the contrary, such administrative interventions would be much easier if real-economy enterprises and households put their cash in commercial banks and other financial institutions under the deposit and loan mechanism. In this sense, "bringing finance back to the real economy" essentially requires straightening out the government-market relationship to give play to the fundamental role of market mechanisms in allocating financial resources. Hence, this task is an essential issue to be addressed in China's financial reforms.

Reform involves readjustment of institutional systems and vested interests. Aside from differences of understanding, other barriers include differences in preferences, path dependence and habitual forces. From the perspective of financial reforms, expanding the real economy's financial options will inevitably create fundamental shocks to the existing financial system with a severe impact on China's financial operation and regulation modes underpinned by commercial banks' deposit and loan business, and substantially promote the fundamental shift from the externally embedded financial system to an endogenous one. Hence, it is arduous and complicated process. The purpose of this reform is to overcome the drawbacks of the externally embedded financial system and create a new mode of development of China's sound and sustainable financial system. In this sense, the process of "bringing finance back to the real economy" is a process re-creating China's financial system.

8.5 Financial System Reform with Corporate Bonds as Entry Point

Judging by their objectives, financial reforms can be divided into piecemeal reforms and systemic reforms. Since the start of the twenty-first century, a series of piecemeal reforms has been enacted, including Renminbi deposit and lending interest rate liberalization reforms, the establishment of the deposit insurance system, the business model transformation of commercial banks, asset securitization, accelerated development of capital markets, increasing capital account openness and Renminbi exchange rate reforms. Yet each of these reforms targeted one aspect or another of the financial system, instead of the institutional infrastructure of the system itself. One striking example is that Renminbi exchange rate reform, which does not lead directly to institutional reforms to the monetary policy regulation mechanism, Renminbi interest rates, business model transformation of commercial banks, financial market structure and financial product innovations. Another striking example is that no substantive change has occurred in the direct regulation mechanism of China's monetary policy and business modes of commercial banks despite the launch of Renminbi interest rate liberalization reforms in 1996 and the PBoC's adjustments of Renminbi deposit and loan benchmark rates to expand the floating band of deposit and lending interest rates since June 2012. These reforms have shown little correlated effect. Compared with individual reforms, it is more complex and challenging to reform the financial system. With commercial banks still comprising a dominant part of China's financial system and the fact that the proportion of deposit and loan financial products to the total product products is considerably higher than the sum of other financial products, any misstep will trigger great turbulence of the entire financial system—and even a crisis to some extent. For this reason, reforms should be carried out with great caution.

Through comparison of various financial products, it has been found that corporate bonds have a host of unique functions in driving the transition of China's financial system.

First, replace deposits and loans. By nature, corporate bonds are credit and debt financial products just like deposits and loans. A corporate bond interest rate is the same for capital suppliers and borrowers, overcoming the difference between deposit and lending interest rates. With the same risk attributes, corporate bond interest rates are smaller than loan interest but higher than deposit rates. Due to the heterogeneous quality of corporate bonds, corporate bond rates are obviously much more complex than deposit and loan rates, which meet the needs of different capital suppliers and borrowers and create conditions for the development and innovation of derivative financial products. With the full development of corporate bonds, commercial banks will receive fewer deposits and issue fewer loans. The associated changes are threefold: 1. Money supply measured by deposits will decrease. By September 2013, the balance of China's broad money (M2) reached 107.74 trillion yuan (twice the amount of GDP), including the balance of Renminbi deposits worth 103.09 trillion yuan. Yet if household deposits are supplanted by corporate bonds, a portion of the

44.31 trillion yuan worth of household deposits will be converted into bond purchase funds, which will not only increase household property incomes but also substantially reduce M2. 2. The monetary policy regulation mechanisms will be transformed. The development of corporate bonds will render the Central Bank's regulation of deposit and loan benchmark rates meaningless and control of newly issued loans ineffective, prompting a transition from administrative regulation to market-based indirect regulation of the monetary policy. 3. Commercial banks will be forced to embark upon a business transition. With the amount of deposits and loans on the decrease, commercial banks will have to vigorously develop non-deposit and non-lending business, improve financial service quality, adjust their asset structure, and transform business model.

Second, mitigate the problem of funding mismatch. A prominent phenomenon in banks' capital operation is to absorb short-term funds while issuing long-term loans. On June 20, 2013, the overnight lending rate in the interbank market spiked due to an excess of mid-and long-term credit issuance by banks (mid-and long-term funds accounted for over 60% of the total). At a deeper level, the problem was a dearth of long-term funds in the operation of real-economy enterprises. This funding maturity mismatch can be effectively mitigated by vigorously developing corporate bonds as a source of mid-and long-term capital for real-economy enterprises (in developed countries, corporate bonds are ranked far above stocks in importance).

Third, reduce the corporate debt ratio. The debt ratio of real-economy enterprises is primarily attributable to the liabilities of bank loans. Considering the quasi-capital functions of long-term bonds, the replacement of bank loans with corporate bonds will substantially reduce the short-term debt ratio (as well as the associated debt risks), which is conducive to the stable operation of real-economy enterprises.

Fourth, advance asset securitization. Asset securitization is predicated upon the sophistication of the bond market. If the massive issuance of corporate bonds helps expedite maturity of the bond market, the basic conditions for asset securitization will improve; otherwise, it would be hard for asset securitization to be fully rolled out.

Fifth, propel business transition of commercial banks. An extensive issuance of corporate bonds will reduce absorption of deposits and issuance of loans by banks. It will also create financial market conditions for banks' business transition and provide such transition with relatively sufficient time.

Sixth, mitigate the problem of financing difficulty of small and micro businesses. As most large and medium-sized enterprises raise funds by issuing bonds, banks have to lend to small and micro businesses, which will help address the shortage and high interest rates of finance currently facing small and micro businesses.

Seventh, iron out stock market volatility. In China's financial system, households have few alternatives except for depositing their consumption surplus funds in banks or investing them in the stock market. The inflow and outflow of these funds have led to stock market boom and bust. With the sufficient development of corporate bonds, household funds will be distributed across a wide range of bonds with different qualities. Meanwhile, bond market interest rates will restrain stock market price volatility, preventing wild swings in the stock market.

Corporate bonds play a pivotal role in China's financial reforms. First, interest rate liberalization reforms: corporate bond rates are substitutes to banks' deposit and lending interest rates. Without the institutional mechanism of corporate bond rates, it is hard for China to complete the deposit and lending interest rate liberalization reforms. Second, the deposit insurance system: it is gravely risky to implement the deposit insurance system when deposits remain the key assets of households and a principal business for the banks. The sufficient development of corporate bonds will diminish the role of bank savings and loans in the financial system, making it less likely for the implementation of the deposit insurance system to cause any significant shock. Third, the openness of transactions under the capital account: in opening the capital account, most financial transactions are focused on corporate bonds and their derivatives, and the backflow of overseas Renminbi also occurs primarily through this conduit. Without a mature corporate bond market, it would be hard to fully open the capital account. Fourth, corporate bonds can facilitate the formation of the Asian Bond: developing the Asian Bond is an option for China to exercise its leadership in Asian financial markets. With an underdeveloped domestic bond market, however, China will not have a sufficient right of discourse in this field (not to mention the power to set rules).

As a direct financial instrument, corporate bonds should be distributed to real-economy enterprises and urban and rural households. Compared with bank loans, this not only provides real-economy enterprises an alternative way for them to borrow funds and handling their idle funds, but also helps raise urban and rural households' property incomes. Concerns over households' lack of financial investment risk tolerance are unnecessary. After two decades of stock market swings, Chinese households are fully experienced in financial investment and much more tolerant of investment risks than before. Besides, individual corporate bonds are issued in limited amounts, representing a drop in the ocean compared to 44 trillion yuan worth of savings deposits from urban and rural households. Some believe that urban and rural households may purchase bonds issued by companies listed at the Shanghai and Shenzhen stock exchanges, and if subscriptions in this market are not vibrant, it can be deemed that there are no sufficient corporate bond subscribers. This plausible argument is far from the reality. Most investors in Shanghai and Shenzhen stock exchanges invest in stocks, and stock price volatility from 1 to 5% appears too small for many investors, who are not sensitive to bond price change by around one percentage point. Such price insensitivity is in sharp contrast to the deposit market. Many depositors including real-economy enterprises and urban and rural households respond strongly to deposit rate volatility by 0.5 percentage points. Stock market investment is unlike household savings deposits. They cannot be confused to deny the role of corporate bonds as an alternative to deposits and loans.

We should focus on the following seven priorities in facilitating the direct issuance of corporate bonds to real-economy enterprises and urban and rural households: first, we should effectively implement relevant rules of the *Company Law* and the *Securities Law* to safeguard real-economy enterprises' lawful rights of bond issuance. After 1994, corporate bond market became an important institutional priority for China's securities market development. Chapter 5 of the *Company Law* effective as of July 1, 1994 prescribes rules on the issuance of corporate bonds. It stipulates that a joint-stock company with net assets worth 30 million yuan or a limited liability company with net assets worth 60 million yuan may issue corporate bonds, and that the balance of corporate bonds may reach 40% of the issuing company's net assets. In 2005, these rules were transferred into the *Securities Law* upon the amendment of the *Company Law* and the *Securities Law*. Over the past 20 years, however, very few corporate bonds have been issued in accordance with these rules. These legal provisions should, therefore, be further implemented. Second, we should establish a nationally unified system for corporate bond issuance and transactions to change the current system where five government authorities are in charge of bond issuance review and approval.[2] Third, we should remove the review and approval system for corporate bond issuance, implement an issuance registration system, and enhance supervision on corporate bond transactions. Fourth, proactive efforts must be made to create market mechanisms for the determination of corporate bond interest rates based on the nature of corporate bonds and the conditions of issuers. On this basis, further efforts should be made to form a yield curve based on corporate bond interest rates and improve the market-based pricing mechanisms for various securities in the securities market. Fifth, the role of credit rating in the securities market should be brought into play to create conditions for the issuance and transactions of corporate bonds of various types and at different levels. Sixth, we should create a multi-tiered market mechanism for the distribution of corporate bonds directly to real-economy enterprises and urban and rural households, expand the scope of corporate bond buyers through various sales channels (including sales counters and networks), diversify the buyers and holders of corporate bonds away from commercial banks and other financial institutions, and restore the nature of corporate bonds as a direct financial instrument. Seventh, we should develop debt acquisition to supplement equity acquisition and defuse risks from the non-payment of principal and interest upon maturity. Meanwhile, we should effectively implement the company bankruptcy system to standardize corporate bond market development and protect investors' interests.

With the return of corporate bonds to direct finance, we should enact the "Lenders Ordinance" to promote lending market development among real-economy enterprises; revise the *Law of Negotiable Instrument* to increase financing commercial bills for real-economy enterprises and increase the currency market's capacity to provide real-economy enterprises with short-term funds; steadily advance the development of financial leasing mechanisms and allow real-economy enterprises to establish

[2] Five competent authorities are in charge of the review and approval of corporate bond issuance, including the National Development and Reform Commission (NDRC) responsible for approving corporate bonds, the Central Bank responsible for approving short-term financing bonds, mid-term notes and debt financing instruments, the China Banking Regulatory Commission (CBRC) responsible for approving financial bonds and various bank bonds, the China Securities Regulatory Commission (CSRC) responsible for approving bonds and convertible bonds issued by listed companies and bonds issued by securities companies, and the China Insurance Regulatory Commission (CIRC) responsible for approving bonds issued by insurance companies. The involvement of multiple competent authorities has resulted in a fragmentation in the corporate bond issuance market.

financial leasing companies or enter the financial leasing market based on the needs of their business operations. Under these conditions, China's financial system will be brought back to the real economy in real earnest.

Reference

[US] Zvi Bodie, et al.: *Finance*, China Renmin University Press, 2000.

Printed by Printforce, the Netherlands